Parent-Child Retreats

Spiritual Experiences for Young Children and Their Parents

Maggie Pike
Lynne Knickerbocker
Eleanor Sheehan, CSJ
Mary Ann Figlino, CSJ

Foreword by
Dolores Curran

We wish to thank Kathy Coffey, Dolores Curran, Dr. Wendy Ebert,
Bob Knickerbocker, and Steve Pike.
To all who supported us with their laughter, loyalty, and love,
we dedicate this piece of our souls.

Living the Good News, Inc.
a division of The Morehouse Group
Editorial Offices
600 Grant Street, Suite 400
Denver, CO 80203

Cover Design and Layout: Val Price

Printed in the United States of America.

ISBN 1-889108-16-2

"People were bringing even infants to him

that he might touch them."

Luke 18:15

Foreword

My first reaction to the idea of a parent-child retreat was one of incredulity. A retreat for three-year olds? Mine didn't retreat for as much as ten minutes at that age.

But God sends us the gift of reflection and the more I pondered the idea, the more I came to believe. Why not toddlers? Insightful parents sense the special transcendence of young children, an awe and trust we spend a lifetime to recapture. Why not nurture it at the time and prevent the struggle later on? Gerald May says, "There is a part of you that has always said yes to God." Why not nurture that part in the earliest years of life?

As the former director of family weekend retreats, I've often remarked that those fifty-five hours did more for family faith than the collective religious education of the family for a year. Parent response is the basis for my remark. Some 200 parents can't be wrong.

Retreats touch the heart. They take faith out of the classroom and transform "head" stuff into "life and heart" stuff. They integrate body, spirit, and soul, offering an ideal opportunity for families to interact and support one another in a largely secular world.

Sadly, most Catholics have never experienced a retreat. The parent-child retreat is a wonderfully non-threatening way to introduce children in their most formative years to an experience of faith which will stand by them when the inevitable doubting stages emerge.

The four pioneers in the parent-child retreat movement are creative, faith-filled, and joyous women. Their energy and enthusiasm are contagious. They don't need to sell the process because parents embrace it as a chance to spend some quiet one-on-one or one-on-two time with their children in a spiritual setting. And these parents are telling their friends about it.

The short block of time required is attractive to time-hungry parents. Young children love the experience and demand more of it—a refreshing change from many children's reaction to religious education.

We know that experiential learning is the only effective learning in the preschool years. We also know that most lifetime attitudes are formed by age five. Yet, we can't seem to put the two together. Bless these four authors who have done so. This is not a book about an idea. It's a description of and a prescription for an effort that works. On behalf of parents and children everywhere who will benefit from this effort, I thank the four creators of *Parent-Child Retreats* for sharing themselves so generously with us.

—Dolores Curran

Contents

1

Overview

The Beginning

It started out like any other day at Sacred Heart Jesuit Retreat House in Sedalia, Colorado.

Retreatants strolled the sprawling grounds in silent, prayerful union with God. The silence within the stately house of prayer, too, spoke of peace, of reverence, whispering praise to our God of serenity.

Then they came. Little retreatants. Lots of them. And they sang and they climbed and they chased and they squealed, shouting praise to our God of joy.

Thus marked the jubilant birth in 1986 of Denver's parent-child retreat movement, although "parent" might be grandparent, godparent, stepparent, aunt, babysitter, or friend. No matter, for this is an opportunity for young children to spend special time with someone who loves them, learning the practice of spending special time with Someone Else who loves them: their best friend, Jesus. They're making a retreat.

We are four women—teachers, religious educators, retreat directors, moms, or a combination thereof—who love children and long to see them grow in intimacy with Jesus. The idea of a parent-child retreat was an outgrowth of our own retreat experience, where we saw the hunger for God in adult peers, yet a reluctance to make a retreat. Some admitted to less-than-pleasant retreat weekends in high school; others felt they weren't spiritually advanced enough to spend all that time alone with God.

What would happen, we wondered, if children started making retreats as tiny youngsters: warm, joy-filled experiences in the security of their parents' laps? What if we used the word *retreat* repeatedly and unabashedly with them from the time they were three years old? And what if they discovered through all this that a retreat is actually an experience of Jesus' friendship? We envisioned retreat houses of the future brimming with excited retreatants who had been enjoying times like this since they were practically babies.

A Word of Reassurance

Many parents look with trepidation upon our call to be our children's first teachers, especially in the area of faith. Understandably. Our own journey to union with God has been marked by both smooth and rutted pavements, occasional detours, and stretches of construction and reconstruction. We have doubts, then, about our ability to pass “religion” on to our children. It may seem formidable to share a spiritual experience with our children if we ourselves “aren’t there” yet.

We share these doubts. But we’ve learned by giving parent-child retreats that God is truly the one at the wheel. God needs us to open the doors, hop in, and enjoy the ride.

Our children are open to friendship with Jesus. Many of us received religious instruction rich with that friendship. We had positive experiences from warm, faith-filled teachers and parents, and we’re excited to pass on to our children the vital faith we’ve come to treasure.

For others, unfortunately, religious instruction was devoid of friendship with Jesus. It may have been, instead, dry, heady, or fear-filled. We might try, therefore, to nervously reassure our children about this retreat experience, thus subtly passing on negativity or doubts.

But our young children don’t have doubts. Since they didn’t experience the religious climate of previous decades, we don’t have to alleviate doubts that are not there. It is the good in our faith experience that we want to pass on. If we show enthusiasm, our children will embrace our enthusiasm.

Who Can Use Parent-Child Retreats?

Our retreats have moved from those isolated grounds of the retreat center into the city and have taken on different forms. Religious education programs and mothers’ groups host parent-child retreats in church halls, sometimes combining with neighboring parishes. We offer a daytime retreat, most often attended by moms and young children, and a bedtime retreat, so that working parents can participate.

But we also envision these same spiritual experiences going on in preschools, in child care homes, in small play groups, in home religious education programs. We see them in two-parent and single-parent homes, in foster families, in non-custodial parent homes—wherever children and parents (or surrogate parents) spend time together. By examining the overview and understanding the focus of each retreat, caregivers themselves can spread the good news to children that Jesus is their best friend. Caregivers might lead their children in one of the prayers one night, do the corresponding craft the next afternoon, and read the book later in the week, filling an entire week with the theme of the closeness of Jesus. Preschools might choose to devote a morning where they invite parents to join their children in a parent-child retreat to provide parents with the richness of a shared experience. Later, the school might choose another retreat to weave throughout an entire month or season with just the children, and send home information about the retreat so the parents can share with their children there. The format need not be formal and structured. A retreat is an experience of Jesus' friendship, more a way of life than a moment in time or a location.

Why Parent-Child Retreats?

It doesn't take a parent or teacher long to realize the great potential children have to grasp faith, both in its simplicity and in its depth. Young children, especially, are fertile in imagination, curiosity, intuition, spontaneity, trust, openness, and friendliness. This is the time to nurture the seeds of faith planted at baptism. Our little ones are ripe for experiencing God. They're eager to make friends with Jesus.

Our parent-child retreats are a vehicle for just this experience. The groundwork has been done: the love, intimacy, and feeling of specialness they've experienced with their parents and other caregivers mirrors what they receive from Jesus. Of course, human love is flawed no matter how hard we try, but for most children, love is their frame of reference. The retreat, therefore, is time spent tuning into their own experience of Jesus' love. It is because of the love the children have received from their parents all along that they are able to move into the love and friendship of Jesus. A retreat for young children, then, derives its power precisely from the presence of the child's parents or caregivers there.

We recognize, however, that not all children are raised in loving homes. Where this is the case, some children may be confused about the nature of love, whether from Jesus or from anyone else, based on the imperfect love they've received from their parents. For these children, it is even more important that they have opportunities to grow in friendship with Jesus. When we speak to young children of this friendship, therefore, we acknowledge that moms and dads sometimes get frustrated and angry. Jesus, however, does not get angry with children. We share regret that parents are sometimes too busy to listen to us. We can, however, always talk to Jesus. We admit that adults aren't always patient with us, especially when we're grumpy or scared, but we can always tell Jesus how we feel, and Jesus understands. The experience of friendship with Jesus in a parent-child retreat is a genuine immersion into the ever-present, all-embracing love of God.

A parent-child retreat lights the fire of spirituality between parent and child. Because they've had this experience together, it remains with them always.
And that same spiritual experience can happen again in other settings. A young mother named Maura had made a parent-child retreat with her four- and six-year-old children, John and Katie. All three had learned the Heart Room Prayer[1], a

quiet and sacred time of encountering Jesus through visualization. Several days later Maura wanted some uninterrupted prayer time, so she told the children she wanted to go to her heart room. "Okay, Mommy," they said. "We'll be quiet." Maura was astounded when she realized an hour had gone by without a peep out of John and Katie. They honored her relationship with God because it was a relationship they shared.

Our retreats are an opportunity to initiate parents and children into sharing faith and prayer with each other. It gives families the time and format to talk about God. By linking the sacred with the secular in our retreats, we attempt to give spiritual meaning to their everyday experiences and thus to open their eyes so that together, parents and children might continue to look for the spiritual in their lives.

Parent-child retreats fill in the sacramental time line. Most of us remember even the most minute details of our first communion, reconciliation, and confirmation, events surely worthy of long-lasting memories. Few of us, though, remember our initiation into the Christian community at baptism. Even more, experiences of God's presence—lively, sacred retreats with Mom and Dad—can, in the time between the sacraments of initiation, link those outward signs, remembered and unremembered.

Parent-child retreats are milestones in a child's life, on a par with the loss of a first tooth, the first day of school, noteworthy trips, honors and awards. As a child looks back on her life, she can know something did happen between baptism and first eucharist: she made her first retreat. We deliberately create and preserve memories for our children to clarify their particular identity, their history. The memory created in a parent-child retreat says clearly: I am a special friend of Jesus—and I always have been.

Parent-child retreats reinforce that we are the Church. If we truly believe this, then we regard even our youngest members not as the future Church, but the Church right now. The children already seem to know it. They want to do what they see others doing. In their minds, there's no reason why they can't make a retreat. Our parent-child retreats respond to their openness and invite them into participation in our faith tradition.

Perhaps the most attractive bonus of making a parent-child retreat is simply time alone with our children. Families today are hungry from the famine of too little "together" time, the result of overworking, overscheduling, and overdoing, albeit well-intentioned. The one-to-one time of a retreat, the quieting and sharing of two people who love each other, can truly be a sacred and intimate time for both.

Parents and children are a presence of God to each other. The mystic Teresa of Avila wrote that just as water helps the flowers grow, prayer helps the virtues grow. Many parents can tell stories of how their children helped them to blossom spiritually and, consequently, grow in virtue. Parent-child retreats nurture that primary relationship, like a watering can—with a pinch of fertilizer in it.

Forming a Team

WANTED: Women and men who love and honor children, to be part of retreat team for three- to six-year-olds. Need not be teachers or parents. Will train. Personal qualities: warmth, humor, and an enthusiasm about their own friendship with Jesus.

Respect for children, born out of the belief that even young children have a spirituality, is the most important quality in the four adults who lead a parent-child retreat. Three will work directly with the children in small groups; the fourth will talk to the parents. Absolutely crucial in all four leaders is a personal spirituality that reflects the consistency of the Word in John and Paul: "God is love" (1 John 4:8) and "Love is patient, love is kind" (1 Corinthians 13:4).

The four of us, the authors of this book, bring a combination of gifts: training in spirituality, background in child development, experience raising children, soothing voices, creativity in designing crafts, imagination, playfulness, and agility on piano keys. None of us has all these qualities, but all of us have one that supercedes all else: each of us is able to see spiritual meaning in the mundane. Thus, a story is not just a story; it carries a message of Jesus' abundant friendship, which we help the children recognize. For the same reason, if a craft flops, it's inconsequential to us. More important is the chance for the leader to talk with retreatants about the joy of spending special time with Jesus as they work on their project. Their creations will serve as reminders of this sacred time long after they return home. Prayer time taps into children's wonderful ability to imagine, providing a rich encounter with Jesus in settings they know well.

It is essential that each member of the retreat team understand the focus of parent-child retreats as explained in this book. Planning meetings will ensure this. We are most careful to emphasize to our team, so that they in turn will convey it to the parents, that this is a retreat for young children. It is not a babysitting session and it is not a retreat for parents. Young retreatants are the VIP's at this event.

In forming a team, we do not understaff. A helper-to-child ratio of 1:4 is ideal for the craft, for example, while less help is needed for the story and prayer. It is always good to have an extra hand for the child who is crying, who needs a trip to the bathroom, or who feels frustration because the scissors won't work. Because we want to sufficiently supervise and nurture our young retreatants, we often ask older children to be helpers, girls and boys over ten years old, some of whom have made parent-child retreats themselves as young children.

Nor do we ever combine groups to make a larger group. Our retreat schedule is based on accommodating ten or fewer children per activity, and adding more children will necessarily require extending the time periods. Each activity should be limited to fifteen minutes, including travel time to the next activity; we honor the attention span of young children.

Finally, we pray together as a team. Prayer renews our own friendship with Jesus. It bonds us in the love, peace and joy of God's Spirit. Acknowledging that we are vessels of God's wisdom and presence, we pray for pureness of heart to be a holy presence to the retreatants. Assisting in the spiritual formation of Jesus' youngest friends is one of the greatest privileges we've ever experienced.

Profiles of Children Ages Three to Six

Children are the VIP's at parent-child retreats. We speak to them and, in the parents' session, *about* them. Therefore, it is important that all team members be knowledgeable about the nature of small children. We keep in mind their developmental level at all times and don't hesitate to make changes, even midstream, if what we're doing isn't working out.

Children learn by seeing, hearing, and touching, and they retain more in their long-term memory if they are active participants rather than passive listeners. We attempt to provide a variety of activities that will appeal to visual, auditory, and tactile learners. In planning and delivering our parent-child retreats, we follow these two rules religiously: Keep it simple and remain flexible.

To assist in planning retreats appropriate to the age level of our retreatants, we include here the profiles of three- to six-year-olds from the curriculum series *This is Our Faith*.

Age 3

- ▲ Most three-year-old children strongly believe that God loves them.
- ▲ They have many questions about God; they are curious and filled with wonder.
- ▲ They tend to be quite egocentric and find sharing difficult.
- ▲ They enjoy adult conversation and attention; they want to please adults.

- ▲ They have strong attachments to the parent of the opposite sex.
- ▲ They love to celebrate special holidays and events.
- ▲ They have short attention spans—four to six minutes. Thus, they need a variety of experiences and physical activities.
- ▲ At times, their need to speak comes faster than their words, so they may stutter.
- ▲ Their large muscles are quite well developed.
- ▲ Because their small muscles are just beginning to develop, most cannot use scissors well or do detailed work with their fingers.
- ▲ They love to climb; they are learning to jump; however, few can skip.
- ▲ Many three-year old children are beginning to use oral threats and become bossy or whiny.

Age 4

- ▲ They are curious and eager learners.
- ▲ They are anxious to display their growing independence and developing skills.
- ▲ They have begun to recognize that living with and being with others requires limitations and rules.
- ▲ They frequently defy parents, testing themselves against siblings and peers.
- ▲ Many four-year-olds appear egocentric, boastful and lacking in social skills. They relate best with a single peer.
- ▲ They look forward to being five and to entering formal schooling.
- ▲ They are reflective and in awe of God's power and greatness.
- ▲ They love to ritualize events, and they enjoy celebrations and special holidays within their respective traditions.
- ▲ They wonder about cause-and-effect relationships.
- ▲ Four-year-olds are wondering persons. Because they wonder about almost everyone and everything, they can be very prayerful.

Ages 5 and 6

- ▲ Kindergarten age children are ready for and eager to participate in learning experiences away from home in a loving, caring environment.
- ▲ They approach new experiences and situations in life with enthusiasm, excitement and wonder.
- ▲ They live in a world of here and now. They cannot grasp historical concepts.
- ▲ They can concentrate on a task for only a short time.
- ▲ They need frequent changes in activities (every five to eight minutes) and require physical movement, games and songs.
- ▲ They are able to focus for a few moments on quiet and reflection.

- ▲ They are naturally curious, creative, and filled with questions.
- ▲ Many of their questions are unanswerable and simply lead to new inquiries.
- ▲ They may be self-centered and somewhat reluctant to get involved in social play or group activities.
- ▲ They need words of positive reinforcement and encouragement to demonstrate the love and care of a loving God.[2]

Tips for Directing Young Children

Through trial and error, we've discovered some tricks which have helped us engage children in large groups, focus the ones who get distracted, and comfort those who are crying. No matter what the child's behavior, we try to discover the need behind it and respond to that need, rather than ignore or reprimand the child.

- ▲ Encourage all retreatants to sit close together, children on their parents' laps or right next to them.
- ▲ Throughout the retreat, inform the children of what's going to happen before it happens.
- ▲ Use the children's names frequently. Read them right off their nametags.
- ▲ Maintain eye contact in both large and small groups.
- ▲ Occasionally change volume or tone, or move about for variety.
- ▲ Include the children's comments in the presentation.
- ▲ Ask the children to repeat a short phrase.
- ▲ Get the group's attention by saying in a hushed voice, "Listen carefully. I have something important to tell you."
- ▲ Ask a distracted child to sit on your lap, help you, or hold something important which you'll be using later.
- ▲ Walk over to a talkative child, put your hand on his shoulder, and continue talking.
- ▲ Comfort a crying child by having a helper take her for a walk, get her a drink, put her hands under cool water, draw pictures on her back, or offer reassuring words.
- ▲ In small groups when children are apart from their parents, remind them to concentrate so they can tell their parents later what they've done.

Guidelines for the Parent Sessions

While the focus of our retreats is on young children, the parents also appreciate their time together, a time to renew their own spirituality. Since our parent session lasts only fifty to sixty minutes, we want to ensure that our adult retreatants gain the most during their brief time together.

In planning our parents' session, therefore, we draw on the advice of adult educator Dolores Curran, who has recorded her experiences and insights from facilitating successful parent groups in her book, *Working with Parents*.[3] The following tips can assist the retreat director in planning the parents' session of a parent-child retreat.

Create a pleasing environment.

We arrange the meeting room in a way that promotes interaction among retreatants. Placing the chairs in a circle or semicircle invites eye contact; encouraging parents to sit close together, filling in empty seats, facilitates bonding within the group.

Since our adult membership is fairly small—twenty-five is the most we've ever had—we don't normally need a microphone. However, when we do use one, we test it ahead of time to make sure we know how it works and whether the volume is adequate for the size of the room.

We also like to create a sacred atmosphere and we do so by designing a focal point, such as a small table with flowers, a picture, the Bible, a candle, or whatever might be aesthetically pleasing to our retreatants. As the eyes rest upon it, the focal point is a reminder of God's gentle presence in the room.

Know the interests and concerns of the group.

Adults have stated a variety of reasons for coming to our parent-child retreats: spiritual nourishment, companionship with other parents who share the same values, uncertainty about how to share their faith with their young children, even concern about their teenager who is rejecting traditional religion. Other reasons may surface with time, and it's the responsibility of the retreat team to listen to the parents' interests.

Our own presentations have developed from the needs of our participants, but our focus is always on young children and on the parents themselves in their call to be their children's first teachers. Within this context, it's important to invite the retreatants' suggestions for topics, either informally in conversation, or by means of a formal survey. The parents' session is enriched by the input of the participants themselves.

Know your subject.

It isn't necessary that the speakers have raised children, but it is essential that they understand and appreciate parenthood, for the retreatants expect them to be knowledgeable about their role in the faith development of their children. Whether from first-hand experience or from extensive talking with parents, as well as from reading, the adult leader must be familiar with family life in order to effectively lead parents in reflection on their own spiritual leadership in the family.

Empower the retreatants.

Like children, adults retain more in their long-term memory if they are active participants rather than passive listeners. While the retreat director is chiefly responsible for the content of the parents' session presentation, the parents add wisdom that enriches the retreat many-fold. The director empowers them to participate, sharing their insight with each other. Sometimes an entire group seems reluctant to speak. At other times, the group is overly chatty, or a few people dominate discussion. One technique to avert either of these situations is to stop the presentation periodically and pose a question, inviting participants to share with the person next to them. A discussion with the larger group might follow, or it might be saved until the end of the talk. This opportunity for paired reflection helps retreatants to focus their thoughts before sharing with the whole group, and empowers those who hesitate to speak before large groups to express their thoughts as well.

Be true to your own personality.

In making a presentation, we are most effective when we use our own unique gift, be it humor, gentleness, visible spirituality, gregariousness, reserve. Some speakers use notes, others don't. It doesn't matter, for it's through our uniqueness that God can work in us. Trying to be something we are not poses a barrier to that.

Control the agenda.

Retreatants expect the director to prevent anyone from monopolizing the discussion, to keep the topic on focus, to prevent digressions into areas unrelated to the retreat and to keep the group from deteriorating into a personal therapy session. A comment like, "I sense the group is ready to get back to the topic. Am I right?" or a light-hearted "Well, time to talk about forgiveness again" (or whatever the day's topic is) can be most effective in regaining control of the agenda.

Use simple language rather than professional jargon.

Using professional language, which is familiar to us, but not to our retreatants, distances us from them. Our goal is not to impress, but to share our insights and to encourage parents to share theirs. Using jargon is counterproductive to this goal. If we can say it more simply, we should do so. Theological terms, for example, are not universally understood and vary among churches. Experience, on the other hand, unites people. So a retreat director will have a better chance of touching common experience if she talks about kids around the kitchen table rather than "the domestic church."

Avoid expressing controversial attitudes.

This is not to say that we cannot hold our own attitudes, but that revealing controversial attitudes early on can evoke irritation in the retreatants and may prevent them from hearing anything more we have to say. Inevitably, controversial statements will come up, but they should not originate with the retreat director. Rather, it's the director's responsibility to handle controversy objectively.

In a parent-child retreat, for example, parents may express discontent with the leadership of their church or with the lack of members' loyalty to church leadership. Sometimes a simple "I hear your concern. Thanks for sharing," from the director is the best response, especially if the comments wander from the focus of the retreat.

Notes

1. Mary Terese Donze, *In My Heart Room* (Ligouri, Mo.: Liguori Publications, 1982), 7.
2. Karl Pfeifer and Janeen Manternach, *This Is Our Faith.* Teacher's Edition (Morristown, N.J.: Silver Burdett and Ginn, 1994), 296-299.
3. Dolores Curran, *Working with Parents* (Circle Pines, Minn.: American Guidance Service, 1989), 41-59.

2 What We Do and Why We Do It

Environment

"In my Father's house there are many dwelling places" (John 14:2a).

Environment is a broad term used to describe the setting of the retreat. We've given parent-child retreats in a variety of settings: a stately retreat house, an ultra-modern meeting center, and many unadorned church halls. It's the environment we create within the building, rather than the building itself, that sets the tone for the retreat. When we refer to the environment of a parent-child retreat, we mean the facilities as well as the decor.

The location of a retreat must be functional. We need a large meeting area where parents and children together can gather. When we use piano accompaniment for our gathering songs, we request a piano in this room. We also need a separate room for each of the three children's activities. The room for the craft group will need tables and chairs; for story and movement, lots of space; and for prayer, a room devoid of distracting toys, decorations or clutter. In addition to these four separate rooms, we need a meeting room for the parent session and a place for the children to eat their snack.

It's possible to double up on room usage. For example, the parents' session might be in the same room where parents and children gathered. Or it might work to serve the snack in a room that was used for an earlier activity. We leave the decision to the parish retreat organizers, who know the set-up of their own church, but we always arrive early enough to preview the facilities and make changes where necessary. It's essential to the smooth flow of the retreat that the team have the accommodations they need and become familiar with them well before the retreat starts. We suggest arriving an hour early to check the facilities, set up the activities, pray together, confer with each other, and otherwise prepare for the arrival of our retreatants.

Environment refers, too, to the visual appeal of the meeting place. We pay particular attention to the gathering room, where we create a display which blends the secular and the sacred. We want the environment to be pleasing to small children and at the same time reflect the theme of the retreat in a concrete way. For example, at our picnic retreat we spread a checkered tablecloth over a nearby table or piano and make an arrangement consisting of a picnic basket, thermos or jug, and teddy bears. The display is simple, but it makes tangible what we will be talking about during our gathering time.

Nametags and Introductions

"I have called you by name: you are mine" (Isa. 43:1b).

Denise was pregnant with her first child, due in two weeks. "I've changed my mind about names," she moaned. "All this time I've wanted to name my first daughter Lisa. But last month a new family moved in next door and their two-year-old is named Lisa. All I've heard for the last four weeks is that mother's shrill voice shrieking, 'Leeeeeesa! Lisa, come here!' I just can't name a child Lisa." Consequently, Denise named her daughter Deanne.

Our names are important to us. The way we hear our names spoken time after time affects the image we have of ourselves. God told each of us through the prophet Isaiah, "I have called you by name: you are mine. You are precious to me...and I love you" (Isa. 43:1-4). Following God's example, then, we can express God's love to our children by using their names with respect, kindness and affection. Imagine what a child feels when she hears her name spoken with harshness and disdain: "Leeeesa, come here." Imagine the same child growing up hearing phrases spoken in gentle tones: "Come here, my Lisa," or even, "Come here, my precious Lisa." It is perhaps no coincidence that Denise, herself a well-loved child, blessed her daughter with a name similar to her own. Recently, a preschooler named Kate brought her doll, Kate, to school for show-and-tell. Her response as to why she gave her doll her own name was quick and direct: "Kate's a nice name."

Therein lies our reason for nametags—big, colorful, beautiful nametags—at our parent-child retreats. Each of our retreatants has a "nice name." Like their friend Jesus, we want to know their names, love their names, and call them by name. They are precious to us.

Regardless of the form of the nametag, we make them in three different colors. Later, when we divide the children into small groups, we ask them to match their nametag to an adult leader's nametag of the same color. The bonding of the community has begun. The same color groups travel together to each portion of the retreat. Nametags are also a vehicle for introducing ourselves to each other. The directors of the retreat make an effort to warmly greet every family, and especially each child, to put them at ease in this new experience. So, too, will the members of this soon-to-be community welcome the opportunity to meet each other.

Gathering Time

"For where two or three are gathered together in my name, there am I in the midst of them" (Mt. 18:20).

We take God's promise of presence seriously as we gather the retreatants to begin our time together. Since the introduction sets the tone for the day, we fill our words and actions with love, peace, joy and excitement.

The children will want to sit in the security of their parents' laps. It's good to gather the participants close together in a semicircle so that they can see each other, hear the speaker and ignore distractions.

In welcoming the parents and children we use the word *retreat* repeatedly, keeping in mind our desire to instill in these little ones a lifelong love of retreats.

We tell the children we're excited they came to our retreat, that this is a day to have "special time" with Mommy or Daddy, and that it's also going to be a day to spend special time with Jesus, who's their best friend. Jesus has loved them since they were tiny babies, and we're going to learn some ways today to show Jesus that we are his best friend, too.

One way we can show Jesus we love him and welcome him into our midst is to sing songs for him. Our team likes to make up lyrics to songs already familiar to the children, but music for young children abounds. Since the retreat is a one-time experience, we suggest teaching them a song that is simple to learn and easy to remember, for both parents and children.

We then introduce the members of our retreat team, saying that we are special friends of Jesus just as they are, and that we want to help them to know Jesus even better. We explain that their parents are going to hear a talk for a little while and, while they're doing that, we're going to play some games, read stories, pray to Jesus, and make something special to show their parents when they come back from the talk.

At this time we focus the retreat on a theme familiar to the children's experience. We explain the focus in detail later in the book, as we describe each retreat.

The core message, regardless of the theme, remains the friendship of Jesus. Jesus has all the qualities a good friend would have: he loves us; he is with us always; he wants to hear about the times we're feeling angry, glad, sad, and scared; he wants to be our friend.

Before parents and children separate for their individual sessions, we explain to the children exactly where they're going, what they'll be doing, what their parents will be doing, and state that when we have our snack, their parents will be there, too, to spend some more time with them. We allow a moment for hugs and goodbyes, then lead the children to their activities. Our best reassurance to these small retreatants is to exude joy and excitement ourselves, encouraging them to smile and wave goodbye.

We dismiss the children before the parents. Each child looks at the color of her nametag and matches it to the color of one of the adult team members' tags. That's the identification of the group the child will join first, but he or she will eventually rotate through each of three activities.

Time to begin our adventure.

Children's Activities

Jesus, however, called the children to himself and said, "Let the children come to me..." (Lk. 18:16a).

Prayer

We provide a prayer experience for the children which complements formal prayer and which is appropriate to their developmental level.

The underlying purpose of the prayer time in each retreat is a personal encounter with Jesus. Tapping children's gift of imagination, we employ all their senses to image their friend Jesus, listen to him, speak to him, and be with him. These steps—becoming familiar, listening, speaking, and being with—reflect the levels of intimacy in any friendship and form the framework for each of our prayer experiences. We weave the theme of the retreat into the children's encounter with Jesus as we lead them through these levels of friendship.

We've found tremendous success in using the term *heart room* as explained by Mary Terese Donze, ASC, in her book, *In My Heart Room.* We ask the children to imagine a room deep inside themselves. Jesus lives there, we tell them, and they can go there to be with Jesus whenever they want. It is in the "heart room" that we help the children visualize their friend Jesus, listen to him, speak to him, and sit with him in silence. Donze gives the following instruction for leading the children into their "heart rooms":

"Before giving directions to the children, make sure they are comfortably seated. If the prayer session is being held in the home or in an area of the school that is carpeted, the children may sit (not lie) comfortably on the floor.

"Help the children relax by taking them through a few breathing exercises. Direct them to breathe deeply and slowly (and silently) through the nose, in and out several times.

"If this is the children's first experience with this type of prayer, be sure they have been prepared beforehand by some short discussion of what they are going to do. Be brief. It is sufficient that the children realize they are praying and that it is a time of quiet.

"After the children have been prepared, begin the instructions. If you are standing, do not move from place to place as you read the prayer directions. Use a calm, quiet tone that is audible without being loud. Try to read as if you were speaking. Appeal to their hearts, but avoid the dramatic. State the direction in a simple, sincere way, keeping in mind your desire to lead the children to God through this prayer. Pause between sentences or parts of sentences where the thought suggests a pause, but avoid prolonged silences. Move through the prayer with a certain deliberateness.

"Finally, begin well. Approach each prayer session asking God to bless you and the children you are trying to lead to [God]."[1]

Craft

The craft is something the children can take home to play with and talk about, reinforcing the message of the retreat in their play. Due to time limitations, simplicity is the key. Therefore, we try to have the craft so well prepared that the children have little to do the day of the retreat. Assembly of the project is merely the medium through which the adult leader talks about and reinforces the theme of the retreat. We offer these basic management details:

- ▲ Have enough helpers to ensure that each child is able to finish her project in ten minutes. We suggest a helper-to-retreatant ratio of 1:4.
- ▲ Write names on the projects so that each child goes home with his or her own.
- ▲ Leave the projects in one place to be picked up at the end of the retreat.
- ▲ Honor what each child has made with lavish praise.

Story and Movement

With each retreat we suggest a book which echoes the theme of the retreat. We look for books that touch children's experience authentically, books which we've found to successfully engage children, the ones they love to hear over and over again. While not religious per se, each book contains a metaphor for friendship with Jesus. As the children listen to the story, and share insights afterwards, they shift in awareness from an abstract Jesus to his human presence.

Reading and storytelling touch the deepest part of ourselves, whether child or adult. Story time at parent-child retreats attempts to assist children on their journey inward, where Jesus dwells. Our goal is to plant the seed for children to look for spiritual meaning in the stories they love. As they grow out of their strictly literal phase, they have the beginnings of a new, deeper way of life.

It also seems appropriate to allow the children time to stretch after they have sat still for so long. We choose from a variety of songs, dances, fingerplays, and exercises, and encourage you to use your favorites.

Snack

When the hour came, [Jesus] took his place at table with the apostles (Lk. 22:14).

Our snack is both practical and spiritual. We serve a snack primarily to meet the physical needs of small children: they need to eat. At the same time, as we eat together we gather as a community not unlike that small group of friends who shared Jesus' Last Supper. The snack coordinates with the theme of the retreat. For example, at our picnic retreat we serve Ants on a Log, celery sticks loaded with peanut butter and sprinkled with raisins.

Note: Extra projects may be used after any of the children's activities if time remains. See Appendix, pages 179-217.

Parent Sessions

"Everyone who listens to these words of mine and acts on them will be like the wise one who built a house on rock. It did not collapse; it had been set solidly on rock" (Mt. 7:24, 25b).

Parents, having lovingly sent their children off to their activities, are ready for their own time of spiritual nourishment. This sixty-minute session, led by one of the retreat directors, embodies five elements:

1. overview
2. group introductions
3. explanation of children's activities
4. prayer
5. presentation

Overview

As the parents gather together for their session, we take care to emphasize why they are here. This retreat, we tell them, is not a retreat for parents. Nor is it a nice program offered by the church, where parents bring their children, let them do something religious, then take them home again, happy to have exposed their little ones to another church activity.

We emphasize this because of an experience that made us realize some of our participants were misunderstanding the purpose of a parent-child retreat. A woman approached us at the retreat house a year after she and her daughter had made a parent-child retreat. Genuinely happy to see us, she exclaimed, "I remember you. You're the ones who did the child care during the moms' retreat at our church." Our hearts sank.

We are careful, therefore, to instill in our adult participants their purpose for making a retreat with their children. This, we explain, is to be a communal, mutual, happy, and holy experience of adults and young children spending "special time with Jesus." This is our definition of a retreat. The parent-child retreat is for young children and their special adult, who together sing, listen, reflect, pray, and share. The main element of the retreat is the communal experience of parent and child spending time together. Parent and child meet Jesus in prayer, then come together to talk about their prayer time. Loved child and loving parent share precious time with each other alone.

The parent-child retreat makes mutual sharing in faith a down-to-earth reality for those who believe in God and want their children to share that belief.

Group Introductions

The leader will want to allow time for the parents to introduce themselves to each other. In our discussion of nametags, we emphasized the importance of each child's name in reflecting the uniqueness and worth of that child. Correspondingly, the leader wants to convey the same attitude of respect for parents by asking them to share something of themselves with each other.

When we take time for this, a group of separate individuals can become a community of adults coming together in warmth and humor. In listening to and receiving one another in God's name, we experience Church; that is, being part of the people of God.

We ask the adults to say their name, then to answer a question. Their responses to the question have the effect of touching each other's common experience. The following questions have successfully elicited sharing at our retreats. Choose one question per retreat:

- ▲ What do you most long for from God?
- ▲ What do you most want for your child?
- ▲ What's the most important thing about God that you want to communicate to your child?
- ▲ Share something your child has said about Jesus.

- Whom/what does your child remind you of?
- What do you want to be when you "grow up"?
- Where did you get your name?
- Why did you name your child as you did?
- What do you like most about young children? least?
- Share something your child taught you about the love/goodness/wisdom of God.

Explanation of Children's Activities

The parents are curious about what their children are doing during this time, so we spend a few minutes explaining the format of the children's activities.
The children will have four twelve- to fifteen-minute sessions:

1. prayer
2. craft
3. story and movement
4. snack

Later, parents will have time alone with their child to talk about the events of the morning/evening. This sharing time is key to the retreat, so it's essential that the parents know it's coming up as well as what their children are experiencing. Parents have found it helpful when the leader gives them a copy of the questions (p. 216) to use with their child during the ensuing parent-child sharing time. The following questions will enable parents to elicit reactions, insights, and experiences rather than yes/no answers:

- Tell me about the story you heard.
- What do you like about the craft you made?
- What was it like when you met Jesus in your heart room?
- What did Jesus look like?
- How did it feel to be with Jesus?
- When I met Jesus in my heart room, he said... I did...
- What did Jesus say to you? What did you do?

Prayer

We teach the parents the Heart Room Prayer following the guidelines outlined in Mary Terese Donze's *In My Heart Room*, and reproduced in this book on pages 15-16.

Because many parents have never experienced this type of prayer and because they'll later be sharing the experience with their children, we are careful to explain it thoroughly.

We begin by leading the parents into quieting, which could sound like this:

- ▲ Close your eyes and place your feet comfortably on the floor, hands relaxed in your lap. *(Pause.)* Pay attention to your breathing. *(Pause.)* As you breathe in, breathe in the love of God. As you breathe out, breathe out anything that might prevent you from focusing on God's love. *(Pause.)* Breathe in God's love; breathe out any barriers to God's love. *(Pause.)* As you breathe in, breathe in God's peace. And as you breathe out, breathe out any anxiety or worry. *(Pause.)* Breathe in God's peace; breathe out anxiety. *(Pause.)*
- ▲ *(Wait 30 seconds, then continue:)* Move down, now, into that most intimate, private place, which is your own heart.
- ▲ You hear a knock on the door of your heart, a door that can be opened only from the inside. You know who is knocking. It's Jesus.
- ▲ Go to the door and welcome Jesus in your own way. *(Wait 30 seconds.)*
- ▲ Invite him into your heart room if you can. If you can't, tell him so, openly and honestly.
- ▲ Sit with Jesus now, or speak to him from a distance if you're more comfortable. Tell him what's in your heart. *(Wait 90 seconds.)*
- ▲ Now close this time with Jesus. Ask him to stay with you, to dwell there in your heart room where you can always meet him.

The leader then asks each person to share with one other person something that happened in their prayer.

For many, this may be the first time they've shared a faith experience. This will help them to share more easily with their child later.

Presentation

The total presentation lasts approximately an hour. It may begin with participants introducing themselves. One technique that helps establish a community among retreatants, set the tone of freedom to participate, and get a sense of where they are on their spiritual journey is to invite the parents to introduce themselves, then answer a question.

The leader might say, for example, "As we go around the room, please introduce yourself, then answer this question: Who is God for you?" The presentation itself is most effective as a combination of lecture and group sharing, thus drawing on the wisdom of the whole group.

The topics of our parent presentations reflect the recommendations of our adult participants through the years. They are subjects in which our retreatants have expressed an interest. Each one addresses an aspect of the call to parents to be their child's first teacher of the good news of Jesus Christ. The wisdom of our presentations is rooted in scripture.

We offer a simple outline for each presentation, for we recognize that it must evolve out of the presenter's personality. While we provide examples, we invite readers to flesh out our outlines with personal experiences, insights, and anecdotes, and to infuse them with the presenter's unique personality.

The presentations are not tied to the themes of the retreats, so any talk can fit into any retreat. The talks for parents contain basic theological truths which help empower parents in their role as primary figures in their child's faith formation. Just as the children's retreats are built on where children are developmentally and experientially, so, too, are the parent retreats designed to address their experience. Each retreat helps parents grow in awareness of their own image of God and deepen their relationship with God. Each centers on two aspects of the spirituality of parenting: parents as a presence of God's love to children, and parents sharing their faith with their youngsters. We would encourage the adult leader to speak on those topics for which he or she has some conviction and with which he or she feels comfortable, even if it means giving the same talks over and over again. It's unlikely that any group would ever hear the same talk twice, given how quickly children grow up. But we've been delighted, too, with the freshness of a repeated presentation because of the diversity in personalities and the input of new participants.

Parent-Child Sharing Time

"[Parents], bring [your children] up with the training and instruction of the Lord" (Eph. 6:4).

Parents and children have been apart for approximately one hour by this time, each being renewed and refreshed in their encounters with God. It is time to share these experiences with each other.

During their own talk, the parents learned what their children would be hearing and doing in the children's activities. They know what story the little ones have heard, what their craft has been, and, like their children, they have encountered Jesus in their "heart room."

The purpose of the sharing time is to discuss each person's retreat experience. Even if a parent found parts of the retreat difficult (entering the "heart room," for example), it's okay to share that with the child. The sharing time can also be one of pointing out the omnipresence of God, in nature, in the church, in special friends. Until we provided parents with a hand-out of questions (p. 216), we were repeatedly frustrated. They would visit with each other, rather than share with their children. We realized they weren't sure what to say to their children.

Closing

Our hope is that, as your faith increases, our influence among you may be greatly enlarged... (2 Cor. 10:15b).

The closing is brief, but summarizes what the retreatants have experienced, re-affirming their friendship with Jesus. This can take the form of eliciting answers to questions, giving a three- or four-sentence statement, singing songs, praying, or a combination of these. Remember, though, to keep it brief. The children are ready to go home.

At the end of each retreat in this book, we include a closing prayer, to be adapted as you see fit. In our retreats, we have all parents and children stand and join hands, then repeat our words, one line at a time. The prayer addresses Jesus, our friend, thanks Jesus for always being with us, and repeats the theme of the day.

Child Care

He said to them, "Come away by yourselves to a deserted place and rest a while" (Mk. 6:31a).

We've found that our retreats draw greater numbers when we offer child care for younger and older siblings. These retreats focus on three- to six-year-olds and we try to ensure that attention is not drawn away from our little retreatants by the distractions of siblings who cannot adequately participate. It's always helpful to parents to provide child-care if facilities permit.

Note

1. Mary Terese Donze, *In My Heart Room* (Liguori, MO: Liguori Publications, 1982), 7.

3

Parent-Child Retreats

Schedule

We offer two types of retreats: a daytime parent-child experience and an evening bedtime retreat. The latter was a response to requests of working mothers and fathers who wanted to share this special time with their spouses and children. We follow these schedules:

Daytime Parent-Child Retreat

9:15 am	Families Arrive (put on nametags, greet each other and the retreat team)
9:30-9:45	Introduction and Focus
9:45-10:45	Parents' Session
9:45-10:30	Children's Activities
10:30-10:45	Children's Snack
10:45-11:15	Parent-Child Sharing Time
11:15-11:30	Closing
11:30	Group Lunch

Evening Bedtime Retreat

5:15-6:15 pm	Potluck Dinner
6:30-6:45	Introduction and Focus
6:45-7:45	Parents' Session
6:45-7:30	Children's Activities
7:30-7:45	Children's Bedtime Snack
7:45-8:15	Parent-Child Sharing Time
8:15-8:30	Closing

1-Fish

Matthew 4:18-20

Focus

Our young retreatants' best friend Jesus did something significant during his life on earth: he chose men and women to help him spread God's love. Many of their names are familiar to the children; others are not so recognizable. Peter, James, John, Andrew, Philip, Bartholomew, Matthew, Thomas, another James, Thaddaeus, Simon, Judas, Mary, Martha, another Mary (the mother of James and Joseph), Mary Magdalene, Elizabeth, and the mother of Zebedee's sons: they were ordinary people like us, but they became Jesus' best friends because they loved him and wanted to help him be a presence of God in the world.

Jesus is still choosing good friends to help him spread God's love, and their names are quite recognizable: Peter, Luz, Matthew, Corey, Jamal, Kelsey, Yumiko, Andrew, Teresa, Shareece, Jill, Jeffrey, Valerie, and all the other children on this retreat.

In this retreat, we introduce the fish as a Christian symbol and add the term "disciples of Jesus" to the children's vocabulary, interchanging "disciples," "friends," and "helpers."

The fish has long been a symbol for discipleship, beginning with Jesus' invitation to the first twelve to follow him and become fishers of all people. The fish continued to be significant following Jesus' death when, during centuries of persecution, Christians communicated to each other their affiliation with Jesus and with one another by means of the *ichthys*. This fish-shaped symbol emerged from the initial letters of the title "Jesus Christ, Son of God, Savior." The first letters of these Greek words spell *ichthys*, the Greek word for "fish."

The Fish Retreat brings awareness to our children that Jesus is inviting them to be fishers, friends, helpers in his work of spreading God's love. They are Jesus' cherished disciples.

Preparations Before the Retreat

1. Meet as a team to pray, read, discuss, understand, and interiorize the focus and scriptural basis of the retreat.
2. Discern which team members will be responsible for the gathering presentation, each of the three children's activities, and the adult retreat session.
3. Choose a topic from the Outlines for Parent Sessions (pp. 143-178).
4. Divide preparation responsibilities. Use the gifts of your community to lighten the load. Parents, teenagers, school children, and senior citizens can all help prepare.

Make the nametags.
Using the fish pattern (p. 184), prepare a different color nametag for each of the four team leaders. Then, using the same four colors, prepare one nametag for each child. You should have an equal number of each color of children's nametags. You will divide into groups by colors. As the children choose their nametags, the groups are formed.

Warning: Use safety pins or tape to attach nametags. For the safety of the children, do not use straight pins or string.

(Note: For an optional nametag, use the footprint pattern on p. 185).

Collect materials for the environment.
To arrange an attractive display on a table or piano in the gathering place, locate an aquarium or fish bowl with goldfish, netting, fishing pole, picture of Jesus.

Prepare for the gathering presentation.

Copy the *ichthys* (fish outline) to posterboard using the pattern on page 184. Make this illustration large.

Prepare the craft (p. 29).

First, gather materials:

▲ dessert-size paper plates, 1 per child
▲ scissors
▲ google eyes or large sequins
▲ glue
▲ collage materials: soda can pull-tabs, colored aquarium gravel
▲ pipe cleaners, 1 per child
▲ hole punch

Second, do the advance preparation:

1. Punch hole in top of each plate.
2. Cut triangular piece from one side of each plate to make a mouth.
3. Glue triangular piece at opposite end to make a tail.

Optional craft: Glitter-Fish Names
Gather materials:

▲ construction paper
▲ glue
▲ glitter

Locate the story.

Obtain *Now One Foot, Now the Other* by Tomie De Paola (New York: Putnam Publishing Group, 1980), or one of the following:

▲ *Swimmy* by Leo Lionni (New York: Knopf Books, 1987)
▲ *Hired Help for Rabbit* by Judy Delton (New York: Macmillan, 1992)
▲ *Rainbow Fish* by Marcus Pfister (Coral Gables, Fla.: North-South Books, 1992)
▲ *Fish is Fish* by Leo Lionni (New York: Random House, 1974)
▲ *It Could Still Be a Fish* by Allan Fowler (Chicago: Children's Press, 1990)
▲ *Fishes* by Brian Wildsmith (New York: Oxford University Press, 1987)

Select a movement activity.

Use Fish in the Ocean (p.31) or another of your choice.

Become familiar with the prayer (p. 31).

Purchase groceries and prepare the snack (p. 34).

▲ gummy worms

▲ fish-shaped crackers
▲ punch

Prepare for the parent-child sharing time (p. 34).
If you wish to present the Hooked on Jesus Fish Pond, you will need the following items:
▲ 1 fishing pole (made with a wooden pointer or yardstick, an 18" length of yarn, and a snap clothespin, paper clip or safety pin attached to the end)
▲ "fish" cut out of cardboard, each with a prize attached to one side and "helping" idea on the other (see list below)
▲ table or similar divider for adult to hide behind to put prizes on fish hook
▲ blue tablecloth to cover table
▲ tape player and children's tape (to distract children who are curious about behind-the-scenes operations)
▲ fish pond prizes: stickers, nickels, pennies, gummy fish, prayer cards, sticks of gum, or bookmarks

Write each of these "helping ideas" (ways to show God's presence) on the back of a different cardboard fish. Add others if you wish:
▲ pray for a sick person
▲ play with a younger brother/sister or neighbor
▲ sing to the baby
▲ hug a sad person
▲ talk to Jesus

Duplicate the Parent-Child Sharing Form (p. 216).

Preparations the Day of the Retreat

1. Gather as a team and pray.
2. Set out nametags and safety pins or tape. (No straight pins or strings!) Have exactly as many nametags as retreatants.
3. Have each retreat team member put on a different color nametag. This will later help the children divide into groups for their activities.
4. Atop a piano or table, create the environment in the gathering room with an arrangement of aquarium or fish bowl with goldfish, netting, fishing pole, and picture of Jesus.
5. Also in the gathering room, place a sample of the fish craft, a copy of *Now One Foot, Now the Other* or a book of your choice, and a Bible.
6. Gather all the materials for the craft and set out on tables in the room to be used for this activity.
7. Spread out so that at least one team member is greeting the retreatants as they

arrive, one is directing parents and younger siblings to the nursery, one is bringing retreatants and parents to the gathering room, and one is waiting in the gathering room.

8. Begin the retreat by warmly greeting the retreatants, then introducing the team members.
9. Sing together the gathering song "J-E-S-U-S" (p. 180).

Gathering Presentation

Look at these beautiful fish! *(Point to the fishbowl.)* How many do you think are in there? *(Take guesses.)* Let's count them together. *(Count with the children.)*

I'm going to tell you two important things about fish. Are you ready?

When our best friend Jesus lived on this earth, he often invited good friends to go fishing with him. One day he said to the best of his friends something like, "Instead of catching fish all the time, let's catch people, too. Not with our nets, of course. Let's catch people for God by our goodness and kindness and love." That's a strange idea, isn't it? How can we "catch" people?

What Jesus was asking his friends to do was to love God and share their excitement about loving God with their family and friends. He was asking them to be good, kind, and loving so people would know that God is good, kind, and loving, too.

Would you like to know what their names were, these special friends of Jesus? Some of them are names you know. I'll tell you, and if it's your name, too, or the name of someone in your family or of one of your friends, raise your hand, okay? Here they are.

(Say each name and give the children time to raise their hands.) Peter. Does anyone know someone named Peter? That's right. We know a lot of Peters, don't we? James. John. Elizabeth. Mary. Jesus had several friends named Mary. Andrew. Philip. Bartholomew. Matthew. Thomas. Martha. Another James. Thaddaeus. Simon. Judas.

But you know what? I know some more of Jesus' best friends, and they're right here in this room. Raise your hand if you're Jesus' friend.

That's right. Kristen is Jesus' friend, and so is Antonio. *(Continue reading the children's nametags until each child hears his or her name.)*

There's a word we use that means we're Jesus' friend. Are you ready to hear it? *Disciple. Disciple.* Can you say that with me? *Disciple.*

We're disciples of Jesus, boys and girls, and that means we're his friends. But it also means we're Jesus' helpers, because friends help each other, don't they? Jesus was trying to spread God's love all around and he is inviting each one of us to help him do that. It's not very hard. All we have to do is love Jesus and show everybody how excited we are that he's our best friend. We spread God's love all around by being good and kind and loving, just like Jesus. Do you think you can do that? So I told you the first thing about fish. Jesus asked his friends to "catch" people for God by being good and kind and loving. The second thing I want to show you is this. *(Hold up large illustration of ichthys.)*

What is this? That's right. A fish. After Jesus died, his friends told people about what a good person Jesus was, and before long he had lots more friends. But for a long time, some mean people were hurting Jesus' friends so Christians began drawing a fish for each other. The fish meant they were friends of Jesus, but the mean people didn't know what it meant. So for hundreds of years people drew fish for each other and then they knew the secret: who Jesus' friends were. We're Jesus' friends and helpers, girls and boys.

We're Jesus' disciples. Let's say that word again. *Disciples. Disciples.*

We have some fun activities to do now while your moms and dads listen to a talk for parents.

Let me show you what we'll be doing. *(Show the children the craft and tell them they'll also be talking to Jesus.)*

Mommy or Daddy will pick you up when we have our snack. Time to give each other a big hug. *(Allow time for hugs.)*

Now look at the color of your nametag. *(Have the children leave the room with the team leader who has the same colored nametag.)* Wave goodbye.

Children's Activities

The following three children's activities run simultaneously, and the children rotate through them until they've been to all three.

Activity 1: Craft

As the children work, we talk in our own words about how Jesus is their best friend and because of that, how he has invited them to come and help him spread God's love all around. They are Jesus' disciples, or helpers.

Remember, craft time is a time of reinforcing the theme of the retreat. Far more important than what we say or do is that we share our sense of wonder, conveying our awe that Jesus is with us always. Construct a Paper-Plate Fish Collage with the children (see illustration):

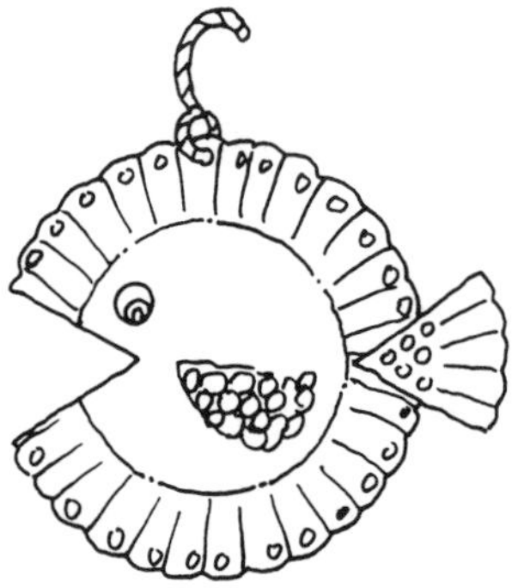

1. Help children write names on back of paper plate.
2. Generously apply glue over entire front of plate.
3. Instruct children to place google eye in appropriate place.
4. Glue soda can tabs onto remaining glued surface.
5. Add multi-colored aquarium rocks, making a rainbow design.
6. When dry, bend pipe cleaner through hole for hook hangers.

To simplify the craft:
Children can simply paint their fish with watercolors, make scales by applying inked fingerprints to fish, or sprinkle glitter onto glued surface of fish.

Optional craft: Glitter-Fish Names (see illustration):

1. On a sheet of construction paper, trace a fish-outline and the child's name in glue.
2. Allow each child to sprinkle glitter over the picture.
3. After glue dries, help children shake off excess glitter from pictures.

Announce to the children: Let's put your fish on this table. When you and Mommy or Daddy are ready to go home, you can come in here and get them. It's time now to go to Prayer *(or Story or Snack).* I *(or our helper)* will walk with you.

Activity 2: Story and Movement

Story: *Now One Foot, Now The Other* by Tomie De Paola (New York: Putnam Publishing Group, 1980)

Introduce the story.
We've talked today about being Jesus' disciples, his helpers. In this story, Bobby and his Grandpa Bob are both Jesus' helpers. Listen now as I read about these friends of Jesus and how they help each other.

Read the story.

Talk about the story.

▲ Do you remember what Grandpa Bob helped Bobby learn? *(to walk and build with blocks)*

- ▲ And how did Bobby help Grandpa Bob? *(He helped him eat, walk, and build a block tower after his stroke.)*
- ▲ There were some sad parts in this story, too. Do you remember any? *(When Grandpa was sick, he couldn't talk or walk.)*
- ▲ Did you notice that when Bobby was little, Grandpa Bob spent a lot of time with him? By helping Bobby learn, Grandpa Bob was being a friend like Jesus. He was being Jesus' helper. How was Bobby a helper for Jesus? *(He remained with his Grandpa throughout his recovery.)*
- ▲ You can be a helper for Jesus, too. When we go home, let's all look for ways we can be one of Jesus' helpers in our family. Come on over to the fishing pond and we'll try to catch something to remind us about Jesus' helpers. Jesus' helpers catch people for God by their goodness and kindness and love.

Do the movement: Fish in the Ocean.
Let's pretend we're fish swimming in the ocean. Listen to my song.

I'm a Little Fish
(Tune: "I'm a Little Teapot")
I'm a little fish and I can swim,
Here is my tail and here is my fin.
God wants me to have fun with my friends,
Just wiggle my tail and dive right in.

Let's lie down on our tummies and be fish. *(If there is no carpet, swim standing up.)* Let's pucker up our mouths like fish and blow bubbles up through the surface of the water. Ooh, this is fun. *(Do a few funny strokes—backstroke, sidestroke, breaststroke—for variety.)* Now let's swim in a school. All together.

(Sing song again while swimming.)

It's time now to move to Craft *(or Prayer, or Snack)*. I *(or our helper)* will walk with you.

Activity 3: Prayer

Note: Lead the children into a personal encounter with Jesus in the setting of a fishing trip. By tapping into their senses and imaginations, you transform the room into a lake shore, a favorite place that becomes more alive as the children's imaginations take over. Here they will meet Jesus, and during their prayer their friendship with him will deepen as they become familiar with him, listen to him, speak to him, and spend quiet time with him.

Lead the children.

On this retreat we've been talking a lot about fish. Look at your nametags. They're in the shape of a fish. How many of you have ever been fishing? I see Isabelle has. Isabelle, did you catch a fish or did it get away? It's exciting when you feel the fish on the end of your line, isn't it?

Let's pretend we're going on a fishing trip. First, we have to put on our big fishing boots. Let's bend down and pull the boots over our legs. Good job. Now let's tighten the straps on the top so they won't fall down in the water. Bend over again and pick up the pole. Is the string tight?

We can't go fishing without bait, can we? Look, I've got some worms in my bag. *(Open an imaginary bag and take out a worm for each child.)* When I hand you your worm, put it on the end of your line, okay? *(As you hand each child the worm, call that child's name out loud.)*

You're all great fisher people, I can tell. Now hold your fishing pole and don't let it drag. We don't want to lose our worms, do we? Follow me as I go down toward the water. Step over this tall grass here...take giant steps. Now we're near the water. Let's step on these rocks as we walk along the water's edge. *(Walk balancing with arms outstretched to the side.)* Be careful not to fall in. Good going. You're great at stepping on the rocks without falling in the water. Oh, look, do you see the bubbles on the water? I bet there are some fish over there. Let's go find out.

I have an idea. Let's all sit in a circle here by the edge of the water. Put your fishing pole behind you...watch out for the worm. I have something important to tell you.

This fun we're having on our fishing trip reminds me of a time Jesus was with his disciples. Ben, do you remember what a disciple is? That's right. A disciple is a friend of Jesus. A disciple is someone who helps Jesus. Cassie, do you think we can call ourselves Jesus' disciples? Yes. We're disciples, too, because disciples are Jesus' friends and helpers.

Some of Jesus' disciples were in a boat one day, trying to catch fish. They were out in that boat all day, but they couldn't catch any fish. They even stayed until after dark, and still no fish. Jesus knew these disciples were good people and that they wanted to help him, so he said, "Would you like to be fishers of people?" They were mixed up. "How can we catch people?" they asked Jesus. "Are they in the water with the fish? Do we have to use a worm?"

Jesus explained to his friends and helpers that we catch people by being good to them. We show people what Jesus is like every time we're kind. Can you think of a time when you did something helpful for someone else? *(Listen to answers.)* Sure. Those were the times you helped catch people for Jesus. Can you think of a time Mommy or Daddy did something good-hearted for you? *(Listen to answers.)* Those were times Mommy and Daddy showed you what Jesus is like. They're Jesus' disciples, too.

Before we go, let's become quiet and think of our friend Jesus.

(Invite the children to close their eyes and listen to the sounds of the boat and the lake. Allow 30-45 seconds, using this time to shift into quiet and calm.)

We are in our heart rooms, children. This is a place deep inside ourselves, and Jesus lives here. Imagine Jesus walking towards you. He's smiling and holding his arms out to you. Spend a little time looking at him. Notice what he looks like.

Jesus wants to say something to you. Listen...listen. What is he saying? *(Allow 45 seconds.)*

Now think of what you'd like to say to Jesus. You can tell him he's your best friend. Good. Tell Jesus how you would like to show others how Jesus loves them by being kind to them. Ask Jesus to help you be kind. Talk to Jesus now in your heart room. Don't say the words out loud. *(Allow 45 seconds.)* Jesus wants to hold you now. If it's all right with you, sit quietly with Jesus while he holds you. Know you are safe in his arms.

(Say softly:) You can open your eyes now, children.

(If the children are comfortable and can verbalize their prayer, ask them to share their talk with Jesus.)

What did Jesus look like? What did he say to you? Since Jesus is your best friend, what did you say to him?

(If time allows, retrace the trip back to the door of the room.)

Let's pick up our fishing poles. Follow me down the path next to the water. Be careful not to fall in. We don't want to scare those fish. Now let's take off our long fishing boots, fold them, and leave them on the ground to dry.

Thanks for fishing with me. Remember, we're fishers of people and helpers for Jesus every time we do something good for someone else. I think each time I see a fish, I'll remember that Jesus is my best friend and I'm his disciple. How about you?

It's time now to move to Craft *(or Story or Snack).* I *(or our helper)* will walk with you.

Snack

After the children have rotated through all three activities, lead them to the snack room to feast on gummy worms candy, fish-shaped crackers, and punch. Their parents will meet them here after the children finish eating.

In the event the parents are delayed, use the Hooked on Jesus Fish Pond (below), or do either of the Fish Retreat Activities, pages 186 and 187.

Parent-Child Sharing Time

After the adult session, parents pick up their children in the snack room to begin their sharing time. Distribute the Parent-Child Sharing Time Form (p. 216). Have the Hooked on Jesus Fish Pond set up nearby for parents and children to enjoy.

Introduce this activity by saying: Remember how Jesus invited his friends to go fishing with him? He said, "Come with me, friends." When we're Jesus' disciples, we find lots of surprises as we help Jesus spread God's love all around. Let's fish for some of those surprises.

Give each child a turn to hold the fishing pole and drop the line behind the table where a helper is hiding. The helper puts a cardboard "fish" (to which both a prize and a "helping idea" have been attached) on the end of the line, then tugs the line to signal the child to pull it up.

Parents can read the helper idea to the child and talk about it.

If you choose not to offer this activity, retreatants can go outside for a nature walk. If not, they might want to find a corner to sit in, parent and child together; take a walk through the church; or even spread out blankets throughout the room. We allow approximately twenty minutes, asking parents and children to return to the gathering room at the appointed time for our closing. During the parent presentation, the adult leader has suggested several questions designed to facilitate parent-child sharing:

- ▲ Tell me about the story you heard.
- ▲ What do you like about the craft you made?
- ▲ What was it like when you met Jesus in your heart room?
- ▲ What did Jesus look like?
- ▲ How did it feel to be with Jesus?
- ▲ When I met Jesus in my heart room, he said...I did...
- ▲ What did Jesus say to you? What did you do?

As retreatants are returning from sharing time, gather together and sing "J-E-S-U-S" (p. 180).

When all have arrived, begin the closing prayer.

Closing Prayer

Join hands in a circle and have parents and children repeat each line.

> Jesus,
> whenever I see a fish I'll remember
> that I'm your disciple.
> I want to help you
> spread God's love
> all around.
> We're best friends.
> *Amen.*

Remind the children to take their craft home with them.

Playing Follow-the-Leader, swim like fish to the door.

2-Bubbles

(Luke 10:21; Matthew 19:13; Matthew 18:1-4)

Focus

We share children's fascination with bubbles, comparing them with the joyful feeling that bubbles up within us when we hear good news. "Good news" is an expression they'll hear throughout their spiritual journey, so we introduce it to them in this retreat.

We tell the children about good news we've received recently (e.g., our family is expecting a baby, our grandparents are coming to visit), then ask one or two to share their own good news (e.g., they found the toy they thought they'd lost, their mom isn't sick anymore). Then we announce some extraordinarily good news: Jesus is our best friend.

But the good news gets better. Jesus really loves children and wants to spend time with them. In fact, during his life on earth, he repeatedly told adults to be more like children. Children bubble over with fun, excitement, and laughter.

And, most important of all, children know how to be friends.

Adults sometimes forget how to be friends with Jesus. They become goal-oriented, heady, and independent. But Jesus wants adults to let go and enter into a trusting love relationship with him.

The good news that Jesus has a special place in his heart for children means that all the youngsters at this retreat can help grown-ups remember how to be Jesus' friend by telling the adults in their lives how excited they themselves are to be Jesus' friend.

Preparations Before the Retreat

1. Meet as a team to pray, read, discuss, understand, and interiorize the focus and scriptural basis of the retreat.
2. Discern which team members will be responsible for the gathering presentation, each of the three children's activities, and the adult retreat session.
3. Choose an adult retreat topic from the Outlines for Parent Sessions (pp. 143-178).
4. Divide the following preparation responsibilities. Use the gifts of your community to lighten the load. Parents, teenagers, school children, and senior citizens can all help prepare.

Make the nametags.
Using the balloon pattern (p. 188), prepare a different color nametag for each of the four team leaders. Then, using the same four colors, prepare one nametag for each child. On the bottom of each balloon, tie a 6" thin ribbon, scissor-curled. You should have an equal number of each color of children's nametags. You will divide into groups by colors. As the children choose their nametags, the groups are formed.

Warning: Use safety pins or tape to attach nametags. For the safety of the children, do not use straight pins or string.

(Note: For an optional nametag, use the bubble pattern, p. 189. Duplicate it on pink paper to resemble bubble gum.)

Collect materials for the environment.
To arrange an attractive display on table or piano in gathering room, locate several colorful bottles of bubble solution, bubble makers of your own, bubble bath, balloons (as translucent as possible), and large posters and framed pictures of children of all ages and races.

Prepare the craft (p. 42).

First, gather materials for Bubble Cans:

▲ empty soda pop cans, rinsed, 1 per child
▲ one funnel
▲ blank white paper, one sheet per child
▲ 4" squares of aluminum foil, 1 per child
▲ rubber bands, 1 per child
▲ ingredients for bubble solution: dishwashing liquid, glycerine (available at drugstores), sugar or corn syrup, water
▲ measuring cup
▲ bubble wands: strawberry mesh baskets, bathroom tissue tubes, 6-pack plastic can holders, bent clothes hangers or pipe cleaners, plastic drinking straws connected with 36" string (see illustration), or your own
▲ crayons or markers
▲ clear tape
▲ paper towels

Second, do the advance preparation:

1. Make bubble solution, one cup per child: gently stir together 1 cup dishwashing liquid, 2 cups warm water, 3-4 tablespoons glycerine, and 1 teaspoon sugar. (Or 1/2 cup dishwashing liquid and 5 cups clean cold water.) Remove any small bubbles from the top.
2. Cut white paper to cover the aluminum cans as wrap-around labels.

Bubble tips:

Bubbles work best on moist, cloudy days. On dry days, the moisture from nearby grass, trees, or bushes might be helpful. The longer the bubble solution sits, the better the bubbles it makes.

Optional craft: Love Bubbles

Love Bubbles is a paper-chain craft. Photocopy for each child the pattern on page 190; precut eight strips with one phrase on each strip: *parent-child retreat, Jesus, love, just, bubbles, me, over, [child's name].*

Locate the story.

Obtain *Bubble, Bubble* by Mercer Mayer (Roxbury, Conn.: Rain Bird Products, 1992), or one of the following:

▲ *The Relatives Came* by Cynthia Rylant (New York: Scholastic Books, 1985)
▲ *I Hate to Take a Bath* by Judith Barrett (New York: Four Winds Press, 1975)
▲ *Bubbles, Bubbles Everywhere* by Melvin Berger (New York: Newbridge Early Science Big Books, 1994)

Select a movement activity.
Use "Balloon Bubble Ball" (p. 44) or one of your choice. To prepare Balloon Bubble Ball: Blow up half as many balloons as children, plus 3-4 extras in case some of them pop. Store in a plastic trash bag.

Become familiar with the prayer (p. 45).
Gather materials:
▲ 2 large towels

Purchase groceries and prepare the snack.
Root Beer Floats:
▲ vanilla ice cream
▲ root beer
▲ cups
▲ spoons
▲ straws
▲ napkins or paper towels to wipe up overflowing foam!
or
Jello Bubbles:
▲ 4 3-oz. packages of blue or red Jello
▲ 2-1/2 cups water or apple juice

Prepare the snack:
In large bowl, stir 2-1/2 cups boiling water or boiling apple juice into Jello until completely dissolved. Pour into 13" x 9" pan. Do *not* add cold water. Refrigerate at least 3 hours or until firm. Dip bottom of pan in warm water for 15 seconds. Cut into "bubbles" (circles) with cookie cutter. Lift from pan. Makes about 24 bubbles.

Take-Home Treat:
▲ bubble gum

Duplicate the Parent-Child Sharing Form (p. 216).

Preparations the Day of the Retreat

1. Gather as a team and pray.
2. Set out nametags and safety pins or tape (warning: no straight pins or strings). Have exactly as many nametags as retreatants.
3. Have each retreat team member wear a different colored nametag. This will later help the children divide into groups for their activities.
4. Atop a piano or table, create the environment in the gathering room with an arrangement of colorful bottles of bubble solution, bubble makers of your own, bubble bath, clusters of translucent balloons, and large posters and pictures of children of all ages and races.
5. Also in the gathering room, place a sample of the picnic basket craft, a copy of *Bubble, Bubble* or an optional book, and a Bible.
6. Gather all the materials for the craft and set out on tables in the room to be used for this activity.
7. Spread out so that at least one team member is greeting the retreatants as they arrive, one is directing parents and younger siblings to the nursery, one is bringing retreatants and parents to the gathering room, and one is waiting in the gathering room.
8. Begin the retreat by warmly greeting the retreatants, then introducing the team members.
9. Sing together the gathering song "J-E-S-U-S" (p. 180).

Gathering Presentation

Girls and boys, watch this. *(Blow some bubbles.)* Raise your hand if bubbles make you feel happy inside. *(Pause.)*

Now, this time when I blow bubbles, everyone say "ooh" *(long and drawn out).*

This time, everyone say "oh" *(long and drawn out).*

And now let's all say "ah" *(long and drawn out).*

We sure like bubbles, don't we? Bubbles always remind me of joy and fun and happiness. When I feel really happy, it makes me feel like I have bubbles inside me. I really don't; it just feels like I do.

I feel happy and bubbly inside when I hear good news. How about you? In fact, I just got some good news that makes me really happy. *(Share some good news with the children.)*

What kind of good news makes you happy? Who would like to share some good news with us?

Well, now I have some more good news for you, the most exciting news I've ever heard. The good news is that Jesus is our best friend.

This good news gets even better. Not only is Jesus our best friend, but Jesus is always telling grown-ups to be more like children. Jesus loves children so much. Listen to what Jesus told the grown-ups. It's right here in his special book, the Bible. He said, "I give praise to you, Father, Lord of heaven and earth, for although you have hidden these things from the wise and the learned you have revealed them to the childlike" (Mt. 11:25b). Jesus was saying, "Good for you, God. You tell children things you can't tell adults because you know the children will understand."

Or how about this one: "Then children were brought to him that he might lay his hands on them and pray. The disciples rebuked them, but Jesus said, 'Let the children come to me, and do not prevent them; for the kingdom of heaven belongs to such as these'" (Mt. 19:13-14). Moms and dads, can you show your little ones how Jesus laid his hands on the children? *(Pause.)* Jesus sure does love children, doesn't he?

And listen to this *(read slowly, with emphasis)*: "At that time the disciples approached Jesus and said, 'Who is the greatest in the kingdom of heaven?' He called a child over *(ask one child to come forward and stand before the group),* placed it in their midst, and said, 'Amen, I say to you, unless you turn and become like children, you will not enter the kingdom of heaven. Whoever humbles himself like this child is the greatest in the kingdom of heaven'" (Mt. 18:1-4).

Children are important to Jesus, and he wants to spend time with you. Do you know why? Because children like you bubble over with fun, excitement, and laughter. And you know how to be friends.

Some grown-ups have forgotten how to be friends with Jesus. And Jesus tells them that if they would let themselves bubble over with fun, excitement, and laughter—if they would just be more like children—then they could be good friends with Jesus, too.

You know what? There's more good news. You can help adults remember how to be Jesus' friend by telling them how excited you are to be his friend.

Let's all sing a song about how the good news that Jesus is our best friend feels like bubbles inside us.

(One or more team members blow bubbles while all are singing.)

The Bubbles Song
(Tune: "My Bonnie Lies Over the Ocean")

My bubbles mean Jesus lives in me.
My bubbles mean Jesus loves me.
My bubbles mean he is my best friend.
My bubbles are good news to me.
Bubbles, bubbles,
My bubbles are good news to me, to me.
Jesus, Jesus,
Jesus is good news to me.

What great singing! We have some fun activities to do now while your moms and dads stay here and listen to a talk for parents.

Let me show you what we'll be doing. *(Show the children the craft and story, and tell them they'll also be talking to Jesus.)*

Mommy or Daddy will pick you up when we have our snack. Time to give each other a big hug. *(Wait)*

Now look at the color of your nametag. *(Have the children leave the room with the team leader who has the same colored nametag.)* Wave goodbye.

Children's Activities

The following three children's activities run simultaneously, and the children rotate through them until they've been to all three.

Activity 1: Craft

Warning: For the children's safety, bubbles are best demonstrated outdoors. Spilled solution makes for slippery floors and can be dangerous. If weather does not permit outdoor craft time, carefully blow bubbles onto an area where children will not walk. Mention that each child will have his or her own container of bubbles and a tool to take home. Insist they save their bubbles to try at home by placing them in the hands of the adults as they leave after the final prayer.

We demonstrate how to blow bubbles from a large bowl of bubble solution and one or more homemade bubble tools. Remembering the time limit, we invite each child to take a turn blowing one each. As the children work, we talk in our own words about how Jesus is their best friend and how Jesus would love to be invited next time they blow bubbles.

Remember, craft time is time of reinforcing the theme of the retreat. Far more important than what we say or do is that we share our sense of wonder, conveying our awe that Jesus is with us always.

Decorate Bubble Cans with the children:

1. Children decorate their white label with markers.
2. Children dip measuring cup into large container of bubble solution and funnel it into their can.
3. Helper blots children's cans dry.
4. Helper tapes labels to children's cans.
5. Children or helpers write names on cans.
6. Children or helpers fold foil over tops of cans and secure with rubber band.
7. Helper sets a bubble tool next to each can.

Optional craft: Love Bubbles
To make Love Bubbles, have children bend the labeled strips in circles and link them into a chain. (See illustration on page 190.)

Announce to the children: Let's put your Bubble Cans on this table. When you and Mommy or Daddy are ready to go home, you can come in here and get it. It's time now to go to Prayer *(or Story or Snack)*. I *(or our helper)* will walk with you.

Activity 2: Story and Movement

Story: *Bubble, Bubble* by Mercer Mayer (Roxbury, Conn.: Rain Bird Products, 1992)

Introduce the story.

▲ Do you believe in magic bubbles?

▲ Listen to what happens when the child in this story buys a magic bubble maker.

Read the story, taking ample time to show the pictures.

Talk about the story.

▲ How did the child bubble his troubles away? *(He blew bubbles in shapes of things that could "take care of them.")*

▲ Wouldn't it be nice if we could bubble our troubles away? Just imagine if you could blow a bubble in the shape of a bicycle and magically ride to the park to play. Or what if someone were bothering you and you could blow such a huge bubble around him that he wouldn't bother you anymore?

▲ What kind of bubble would you like to magically blow?

▲ Well, the good news is that even if we can't magically blow bubbles to take away our troubles, our friend Jesus is always there for us. You know how you feel when bubbles are floating around you? Do you feel happy inside? Jesus talks in his special book, the Bible, about how happy he feels because children are his special friends.

▲ He wants grown-ups to be his friends, too. I'll bet you could help grown-ups remember the good news that Jesus is their friend. When you take your bubbles home today, your parents will see how Jesus' love bubbles over in you, and maybe they'll remember to meet Jesus in their heart room to talk with him about their friendship.

Do the movement: Balloon Bubble Ball.

Say: We have a game to play with these balloons. They remind me of bubbles.

Decide who will be partners by saying, "Double, bubble, double, bubble" while touching each child on the shoulder. Give each child to whom you say "double" a balloon. Pair the remaining children with those who have balloons, facing each other three to five feet apart. Tell *doubles* to tap their balloon gently in the air to *bubbles,* their own partner. The object of the game is to keep the balloons in the air.

Enjoy the glee that Jesus spoke of, which children know so well. Encourage positive remarks to each other, such as "almost," "nice try," and "good job."

Say: Now it's time to move to Craft *(or Prayer or Snack)*. Let's walk together.

Activity 3: Prayer

Note: We lead the children into a personal encounter with Jesus in the setting of a swimming pool. By tapping into their senses and imaginations, we transform the room into a pool, a wonderful place that becomes more alive as the children's imaginations take over. Here they will meet Jesus, and during their prayer their friendship with him will deepen as they become familiar with him, listen to him, speak to him, and spend quiet time with him.

Lead the children.

We've been talking about bubbles this morning, haven't we? I know a fun place where we see all kinds of bubbles in the water. Do you remember when you were at a swimming pool? I remember jumping in, putting my face in the water, and blowing out bubbles. Come follow me and we'll pretend we're going to the pool with our friends. We'll have a chance to talk to Jesus there. It's surprising to think we could talk to Jesus at a swimming pool, but we can.

Daniel, you carry this beach towel and Angie, you bring this one. *(Hand out two large beach towels for all the children to sit on later.)* Let's go past the gate. Give the lady your money. Good, now we have to find a place where we can spread the towels out and sit after we get out of the water. Follow me. Be careful as we walk among these people lying out in the sun. Good job.

Let's wind through these picnic tables. Great. Oh, look. Slices of watermelon! Help yourself, and be sure to say thank you. I have an idea. Let's see who can spit the seeds the farthest...aim for the lawn.

Look over there. I see a great place to sit right under that big tree. *(Name)* and *(Name),* would you spread the towels for us? Thanks. Let's all sit down right here.

Look at those boys and girls in the shallow end throwing the big red ball. I bet they'd let us play with them later on. Oh, look at the deep end. See that girl on the diving board? Watch her jump up and down. Wow, now she's diving into the water. What a big splash! Did you get wet?

Let's jump in, girls and boys. Now put your face in the water and blow out air. Look at the bubbles you just made. Let's do it again. We made some great bubbles, didn't we? Bubbles always remind me of good news because they're kind of tickly. And the good news I know is that Jesus is our best friend. Jesus loves children so much.

Let's get out now and go dry off on our towels. Everyone find a place just for you on one of these towels.

(After the children have settled on the beach towels, invite them to close their eyes and listen to the sounds of people having fun at the swimming pool. Allow 30-45 seconds, using this time to shift into quiet and calm.)

We are in our heart rooms, children. This is a place deep inside ourselves, and Jesus lives here. See Jesus walking towards you. He's smiling and holding his arms out to you. Spend a little time looking at him. Notice what he looks like.

Jesus wants to say something to you. Listen...listen. What is he saying? *(Allow 45 seconds.)*

Now think of what you'd like to say to Jesus because he's your best friend and he loves you so much. Talk to Jesus now in your heart room. Don't say the words out loud. *(Allow 45 seconds.)*

Jesus wants to hold you now. If it's all right with you, sit quietly with Jesus while he holds you. Know you are safe in his arms.

(Say softly:) You can open your eyes now, children.

(If the children are comfortable and can verbalize their prayer, ask them to share their talk with Jesus.)

What did Jesus look like? What did he say to you? Since Jesus is your best friend, what did you say to him?

(If time allows, retrace the trip from the pool back to the door of the room.)

Let's pick up the towels. Walk past the picnic tables. Hey, the watermelon's all gone. Walk past these people. Watch out not to step on anyone. Wave goodbye to the ticket lady. What a wonderful, fun place to be able to talk to Jesus. We can come back anytime we want.

It's time to go to Story *(or Craft or Snack)* now. I *(or our helper)* will walk with you.

Snack

After the children have rotated through all three activities, lead them to the snack room. Their parents will meet them here after the children finish their root beer floats or Jello Bubbles.

In the event the parents are delayed, create the Jesus Friendship Hats found on page 183.

Parent-Child Sharing Time

After the adult session, parents pick up their children in the snack room to begin their sharing time. Distribute the Parent-Child Sharing Time Form (p. 216). If weather permits, retreatants can go outside for a nature walk. If not, they might want to find a corner to sit in, parent and child together; take a walk through the church; or even spread out blankets throughout the room. We allow approximately twenty minutes, asking parents and children to return to the gathering room at the appointed time for our closing.

As retreatants are returning from sharing time, gather together and sing "J-E-S-U-S" (p. 180) or the "The Bubbles Song" (p. 41).

When all have arrived, begin the closing prayer.

Closing Prayer

Join hands in a circle and have parents and children repeat each line.

Jesus,
help me to remember
each time I play with bubbles
that you live in me,
that you love me,
and that we're best friends.
This good news
is bubbly good news.
Amen.

Remind the children to take their craft home with them. Invite the parents and children to take a piece of bubble gum as they leave.

3-Valentine's Day

(John 15: 15-16; 1 John 4:19; Matthew 22: 37-39)

Focus

On Valentine's Day, we celebrate our ongoing Christian call to love God, ourselves, and each other. The children will undoubtedly have parties and the exchange of valentines in their neighborhoods, preschools, or kindergartens. But in this retreat, we provide our young retreatants an understanding of why we celebrate a day of love. We love because God loved us first.

First, we love Jesus. Our friendship is important to him. He loves us, and as our best friend, he wants us to love him in return. Just being at this retreat is one way of loving Jesus, because we're spending time with him. So, too, is talking to Jesus whenever we're angry, sad, glad, or scared. And, as the children will learn today, going to our "heart room" in prayer and listening to Jesus there is another way of loving him.

We love ourselves, too. Loving ourselves involves taking care of ourselves as well as appreciating who we are. When we brush our teeth or go to bed when our parents tell us to, we're loving ourselves. When we look in the mirror and notice how wonderfully we are made—with eyes to see and ears to hear—we're loving ourselves. We love ourselves, too, when we give ourselves a big hug.

And we love each other, the third element of the Great Commandment. Sending valentines to our friends is a sign of our love. Inviting them to play, and sometimes even letting them be first, also shows our friends we love them. But perhaps the most important way to love others is to tell them how much we like them—right out loud.

Jesus' message of love points to the reason valentines are shaped like hearts. We love with all our hearts because Jesus loved us first.

Preparations Before the Retreat

1. Meet as a team to pray, read, discuss, understand, and interiorize the focus and scriptural basis of the retreat.
2. Discern which team members will be responsible for the gathering presentation, each of the three children's activities, and the adult retreat session.
3. Choose a topic from the Outlines for Parent Sessions (pp. 143-178).
4. Divide preparation responsibilities. Use the gifts of your community to lighten the load. Parents, teenagers, school children, and senior citizens can all help prepare.

Make the nametags.
Using the heart pattern (p. 191), prepare a different color nametag for each of the four team leaders. Then, using the same four colors, prepare one nametag for each child. You should have an equal number of each color of children's nametags. You will divide into groups by colors. As the children choose their nametags, the groups are formed.

Warning: Use safety pins or tape to attach nametags. For the safety of the children, do not use straight pins or string.

(Note: For an optional nametag, use the "Sonshine" pattern on p. 192.)

Collect materials for the environment.
To arrange an attractive display on a table or piano in the gathering place, locate pink, red and white balloons, various sizes of hearts and valentines, a picture of Jesus, large ball, and a mirror.

Prepare the craft (p. 53).
First, gather materials for Heart Room Crafts:
▲ white paper doilies, 1 per child

- ▲ red construction paper, 1 sheet per child
- ▲ 1-1/2" wide red velvet, satin, or craft ribbon, 18" per child
- ▲ glue
- ▲ narrow-tipped black marker
- ▲ gold braid or thin white lace, 10" per child

Second, do the advance preparation:

1. On each doily, write *JESUS* exactly in center with black marker, filling a space no more than 1" high and 2" wide.
2. Cut paper hearts, 1 per child.
3. With craft knife or very sharp scissors, cut "window" in center of each heart, 2-1/2" wide by 2" tall.
4. Fold top end of ribbon under 1" and glue or staple shut, leaving an opening for stringing lace.

Optional craft: "I Am Wonderfully Made" Mirror
Gather materials:

- ▲ construction paper
- ▲ Mylar or aluminum foil
- ▲ glue

Locate the story.
Obtain *Guess How Much I Love You* by Sam McBratney (Cambridge, Mass.: Candlewick Press, 1994) or one of the following:

- ▲ *Will I Have a Friend?* by Miriam Cohen (New York: Macmillan Child Group, 1989)
- ▲ *My Friend John* by Charlotte Zolotow (New York: Harper Junior, 1968)
- ▲ *Wilfrid Gordon McDonald Partridge* by Mem Fox (Brooklyn, N.Y.: Kane Miller, 1985)
- ▲ *Hello, Amigos!* by Tricia Brown (New York: Holt, 1992)
- ▲ *Rosie and Michael* by Judith Viorst (New York: Macmillan, 1974)

Select a movement activity.
Use Here We Go Hopping Round the Room (p. 55) or one of your choice.

Become familiar with the prayer (p. 56).
Cut one strip of red construction paper (2" x 8") per child, one for the adult prayer leader, and one with *Jesus* printed on it.

Purchase groceries and prepare the snack.
Heart Waffles:

▲ round frozen waffles (remove a small wedge to make each waffle heart-shaped.)
▲ milk

or

Heart Pretzels:

▲ knotted pretzels (point out that pretzels are shaped like hearts)
▲ juice

Duplicate the Parent-Child Sharing Form (p. 216).

Preparations the Day of the Retreat

1. Gather as a team and pray.
2. Set out nametags and safety pins or tape (warning: no straight pins or strings). Have exactly as many nametags as retreatants.
3. Have each retreat team member put on a different colored nametag. This will later help the children divide into groups for their activities.
4. Atop a piano or table, create the environment in the gathering room with an arrangement of balloons, hearts and valentines, hand mirror, and picture of Jesus.
5. Also in the gathering room, place a sample of the Heart Room Craft, a copy of *Guess How Much I Love You* or optional book, and a Bible.
6. Gather all the materials for the craft and set out on tables in the room to be used for this activity.
7. Spread out so that at least one team member is greeting the retreatants as they arrive, one is directing parents and younger siblings to the nursery, one is bringing retreatants and parents to the gathering room, and one is waiting in the gathering room.
8. Begin the retreat by warmly greeting the retreatants, then introducing the team members.
9. Sing together the gathering song "J-E-S-U-S" (p. 180).

Gathering Presentation

Look at all these hearts! It makes me think about Valentine's Day. What about you? How many of you have seen valentines before? Who knows why we give our friends valentines? *(Wait for responses.)* That's right. We give valentines to show we love our friends. Do you know why valentines are shaped like hearts? It's because we love with our heart. Now I have something very important to tell you. Are you ready? I'm going to tell you why we love our family and friends. Listen. We love because God loved us first. God loved us first, girls and boys. Can you say that with me? Say, "God loved me first." *(Wait for echo.)*

In God's special book, the Bible *(hold up Bible),* Jesus told us that we're his friends, and then he told us whom we should love. This is what he said: "You shall love the Lord, your God, with all your heart, with all your soul, and with all your mind. This is the greatest and first commandment. The second is like it: You shall love your neighbor as yourself" (Mt. 22:37-39).

Jesus told us to love three groups of people: Jesus, each other, and ourselves. Let's count on our fingers: Jesus, each other, and ourselves. Jesus told us to love him because he loved us first. We're best friends, right? Anytime we want, we can say, "I love you, Jesus." Another way we're showing Jesus we love him is by coming to this retreat and spending special time with Jesus. And I know of another way we can tell Jesus we love him. We can talk to Jesus anytime we feel angry, glad, sad, or scared. He wants to know about it. Our friendship is important to Jesus. *(Lower the volume of your voice, drawing the children in more intimately.)* Now I have a secret for you, children. Can you hear me? Did you know that Jesus lives inside your heart? He really does. Right here inside your heart. Let's all put our hands on our hearts. *(Remember to put your left hand on your right chest so that the children will mirror you accurately.)* Jesus lives right here. And you know what else? You can visit him there anytime you want. We're going to learn how to do that today—to visit Jesus in our heart room—and that's one way we can show Jesus we love him.

Jesus also told us to love each other. That's why we send valentines to each other. It shows we love. We also show our friends and family that we love them by playing with them. Sometimes we can even let them choose what to play, and that would be a loving thing, right? And you know what? We can tell our friends and family we love them—right out loud. Let's try that right now. How loud can you say it? Let's go. "I LOVE YOU." *(Wait for echo.)*

Jesus told us to love *(count on fingers)* Jesus, each other, and...who else? That's right: ourselves. Can anybody think of a way you can love yourself? *(Welcome ideas.)* Well, we could give ourselves a great big hug. Let's all do that right now. We sure do love ourselves! We also love ourselves when we take care of our bodies. We go to sleep when we're told to, or brush our teeth so they stay healthy. *(Hold up hand mirror.)* Even just looking in the mirror and saying, "I sure like my eyes," or "It's nice to have two ears," is loving ourselves. We really are wonderful children, aren't we? Just look in this mirror and you'll see a wonderful, wonderful child. *(Hold mirror in front of each child so he or she can see him/herself.)* Let's see if we can remember whom Jesus told us to love. *(Count on fingers:)* We love Jesus...each other...and ourselves. Would you like to sing a song about this?

Friend Song

(Tune: "Here We Go Round the Mulberry Bush")

Who will be a friend of mine, friend of mine, friend of mine?
Who will be a friend of mine
On this special day?

I will be your loving friend, loving friend, loving friend,
I will be your loving friend
On this special day.

Jesus is our best friend, too, best friend, too, best friend, too.
Jesus is our best friend, too,
On this special day.

What great singing! We have some fun activities to do now while your moms and dads stay here and listen to a talk for parents. Let me show you what we'll be doing. *(Show the children the craft and story, and tell them they'll also be talking to Jesus.)* Mommy or Daddy will pick you up when we have our snack. Time to give each other a big hug. *(Wait.)* Now look at the color of your nametag. *(Have the children leave the room with the team leader who has the same colored nametag.)* Wave goodbye.

Children's Activities

The following three children's activities run simultaneously, and the children rotate through them until they've been to all three.

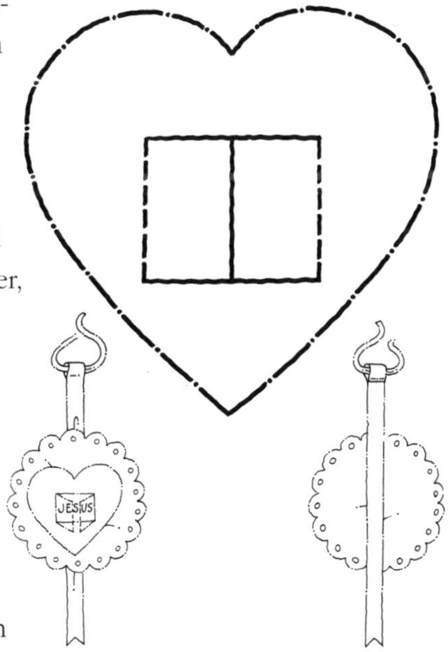

Activity 1: Craft

As the children work, we talk in our own words about how Jesus is our best friend and how he told us to love him, to love each other, and to love ourselves. We love because Jesus loved us first. Remember, craft time is a time of reinforcing the theme of the retreat. Far more important than what we say or do is that we share our sense of wonder, conveying our awe that Jesus is with us always.

Construct Heart Room Crafts with the children (see illustration, right):

1. Glue red heart on top of doily, making sure "window" lands directly over the word *JESUS.* (Children may need assistance.)
2. Glue doily to ribbon.
3. String 10" piece of gold cord or narrow lace through opening at top of ribbon and tie ends together.

To simplify the craft:
On an 8" strip of red ribbon, children glue three 2-1/2" x 2" pink or white paper hearts vertically. On the top heart are the words *Jesus is*; the middle heart is blank; and the bottom heart reads *friend*. The children can print their names in the middle heart. Take time to read the finished product aloud to the children.

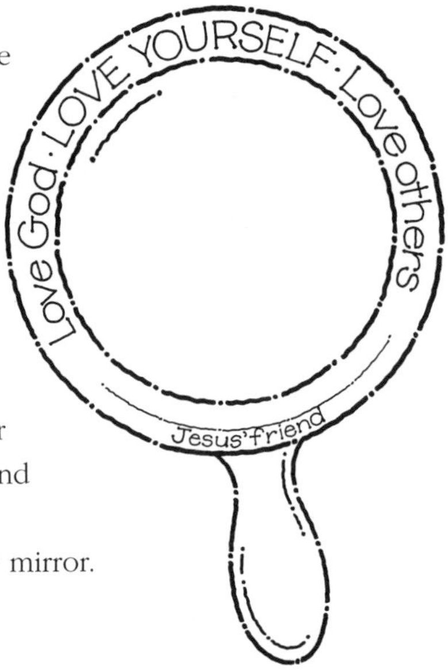

Optional craft: "I Am Wonderfully Made" Mirror
1. Cut mirror-shapes from construction paper and circles from Mylar or foil.
2. Children glue mylar circle in center of paper mirror.
3. Children write names on mirror handle as a reminder to love themselves.

Announce to the children: Let's put your Heart Room Craft on this table. When you and Mommy or Daddy are ready to go home, you can come in here and get it. It's time now to go to Prayer *(or Story or Snack).* I *(or our helper)* will walk with you.

Activity 2: Story and Movement

Story: *Guess How Much I Love You* by Sam McBratney (Cambridge, Mass.: Candlewick Press, 1994)

Introduce the story.
In this story, Little Nutbrown Hare is going to bed. Big Nutbrown Hare listens carefully as Little Nutbrown tells him a very important message. As I read, listen for the message, "Guess how much I love you."

Read the story.

Talk about the story.
- ▲ What words did Little Nutbrown want Big Nutbrown to hear? *("Guess how much I love you?")*

- ▲ What did Big Nutbrown say back to him? *("Oh, I don't think I could guess that.")*
- ▲ Little Nutbrown tries to show how much by stretching his arms as wide as they can go. How would this look?
- ▲ Little Nutbrown tries some other ways to show how much he loves Big Nutbrown. Raise your hand if you remember some of them. Now don't use any words; show us what they did together. *(He reached as high as he could reach, stood on his hands, and reached up the trunk with his feet, hopped as high as he could. If necessary, whisper a clue into a retreatant's ear and help him/her pantomime it.)*
- ▲ Little Nutbrown and Big Nutbrown loved each other very much, didn't they?
- ▲ When they ran out of ways to tell about their love using their bodies, they talked about it using God's creation *(as far as the river, over the hills, right up to the moon)*. Their love is so big it can't be measured. As the story ends, Big Nutbrown settles Little Nutbrown into his bed of leaves and leans over and kisses him goodnight. However much Little Nutbrown loves, Big Nutbrown loves him more.
- ▲ I'll bet none of you has a friend named Little Nutbrown. Tell us the names of some of your friends and people you love. Raise your hand and I'll call your name. *(Listen to three or four.)*
- ▲ And what do you like to do with these special people? *(Listen to two or three.)*
- ▲ Well, whenever we're with our friends, our best friend Jesus, who always loves us more, is right there with us. Having friends and being a good friend were important to Jesus, too. Come over here and we'll play a game with our friends from this retreat.

Do the movement: Here We Go Hopping Round the Room.
Let's play a moving game. Remember our song, "Who will be a friend of mine"? Let's sing the same tune, but change the words. First we'll hop, then we'll jump, then we'll do whatever we think of. Ready? Let's play:

> Here we go hopping round the room,
> Round the room, round the room.
> Here we go hopping round the room
> On this special day.
>
> Here we go jumping... *(skipping, crawling, etc.)*

It's time now to move to Craft *(or Prayer or Snack)*. I *(or our helper)* will walk with you.

Activity 3: Prayer

We lead the children into a personal encounter with Jesus. During their prayer, their friendship with him will deepen as they become familiar with him, listen to him, speak to him, and spend quiet time with him.

Lead the children.

Today we've been thinking about hearts and Valentine's Day. You know, there are lots of things we can do to make our hearts strong and healthy. For one thing, we can walk. Why don't you line up behind me and we'll walk around the room? Follow me as we walk slowly...now let's walk faster. Try to stay behind me. Can you feel your heart beating? Put your hand here on your chest and you can feel it beating. *(Demonstrate.)*

Something else we can do to keep our hearts strong is to run. Let's get in a big circle. Now, stay where you are and run in place. *(Demonstrate.)* Let's pretend we're running up a hill. We'll have to run slowly because it's a steep hill. Now let's pretend we've reached the top and we're going down the hill. We'll be running faster because it's so much easier to run downhill. That's great. You are super runners!

Feel your heart beating in your chest now. Is it beating fast? Let's sit down and give our hearts a rest after all that fast running. There are other ways to help our hearts stay strong. We need rest at night and we also need to eat good food.

But Jesus knows that we need something else to keep our hearts healthy. We need love. We have family and friends to love us, and we also have Jesus. Jesus is our best friend and he loves us no matter what.

I'd like to give you each something. See these red strips of paper? I'm going to put your name on one and ask you to hold it. *(Print each child's name on a strip and place it in the child's hands.)* Now I'm going to make a chain out of our names to remind us that we're all connected to each other and most important of all, that we're connected to Jesus. Let's start with this strip that has Jesus' name on it. As I staple your paper onto the chain, we'll say, "Jesus loves _______." And we'll all say your name. *(Staple each child's strip to the chain and lead the children to respond, "Jesus loves _______.")*

Let's pray to Jesus now as we sit here thinking about him. *(Invite the children to close their eyes and listen to the silence. Allow 30-45 seconds, using this time to shift into quiet and calm.)*

We are in our heart rooms, children. This is a place deep inside ourselves, and

Jesus lives here. See Jesus walking towards you. He's smiling and holding his arms out to you. Spend a little time looking at him. Notice what he looks like. Jesus wants to say something to you. Listen...listen. What is he saying? *(Allow 45 seconds.)*

Now think of what you'd like to say to Jesus because he's your best friend and he loves you. Jesus wants to hold you now. If it's all right with you, sit quietly with Jesus while he holds you. Know you are safe in his arms. Talk to Jesus now in your heart room. Don't say the words out loud. *(Allow 45 seconds.) (Say softly:)* You can open your eyes now, children. *(If the children are comfortable and can verbalize their prayer, ask them to share their talk with Jesus.)*

What did Jesus look like? What did he say to you? Since Jesus is your best friend, what did you say to him?

Our time is just about up, but remember that we keep our hearts strong by eating good food and by exercising. We also keep our hearts healthy by loving our best friend Jesus and our friends and family. Let's thank Jesus for living in our hearts.

It's time now to move to Craft *(or Story or Snack)*. I *(or our helper)* will walk with you.

Snack

After the children have rotated through all three activities, lead them to the snack room to share waffles or pretzels. Their parents will meet them here after the children finish eating.

If parents are delayed, use the Valentine's Day Retreat Activity (p. 193).

Parent-Child Sharing Time

After the adult session, parents pick up their children in the snack room to begin their sharing time. Distribute the Parent-Child Sharing Time Form (p. 216). If weather permits, retreatants can go outside for a nature walk. If not, they might want to find a corner to sit in, parent and child together; take a walk through the church; or even spread out blankets throughout the room. We allow approximately twenty minutes, asking parents and children to return to the gathering room at the appointed time for our closing.

During the parent presentation, the adult leader has suggested several questions designed to facilitate parent-child sharing:

▲ Tell me about the story you heard.

▲ What do you like about the craft you made?

- ▲ What was it like when you met Jesus in your heart room?
- ▲ What did Jesus look like?
- ▲ How did it feel to be with Jesus?
- ▲ When I met Jesus in my heart room, he said... I did...
- ▲ What did Jesus say to you? What did you do?

As retreatants are returning from sharing time, gather together and sing "J-E-S-U-S" (p. 180) When all have arrived, begin the closing prayer.

Closing Prayer

Join hands in a circle and have parents and children repeat each line.

> Jesus,
> you loved me first.
> I love you
> just like you told me to,
> I love my family and friends,
> and I love myself.
> You're my best friend.
> *Amen.*

Remind the children to take their craft home with them. Lead the retreatants to the door while singing the last verse of the Friend Song: "Jesus is my best friend too, my best friend too, my best friend too. Jesus is my best friend too, on this special day."

4-Kites

(Matthew 18:10-14; Isaiah 43:1-4)

Focus

When Jesus lived on this earth, sheep were a common sight. He told the story of the lost sheep to reinforce the message of caring, which God gave us through the prophet Isaiah: You are mine...you are precious to me...and I love you. In describing the shepherd who would leave ninety-nine sheep to find the one that had wandered away, Jesus assured us we're safe in God's hands.

If Jesus lived among us today, he would adapt to our time and culture and might even shift his story from sheep to kites. But the message is the same. Some young retreatants will not have had the experience of kite-flying, but in the events of this retreat, they will.

We show the children several beautiful, colorful kites and ask them to imagine ninety-nine of them flying freely in the blue sky. Then we bring out our favorite kite, the one we made out of newspaper, twigs, and torn-up sheets. This one is precious to us, because we made it ourselves, investing much time and effort. If it were to get stuck in a tree or wire, it would be a great loss because it's the most special one of all. We'd do everything possible to retrieve it. And no matter what, we'd never let go of the string. That string links us to the kite.

We're as special to Jesus as that homemade kite is to us. If we were to wander off, Jesus would leave all the other ninety-nine kites and concentrate on bringing us back. That's how much he cares about us.

Sometimes the wind gets too rough and kites do stray into trees, or even crash. But Jesus never lets go of the string. We ask the children to hold their parent's hand and try to pull away. The tug they feel is like the security of Jesus' grip on our kite string. That string links us to Jesus.

Preparations Before the Retreat

1. Meet as a team to pray, read, discuss, understand, and interiorize the focus and scriptural basis of the retreat.
2. Discern which team members will be responsible for the gathering presentation, each of the three children's activities, and the adult retreat session.
3. Choose a topic from the Outlines for Parent Sessions (pp. 143-178).
4. Divide preparation responsibilities. Use the gifts of your community to lighten the load. Parents, teenagers, school children, and senior citizens can all help.

Make the nametags.
Using the kite pattern (p. 194), prepare a different color nametag for each of the four team leaders. Then, using the same four colors, prepare one nametag for each child. You should have an equal number of each color of children's nametags. You will divide into groups by colors. As the children choose their nametags, the groups are formed.

Warning: Use safety pins or tape to attach nametags. For the safety of the children, do not use straight pins or string.

Collect materials for the environment.
To arrange an attractive display on a table or piano in the gathering place, locate two or three different types of brightly colored kites. In addition, construct a homemade kite out of newspapers and long twigs, with fabric swatches or sheets as a tail.

Prepare the craft (p. 65).
First, gather materials for Cellophane Kites:
▲ 9" x 12" construction paper, 2 sheets per child

- ▲ 8-1/2" x 11" strips of heavy plastic clear wrap, 2 per child
- ▲ 1"-2" cut-outs, any shape, of art tissue paper, 10 per child
- ▲ 3" x 12" crepe paper streamers, 1 per child
- ▲ pre-cut construction-paper kite bows, 3 per child
- ▲ glue

Second, do the advance preparation:

1. Cut two kite frames per child.
2. Glue clear plastic wrap onto each frame, covering the empty middle space and folding over the edges.

Optional craft: Cardboard-Tube Windsock

Gather materials:

- ▲ pre-cut 4-1/2" x 6" pieces of white paper with *Jesus is my Friend* written on them, 1 per child
- ▲ bathroom-tissue tubes, 1 per child
- ▲ yarn, 3 8" strings per child
- ▲ 4" paper ribbons in 2 colors, 6 per child (or 1/2" x 4" construction-paper strips)
- ▲ hole punch
- ▲ glue
- ▲ stapler
- ▲ crayons or markers

Preassemble:

1. Punch three holes, equidistant, in top of cardboard tube 3/4" from top.
2. Tie yarn through each hole by looping end around tube and knotting tightly.
3. Gather the three lengths of yarn at the top and knot them together for a hanger.
4. Attach the six ribbon streamers to bottom of tube with glue.

Locate the story.

Bear's Bargain by Frank Asch (New York: Scholastic, 1989), or one of the following:

- ▲ *The Sea-Breeze Hotel* by Marcia Vaughan and Patricia Mullins (New York: Harper Collins Children's Books, 1992)
- ▲ *Gilberto and the Wind* by Marie Hall Ets (New York: Puffin, 1978)
- ▲ *Rabbit's Birthday Kite* by Maryann MacDonald (New York: Bantam Books, 1991)
- ▲ *Merle the High Flying Squirrel* by Bill Peet (Boston: Houghton Mifflin, 1983)

Gather materials for the movement activity.

▲ large fan

▲ 24" crepe paper streamers, 1 per child

Become familiar with the prayer (p. 67).

Purchase groceries and prepare the snack (p. 69).

Graham-Cracker Kites:

▲ graham crackers

▲ frosting

▲ juice

or

Saltine Kites:

▲ saltines

▲ American cheese

▲ juice

Duplicate the Parent-Child Sharing Form (p. 216).

Preparations the Day of the Retreat

1. Gather as a team and pray.
2. Set out nametags and safety pins or tape (warning: no straight pins or strings). Have exactly as many nametags as retreatants.
3. Have each retreat team member put on a different colored nametag. This will later help the children divide into groups for their activities.
4. Atop a piano or table, create the environment in the gathering room with an arrangement of different types of kites. Include a homemade kite made of newspaper, sticks, and fabric tail. If available, display posters or other pictures of children flying kites.
5. Also in the gathering room, place a sample of the kite craft, a copy of *Bear's Bargain* or book of your choice, and a Bible.
6. Gather all the materials for the craft and set out on tables in the room to be used for this activity.
7. Spread out so that at least one team member is greeting the retreatants as they arrive, one is directing parents and younger siblings to the nursery, one is bringing retreatants and parents to the gathering room, and one is waiting in the gathering room.
8. Begin the retreat by warmly greeting the retreatants, then introducing the team members.
9. Sing together the gathering song "J-E-S-U-S" (p. 180).

Gathering Presentation

Let's talk about kites today. How many of you have ever flown a kite? Raise your hands.

If you haven't, let me tell you about it. *(Explain that it's best to fly kites where there are no trees or power lines. Describe how the wind lifts the kite and takes it away, how the tail stabilizes it so it won't spin out of control, and how the string keeps it anchored to the owner.)*

Look at all these kites. *(Point to display.)* Aren't they beautiful? Which one is your favorite? *(Hold each one up and ask children to raise their hands if it's their favorite.)*

Let me show you my favorite. It's this one *(the homemade kite).* When I was little, I made one exactly like this. See? I made it out of newspaper. I have lots of that at my house. And the sticks are from a tree in my yard. Look: I made the tail out of scraps of material I had around the house. I made it myself and I'm really proud of it. I want to tell you a story about this kite, but first let me tell you a story Jesus told his friends. I found the story in this book. It's the Bible. Do you have this book at your house?

Jesus was trying to tell his friends that God cares about them a great deal. He said that if a person had a hundred sheep, and one of those sheep wandered away, she would leave all those other ninety-nine sheep and go look for the one that was lost. And when this sheep-owner found the sheep, she would be happier about that one than about the others that didn't wander away. God cares about us as much as the sheep-owner cared about her sheep. God doesn't lose us.

Jesus told his friends this story because many of them owned sheep, and he knew they would understand. Well, we're Jesus' friends, too, and Jesus knows most of us don't own any sheep. So I think that if Jesus lived here with us today, he might talk to us about kites instead, because he knows we like kites.

Jesus helped me remember a story about when I was little and made a kite out of newspaper. It looked like this. *(Hold up newspaper kite.)*

One day we went out to fly kites in front of our house with the kids in the neighborhood. All the other kids had beautiful colorful kites from the store, but I liked ours best because we had spent so much time making it. It was really special.

We didn't know you shouldn't fly kites where there are trees, so pretty soon our newspaper kite got stuck in a tree. I started to cry because I loved that kite so much, and I thought I would never get it back. I held onto the kite string while my sisters and brothers tried to climb up the tree. They couldn't get that high, and I started to cry again. Finally, our dad came and brought a ladder with him. He climbed up and loosened our kite from the branches, and I pulled it down with my string. The kite was torn a little bit, and my friend said I could use his colorful kite. But I said "no, thank you" because I was so happy to have our homemade, newspaper kite back again.

Jesus is our best friend. We're as special to Jesus as the lost sheep was to its owner, and we're as special to Jesus as my newspaper kite was to me. God told his friend Isaiah to tell us, "You are mine. You are precious to me, and I love you." Those words are also in the Bible.

Jesus cares about us so much that he won't let us wander away from him. He holds onto us like we hold onto a kite string, to keep it from getting too far away. Try this. Right now, hold onto your mom's or dad's hand. Now, try to pull away. Don't let go, moms and dads. Can you feel how strong your parent's grip is? That's how tightly Jesus holds onto us. He wants us to be with him always.

Let's sing a song about Jesus always holding us.

Kite Song
(Tune: "Farmer in the Dell")

My kite is up so high,
My kite is up so high,
Oh my, watch it fly,
My kite is up so high.

The wind has caught my kite,
The wind has caught my kite,
What fun, I'm on the run,
The wind has caught my kite.

Jesus holds the string,
Jesus holds the string,
Oh my, watch us fly,
Jesus holds the string.

What great singing! We have some fun activities to do now while your moms and dads stay here and listen to a talk for parents. Let me show you what we'll be doing. *(Show the children the craft and story, and tell them they'll also be talking to Jesus.)*

Mommy or Daddy will pick you up when we have our snack. Time to give each other a big hug. *(Wait).*

Now look at the color of your nametag. *(Have the children leave the room with the team leader who has the same colored nametag.)* Wave goodbye.

Children's Activities

The following three children's activities run simultaneously, and the children rotate through them until they've been to all three.

Activity 1: Craft

As the children work, we talk in our own words about how Jesus is their best friend and how he would love to be invited next time they fly a kite. When they do, remember that Jesus will never let them go, just as they will never let their kite get away.

Remember, craft time is time of reinforcing the theme of the retreat. Far more important than what we say or do is that we share our sense of wonder, conveying our awe that Jesus is with us always.

Construct Cellophane Kites with the children (see illustration):

1. Place one kite frame and ten tissue-paper cut-outs on table in front of each child.
2. Dot clear-wrap cover with glue.
3. Allow children time to place their tissue cut-outs on glue dots.
4. Glue along edge of kite frame.
5. Carefully place second frame on top of first.
6. Quickly slip one end of crepe paper streamer between the two kite frames.
7. Press together and let dry.
8. Dot kite tail with glue. Have children place three paper bows onto tail.
9. Write names on kites.

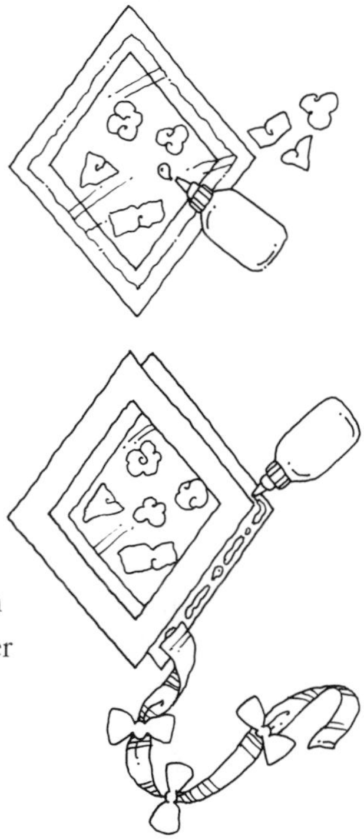

To simplify the craft:
Make a plain construction paper kite and decorate with colored paper cut-outs or markers. Attach a crepe paper tail.

Optional craft: Cardboard Tube Windsocks (see illustration)

1. Have children decorate the white paper with crayons or markers, encouraging them not to cover the words *Jesus is my Friend.*
2. Glue paper on the tube (which has been preassembled with the three lengths of yarn knotted at the top to make a hanger).
3. Fly when dry. (The six pre-attached ribbon streamer ends will add to the effect.)

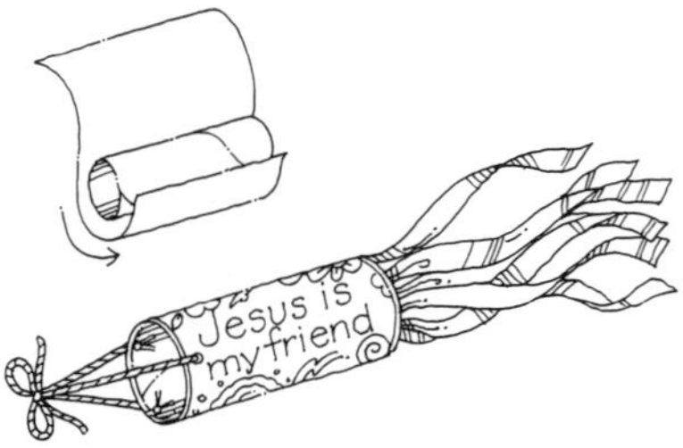

Announce to the children: Let's put your kites *(windsocks)* on this table and when you and Mommy or Daddy are ready to go home, you can come in here and get them. It's time now to go to Prayer *(or Story or Snack).* I *(or our helper)* will walk with you.

Activity 2: Story and Movement

Story: *Bear's Bargain* by Frank Asch (New York: Scholastic, 1985)

Introduce the story.

In this story Bear wants to fly like a kite. Look and listen to see how he gets to do it.

Read the story.

Talk about the story.

▲ Have you ever flown a kite? Tell us what it looked like. *(Pause.).*

▲ Why was bear's kite so special? *(His picture was on it.)*

▲ Did we find out how bear was able to fly? *(It was his picture on the kite that actually flew.)*

▲ If Jesus made himself a kite, I think he would draw a picture of *you* on it, don't you? That's how much he loves each one of us. And I know Jesus would hold onto the string as tightly as he could so we wouldn't get too far away.

▲ When we fly kites, sometimes the wind blows so hard it feels like our kites might blow away. Sometimes a kite does that. The string comes off the reel and—poof—it's gone. But the good news about our friend Jesus is that he never lets go of us. He's never gone.

▲ You know how good it feels to hold the hand of a grown-up who loves you? Our friend Jesus loves us so much that he holds onto us as we hold a kite or someone's hand.

▲ Kites can get away from us sometimes, but Jesus' love is forever.

Do the movement: Kite Dance

(Turn the fan on and show the children how wind lifts crepe paper streamers. Give each child a streamer.)

Let's pretend we're kites, boys and girls. When the music starts, we'll move up and down and all around and watch our streamers do the same. When you get near the fan, see what the wind does to your streamer. Don't stay near the fan too long, though, because we want to let everyone have a chance. Now we're kites, children, and Jesus is holding our string. *(Turn on the music and dance with the children.)*

It's time now to move to Craft *(or Prayer or Snack).* I *(or our helper)* will walk with you.

Activity 3: Prayer

Note: We lead the children into a personal encounter with Jesus in the setting of a kite-flying outing. By tapping into their senses and imaginations, we transform the room into a park, meadow, or playground, a favorite place that becomes more alive as the children's imaginations take over. Here they will meet Jesus, and during their prayer their friendship with him will deepen as they become familiar with him, listen to him, speak to him, and spend quiet time with him.

Lead the children.

Have you ever flown a kite before? Some of you have, I see, but if you haven't, you'll get to take a kite home today—the one you're making at this retreat—and fly it around a little bit.

But let's do something different right now for our prayer. Let's pretend we're kites and Jesus is holding our string. We're with our forever friend Jesus at the park, so let's fly around like kites. Ready? Follow me. *(Hold arms out to side and glide.)* See if you can stay behind the person in front of you.

Imagine what you look like as a kite. *(Name),* what color are you? *(Name),* how about you? Is anyone made out of newspaper? You look great!

Can you feel that, boys and girls? The wind is starting to lift us into the air. *(Lift arms above head and sway left and right.)* Up we go...slowly...slowly...up...up... up. A gentle breeze is blowing our whole body into the air. Feel our tail following us wherever we glide and soar...glide and soar. Are you still following? Stay behind the person in front of you.

Enjoy the feeling of being blown by the wind. We can't blow away because our friend Jesus is down on the ground holding our string. Look down, girls and boys. Can you see Jesus? Look, he's smiling. He likes watching us fly around. He loves us so much. Keep flying, girls and boys. We're safe and secure because Jesus is holding our string.

Look how blue the sky is. We're dancing in the wind. *(Sway.)* Fly, girls and boys. Safe and secure, we're gliding...soaring...rising in the sky. *(Continue flying for 30-45 more seconds.)*

Can you feel that? Jesus is reeling in our string. He's pulling us closer to him...slowly...slowly. We're still high in the sky, but we're on the way slowly... gently toward the ground. Feel the gentle tug toward the grassy park below.

We're enjoying the sunny day, blowing in the wind, aren't we? Let's swirl and twirl in the breezes as Jesus brings us close to him. Softly, gently, our friend Jesus pulls on the string, shortening the distance to the ground. *(Put arms down.)*

We're almost back now, children. Our tail is touching the ground. slowly... slowly ...let's sway in the last gust...slowly...slowly...slowly. Let's lie down on the grass

now and look up at the sky where we were sailing so happily in the blue and the clouds. What a day this has been.

(After the children have settled on the grass, invite them to close their eyes and listen to the sounds of the park and the wind. Allow 30-45 seconds, using this time to shift into quiet and calm.)

We are in our heart rooms, children. This is a place deep inside ourselves, and Jesus lives here. See Jesus walking towards you. He's smiling and holding his arms out to you. Spend a little time looking at him. Notice what he looks like.

Jesus wants to say something to you. Listen...listen. What is he saying? *(Allow 45 seconds.)*

Now think of what you'd like to say to Jesus because he's your best friend and he loves you so much. Talk to Jesus now in your heart room. Don't say the words out loud. *(Allow 45 seconds.)*

Jesus wants to hold you now. If it's all right with you, sit quietly with Jesus while he holds you. Know you are safe in his arms.

(Say softly:) You can open your eyes now, children.

(If the children are comfortable and can verbalize their prayer, ask them to share their talk with Jesus.)

What did Jesus look like? What did he say to you? Since Jesus is your best friend, what did you say to him?

(If time allows, retrace the trip through the park back to the door of the room.)

It's time now to move to Craft *(or Story or Snack)*. I *(or our helper)* will walk with you.

Snack

After the children have rotated through all three activities, lead them to the snack room. Their parents will meet them here after the children finish eating.

Distribute one square graham cracker per child. Provide small bowls of white or colored frosting and plastic knives. Demonstrate how the cracker can become a kite by holding it with a corner at the top. Spread a line of frosting from top to bottom and another from left to right.

If using saltines, substitute cheese strips for frosting.

In the event the parents are delayed, use the Kite Retreat Activity (p. 195).

Parent-Child Sharing Time

After the adult session, parents pick up their children in the snack room to begin their sharing time. Distribute the Parent-Child Sharing Time Form (p. 216). If weather permits, retreatants can go outside for a nature walk. If not, they might want to find a corner to sit in, parent and child together; take a walk through the church; or even spread out picnic blankets throughout the room. The children might like to take their kites with them. We allow approximately twenty minutes, asking parents and children to return to the gathering room at the appointed time for our closing.

During the parent presentation, the adult leader has suggested several questions designed to facilitate parent-child sharing:

- ▲ Tell me about the story you heard.
- ▲ What do you like about the craft you made?
- ▲ What was it like when you met Jesus in your heart room?
- ▲ What did Jesus look like?
- ▲ How did it feel to be with Jesus?
- ▲ When I met Jesus in my heart room, he said... I did...
- ▲ What did Jesus say to you? What did you do?

As retreatants are returning from sharing time, gather together and sing "J-E-S-U-S" (p. 180) or the "Kite Song" (p. 64).

When all have arrived, begin the closing prayer.

Closing Prayer

Join hands in a circle and have parents and children repeat each line.

> Jesus,
> you made me special,
> and you love me so much.
> Thank you
> for always taking care of me.
> Whenever I see a kite
> I'll remember
> that you'll always hold onto me.
> We're best friends
> *Amen.*

Remind the children to take their craft home with them. If the children have their kites (or windsocks), we encourage them to fly them home now. We lead the retreatants to the door flying our own kites, or pretending to do so.

5-Easter

(John 20:11-18)

Focus

Many of our retreatants will wake up Easter morning to a basket full of eggs. We hope that this tradition will remind them of their friendship with Jesus. Drawing on the analogy of the mother hen sitting and sitting until her eggs hatch, we explain to the children that Jesus loves us, is with us always, and wants to be our friend. Jesus cares about us that much.

We introduce the concept of faith, encouraging the children to use the word often. Faith means believing. We believe, for example, that when our mom or dad puts a band aid on our scrapes, it will feel better and eventually heal. That's faith. We believe that it will get dark at night, and that after night, it will be day. That's faith. The mother hen believes that if she sits on her eggs long enough, her chickens will hatch. That's faith. We are able to believe because we've seen it happen before, or because somebody told us. We don't know for sure that something's true, but we believe it is. That's faith.

We believe some things about God and God's son, Jesus: that God made us, that God invited us to be Jesus' friend, that Jesus is always with us, that he takes care of us, that we belong to Jesus. Because an egg belongs to the mother hen, she takes care of it. Because our clothes and toys belong to us, we take care of them. And because we belong to Jesus, Jesus takes care of us. We can't know this for sure, but we believe it. That's our faith. God so loved the world that God gave us Jesus to be our best friend. A mother hen so loves her chicken that she sits for days, keeping it warm until it hatches. Once again, we share with our young retreatants our excitement and awe that Jesus is always there, steadfast in his love and care for us. That is our faith.

Preparations Before the Retreat

1. Meet as a team to pray, read, discuss, understand, and interiorize the focus and scriptural basis of the retreat.
2. Discern which team members will be responsible for the gathering presentation, each of the three children's activities, and the adult retreat session.
3. Choose a topic from the Outlines for Parent Sessions (pp. 143-178).
4. Divide preparation responsibilities. Use the gifts of your community to lighten the load. Parents, teenagers, school children, and senior citizens can all help prepare.

Make the nametags.

Using the Easter-egg pattern (p. 196), prepare a different color nametag for each of the four team leaders. Then, using the same four colors, prepare one nametag for each child. You should have an equal number of each color of children's nametags. You will divide into groups by colors. As the children choose their nametags, the groups are formed.

Warning: Use safety pins or tape to attach nametags. For the safety of the children, do not use straight pins or string.

(Note: For an optional nametag, use the flower pattern on p. 197.)

Collect materials for the environment.

To arrange an attractive display on a table or piano in the gathering place, locate a pastel tablecloth, one or two large baskets filled with colorful eggs (at least one should be plastic, with candy inside), toy chickens and hen, a basket containing such "caring" items as band aids, storybooks, and a pair of children's shoes.

Prepare the craft (p. 77).

First, gather materials for Chicks in a Shell:

- ▲ yellow cotton balls, 1 per child (or shake white cotton balls in dry yellow powdered tempera)
- ▲ white poster board
- ▲ metal brads, 1 per child
- ▲ small plastic google eyes, 2 per child (optional)
- ▲ orange or black construction paper
- ▲ glue
- ▲ watercolor paints and brushes
- ▲ 8 paper cups

Second, do the advance preparation:
1. Cut chicks from poster board, 1 per child (see pattern, p. 77).
2. Cut small beaks from orange or black construction paper.
3. Zig-zag cut two half-eggs per child.
4. Connect egg halves with brad.
5. Glue bottom of chick to back of lower egg half.
6. Dye cotton balls yellow, if necessary.

Locate the story.
Obtain *An Egg is an Egg* by Nicki Weiss (New York: Putnam Publishing Group, 1990), or one of the following:
- ▲ *The Chicken or the Egg* by Allan Fowler (Chicago: Children's Press, 1993)
- ▲ *I Know a Lady* by Charlotte Zolotow (New York: Greenwillow Books, 1984)
- ▲ *Easter* by Gail Gibbons (New York: Holiday House, 1989)
- ▲ *Hosanna and Alleluia* by Dina Strong (Denver: Spindle Press, 1997)
- ▲ *The Easter Story* by Brian Wildsmith (New York: Knopf, 1993)

Select a movement activity.
Use Eggsactly Shake, (p. 78) or another of your choice. If you use Eggsactly Shake, prepare the activity: Fill twelve plastic eggs with items familiar to the children: pennies, rice, jingle bells, rocks, cotton balls, salt, jelly beans, etc. Make two eggs of each item. To avoid spilling, tape the eggs around the circumference where the two halves meet. Place in a large basket.

Optional craft: Paper Dolls
Gather materials:
- ▲ pattern (p. 200)
- ▲ newspaper, wrapping paper, or plain white or colored paper
- ▲ markers or crayons
- ▲ scissors

Preassemble:

1. Accordion-fold entire length of paper to accommodate one doll on each fold.
2. Draw (or use pattern provided) a simple person shape on top fold, making sure to extend arms to the edge. The size of the dolls is determined by the width of the paper. The number of dolls is determined by the length. See illustration, page. 77.

Become familiar with the prayer (p. 79).

Purchase groceries and prepare the snack (p. 80).

Easter Eggs:

▲ hard-boiled eggs in dyed shells

▲ pink lemonade

or

Egg-Shaped Crackers:

▲ crackers, oval-shaped

▲ pink lemonade

Alternate suggestion:

This retreat lends itself well to a Saturday morning time slot where families can gather for breakfast or brunch prior to or following the retreat. If your church has staff and facilities, a breakfast of scrambled eggs, oval-shaped pancakes, and juice would be delightful. Equally festive would be a potluck breakfast, with some families bringing egg dishes, and others providing breads, fruits, and beverages.

Prepare take-home treat:

Fill plastic eggs, 1 per child, with jelly beans. To avoid spilling, tape the circumference where the two halves meet.

Duplicate the Parent-Child Sharing Form (p. 216).

Preparations the Day of the Retreat

1. Gather as a team and pray.
2. Set out nametags and safety pins or tape (warning: no straight pins or strings). Have exactly as many nametags as retreatants.
3. Have each retreat team member put on a different colored nametag. This will later help the children divide into groups for their activities.
4. Atop a piano or table, create the environment in the gathering room with pastel tablecloth, baskets of eggs, toy chicks and hen, band aids, cereal box, and children's shoes.

5. Also in the gathering room, place a sample of the Easter craft, a copy of *An Egg is an Egg* or book of your choice, and a Bible.
6. Gather all the materials for the craft and set out on tables in the room to be used for this activity.
7. Spread out so at least one team member is greeting the retreatants as they arrive, one is directing parents and younger siblings to the nursery, one is bringing retreatants and parents to the gathering room, and one is waiting in the gathering room.
8. Begin the retreat by warmly greeting the retreatants, then introducing the team members.
9. Sing together the gathering song "J-E-S-U-S" (p. 180).

Gathering Presentation

Wow, girls and boys, look at all these beautiful Easter eggs. Do you suppose there might be some candy inside these plastic eggs? Let's look. *(Open egg and hold up the candy.)* There sure is. That's how I know these aren't real eggs. Real eggs don't have candy inside.

Who knows what's inside real eggs? *(Let a child answer: yolk or baby chicks.)* That's right. When the mother hen lays her eggs, there's just yellow, sticky yolk inside. You've seen the yolk, haven't you? When you crack an egg open to bake cookies, yellow, sticky yolk comes oozing out. An egg is just a yolk in a shell, but because of the mother hen, a miracle happens. A miracle is something wonderful that Jesus does. Here's what the miracle is: because of the mother hen's love, the yolk in the shell becomes a real chicken. The mother hen sits on her egg to keep it warm. Day after day after day, she sits on it until one day the egg begins to crack. It slowly cracks, and then suddenly...out pops a chicken. It's not a yolk anymore. It's a real, live chicken. Isn't that a miracle? Jesus helped that mother hen create a baby chick, and because the mother loved her baby, she could sit so long and help it hatch.

Jesus loves us even more than that mother hen loves her baby chick. Even more. Can you believe that? When we're happy, Jesus loves us. When we're sad or scared, Jesus loves us. When we're angry, Jesus loves us. There's nothing we can do to make Jesus stop loving us.

I've just told you something important, children. Jesus loves us and loves us forever. Now I have something else really important to tell you. Are you ready? Here it is.

We believe Jesus is our best friend, and that's called faith. Can you say that word with me? *Faith.* Faith means believing. We believe that we'll grow taller and someday be an adult. That's faith. We believe it will get dark at night, and we believe it will be daytime after night. That's faith. The mother hen believes that if she sits on her egg long enough, it will hatch into a baby chick. What is that? Yes, that's faith. Let's say that word again all together. *Faith. Faith.*

We believe, boys and girls, either because we've seen it happen before, so we know it can happen, or because someone told us it was true, so we think it must be true. When we turn on our faucet, we believe water will come out because it usually does. We can't know for sure, though. Believing water will come out of the faucet is faith. When our mommy or daddy kisses our hurt, puts a band aid on it, and tells us it will get better, we believe our hurt really will get better. We can't know for sure, but we believe it because an adult we love told us it would. Believing our scratches will heal is faith.

We don't know for sure that something's true, but we believe it is. That's faith.

Let's sing a song about how loving makes eggs hatch. While we're singing, let's remember that Jesus loves us even more than the mother hen loves her chick.

Egg Song
(Tune: "Pop Goes the Weasel")
(Sing in a crouched position, jumping up on the last line.)
An egg is just a yolk in a shell,
It's yellow and kind of sticky,
But loving makes it crack and hatch—
Out pops the chickie.

What great singing! We have some fun activities to do now while your moms and dads stay here and listen to a talk for parents. Let me show you what we'll be doing. *(Show the children the craft and story, and tell them they'll also be talking to Jesus.)*

Mommy or Daddy will pick you up when we have our snack. Time to give each other a big hug. *(Wait).*

Now look at the color of your nametag. *(Have the children leave the room with* the team leader who has the same colored nametag.) Wave goodbye.

Children's Activities

The following three children's activities run simultaneously, and the children rotate through them until they've been to all three.

Activity 1: Craft

As the children work, we talk in our own words about how Jesus is their best friend and how much he loves them. He loves them even more than the mother hen who sits and sits and sits, keeping her eggs warm until they hatch.

Remember, craft time is a time of reinforcing the theme of the retreat. Far more important than what we say or do is that we share our sense of wonder, conveying our awe that Jesus is with us always.

Construct Chicks in a Shell with the children (see illustration):

1. Give each child one or two yellow cotton balls.
2. Direct children to pull cotton apart to make it thinner, following adult's modeling.
3. Children glue cotton onto chick.

4. When dry, allow children to open and close eggs to make their chicken hatch.

To simplify the craft:
Instead of using cotton, children can color the chicks yellow with markers, crayons, or water colors.

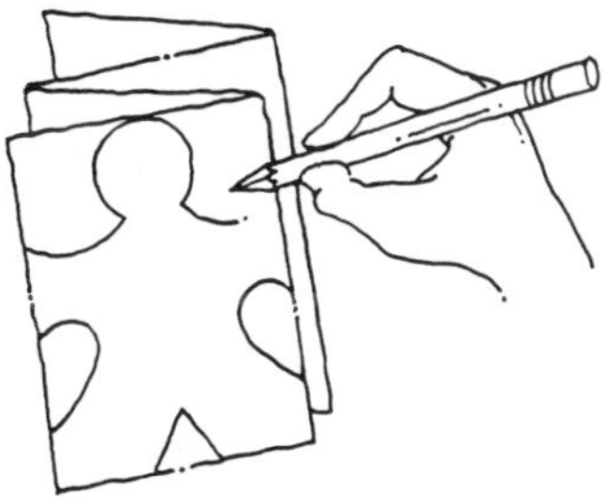

Optional craft: Paper Dolls (see illustration):

1. Instruct children to cut around the outline of doll, leaving the arms and feet attached.
2. Allow children time to play with their string of paper dolls.

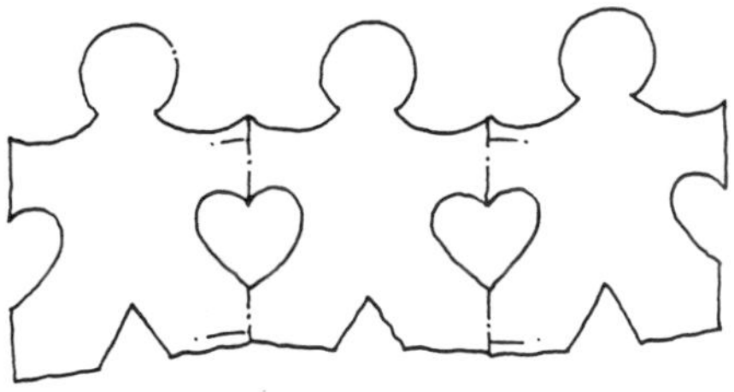

Announce to the children: Let's put your chickies *(or paper dolls)* on this table and when you and Mommy or Daddy are ready to go home, you can come in here and get them. It's time now to go to Prayer *(or Story or Snack)*. I *(or our helper)* will walk with you.

Activity 2: Story and Movement

Story: *An Egg is an Egg* by Nicki Weiss (New York: G.P. Putnam's Sons, 1990)

Introduce the story.

Have you ever wondered which came first, the chicken or the egg? Does there first need to be a chicken so it can lay eggs? Or do there first need to be eggs so they can hatch chickens? Listen while I read this story, then we'll talk about it.

Read the story.

Talk about the story.

- ▲ Notice in the end how the mommy says, "You'll always be my baby." That's sort of like the baby chicken belonging to the mother hen. It's also a lot like us believing we belong to Jesus. We do belong to Jesus. That's something that will never change. What were some of the things in the story that did change? *(Blocks into tower, seeds into flowers, eggs into chickens, etc.)*
- ▲ What do you think about mother hens sitting so patiently on their eggs until they hatch into chickens? *(Listen to several children's ideas. Affirm their contributions.)*
- ▲ I really liked the part where it said, "You are you till I come, then we're 'we.'" That's just how it is being Jesus' friend. If you believe it's "Jesus and me," then you and Jesus belong together.
- ▲ Let's play a game called Eggsactly Shake, and see if we can find some eggs that belong together.

Do the movement: Eggsactly Shake.

Place large basket containing filled plastic eggs in front of the children. Demonstrate the various sounds the eggs make by shaking them, then invite each child to take an egg from the basket and rattle it. Explain that there is one other egg that sounds "eggsactly" like theirs, and their job is to find it by shaking other children's eggs or those remaining in the basket. When they find the match, they sit down by the basket and wait until all the eggs have been matched. One rule: The only noise allowed is that of egg shaking. Feet and voices should not be heard.

Variation: Have the children stand in a circle. Choose someone to be It. Instruct It to walk around the outside and rattle each child's egg until he or she finds the match. Both children then sit inside the "Belonging Basket" (the circle).

Announce to the children: It's time now to move to Craft *(or Prayer or Snack).* I *(or our helper)* will walk with you.

Activity 3: Prayer

Note: Lead the children into a personal encounter with Jesus in the setting of the first Easter. By tapping into their senses and imaginations, you can transform the room into a garden, a favorite place that becomes more alive as the children's imaginations take over. Here they will meet Jesus, and during their prayer their friendship with him will deepen as they become familiar with him, listen to him, speak to him, and spend quiet time with him.

Lead the children.

What do you like best about Easter? *(Wait for answers.)* It seems like we're all excited about Easter and the things we do when Easter arrives. I'd like to think about Easter in another way today while we're here together. Let's go on a pretend trip to the first Easter Sunday and find out what it was like. Follow me.

Come down this path. It's narrow, so get in a line behind me. *(Begin walking slowly as the children follow.)* Walk carefully past this stream. Do you hear the water? Listen to the birds chirping in the trees above us. *(Wait.)* Let's climb up this hill. Take big, gigantic steps. Now we're at the top. Oh, look down there. Can you see the stream we left behind? Listen...I hear the sounds of baby sheep on the hillside. Do you hear them? There's a shepherd taking care of the little sheep. Look, he's leading the sheep to the stream. Why do you think he's doing that? That's right. He's showing them where to get some water to drink.

Let's go over by that garden. Follow me again on the path. Here we are. I wonder what kind of flowers those are. *(Name)* and *(Name)*, can you pick some flowers for us to take home? Here, I'll help you. *(Pretend to pick flowers with two helpers and hand one to each child.)* Let's all sit down under this big tree. I sure do like sitting outside on sunny days, don't you?

You know what? A wonderful thing happened in a garden just like this pretend one. After Jesus had died on the cross, he spoke to some women in a garden. These women were his friends and they remembered how kind he had been to all people, especially people who were poor or sick. They were sad that Jesus had died, and now here he was alive again and visiting with them in the garden. *(Name),* how do you think those women felt when they saw Jesus alive again? Yes, they were so happy. They knew Jesus would always be their friend and that he would take care of them. That was their faith. They had faith in Jesus and here he was spending time with them again. Because we have faith in Jesus, too, Jesus never leaves us. That's our faith.

Let's pray to Jesus now as we sit here thinking about him. Let's pretend it's Easter morning.

(Invite the children to close their eyes and listen to the sounds. Allow 30-45 seconds, using this time to shift into quiet and calm.)

We are in our heart rooms, children. This is a place deep inside ourselves, and Jesus lives here. See Jesus walking towards you. He's smiling and holding his arms out to you. Spend a little time looking at him. Notice what he looks like. Jesus wants to say something to you. Listen...listen. What is he saying? *(Allow 45 seconds.)*

Now think of what you'd like to say to Jesus because he's your best friend and he loves you so much. Talk to Jesus now in your heart room. Don't say the words out loud. *(Allow 45 seconds.)*

Jesus wants to hold you now. If it's all right with you, sit quietly with Jesus while he holds you. Know you are safe in his arms.

(Say softly:) You can open your eyes now, children.

(If the children are comfortable and can verbalize their prayer, ask them to share their talk with Jesus.)

What did Jesus look like? What did he say to you? Since Jesus is your best friend, what did you say to him?

Before we leave this garden let's thank Jesus for being such a good friend to us. Can you repeat after me? "Thank you, Jesus. You are my best friend." And now let's say, "I have faith in you, Jesus."

(If time allows, retrace the trip through the garden back to the door of the room.)

It's time now to move to Craft *(or Story or Snack)*. I *(or our helper)* will walk with you.

Snack

After the children have rotated through all three activities, lead them to the snack room for colored hard-boiled Easter eggs or oval crackers, and pink lemonade. Their parents will meet them here after the children finish eating.

In the event the parents are delayed, use the Easter Retreat Activity on page 198.

Parent-Child Sharing Time

After the adult session, parents pick up their children in the snack room to begin their sharing time. Distribute the Parent-Child Sharing Time Form (p. 216). If weather permits, retreatants can go outside for a nature walk. If not, they might want to find a corner to sit in, parent and child together; take a walk through the church; or even spread out blankets throughout the room. We allow approximately twenty minutes, asking parents and children to return to the gathering room at the appointed time for our closing.

During the parent presentation, the adult leader has suggested several questions designed to facilitate parent-child sharing:

- ▲ Tell me about the story you heard.
- ▲ What do you like about the craft you made?
- ▲ What was it like when you met Jesus in your heart room?
- ▲ What did Jesus look like?
- ▲ How did it feel to be with Jesus?
- ▲ When I met Jesus in my heart room, he said... I did...
- ▲ What did Jesus say to you? What did you do?

As retreatants are returning from sharing time, gather together and sing "J-E-S-U-S" (p. 180) or the "Egg Song" (p. 76).

When all have arrived, begin the closing prayer.

Closing Prayer

Join hands in a circle and have parents and children repeat each line.

> Jesus,
> you made me special,
> and you love me so much.
> Whenever I see Easter eggs
> I'll remember
> how you take care of me.
> I believe
> that we're best friends.
> That is my faith.
> *Amen.*

Remind the children to take their craft home with them. Lead the retreatants to the door and give each child a plastic egg filled with jelly beans.

6-Mother's Day/Father's Day Retreat

(Luke 2:41-48)

Focus

We honor mothers and fathers in this retreat, focusing on the loving relationship between parent and child. Our parents understand and love us even when we're grumpy and not very loving to them. If we're so angry we feel like running away, for example, our mom or dad will come looking for us. Or if we get lost, our parents will search until they find us.

We have a special, loving relationship with Jesus, too. He's our best friend and that means he loves us no matter what we say or do or feel. Angry, sad, glad, or scared—Jesus wraps us in his loving arms regardless of our mood.

There's nothing we can say to Jesus that will make him go away. He is always with us. We can't lose Jesus, and Jesus can't lose us.

We're sensitive to the varying degrees of woundedness in adults and the effect it has on their ability to parent well. Sadly, some of our tiny retreatants won't recognize the tender love and care we ascribe to parents. This needs to be addressed, for a child who has a weak model of love in either parent may project this perception onto Jesus.

Therefore, we explain that our parents love us as best they can, but that sometimes they get tired or feel sick or frustrated, and then they get angry. They still love us, but they can't show us as much as they wish they could.

But God never gets tired or sick or frustrated. If our mom or dad isn't feeling well, we can always talk to Jesus.

The story of Jesus lost in the temple is one of the few stories we know of his childhood, but it shows beautifully the fierceness of love parents have for their children. We retell this story, focusing on how easily Jesus got lost, and how worried Mary and Joseph were, so worried that they wouldn't give up until they found him.

Our parents love us so much. Our best friend Jesus loves us so much, too.

Preparations Before the Retreat

1. Meet as a team to pray, read, discuss, understand, and interiorize the focus and scriptural basis of the retreat. Read Luke 2:39-52, focusing on verses 41-48.
2. Discern which team members will be responsible for the gathering presentation on families, each of the three children's activities, and the adult retreat session.
3. Choose a topic from the Outlines for Parents Sessions (pp. 143-178).
4. Divide the following preparation responsibilities. Use the gifts of your community to lighten the load. Parents, teenagers, school children, and senior citizens can all help prepare.

Make the nametags.
Using the person pattern (p. 199), prepare a different color nametag for each of the four team leaders. Then, using the same four colors, prepare one nametag for each child. You should have an equal number of each color of children's nametags. You will divide into groups by colors. As the children choose their nametags, the groups are formed.

Warning: Use safety pins or tape to attach nametags. For the safety of the children, do not use straight pins or string.

(Note: For an optional nametag, use the smiley-face pattern on p. 200.)

Collect materials for the environment.

To arrange an attractive display on a table or piano in the gathering room, locate three to six framed family portraits; preschool toys in a variety of colors, sizes, and types (e.g., playground ball, doll, building blocks); a picture of the Holy Family.

Prepare the craft (p. 89).

First, gather materials for Love-Coupon Baskets:

- ▲ plastic mesh strawberry produce baskets, 1 per child
- ▲ narrow wooden craft sticks, 4 per child
- ▲ 4 (only) colors of construction paper
- ▲ glue
- ▲ crayons or markers, *optional*
- ▲ green spray paint
- ▲ extra long pipe cleaners, 1 per child
- ▲ computer labels or masking tape for children's names

Second, do the advanced preparation:

1. Cut out flowers in four different colors (see patterns, p. 90), making enough so that every child will get one of each color. *Option:* Make the flowers on white paper so that the children can color their own.
2. Write a love coupon on every flower, with each color carrying the same message, different from those on other colors. The following are possibilities, each one a loving activity which promotes interaction between parent and child:
    - ▲ I'll ask, "Can I help?"
    - ▲ I'll give you a hug.
    - ▲ I'll say, "I love you."
    - ▲ I'll try to do something hard.
    - ▲ We'll say "I'm sorry"/"I forgive you" together.
    - ▲ I'll teach you a song.
    - ▲ I'll pray with you.
3. Spray paint craft sticks green.
4. Weave craft sticks through center of each side of basket so they stand up vertically (see illustration, p. 90).
5. Attach pipe cleaner handle.
6. Affix computer label or masking tape onto pipe cleaner handle (folded in half to stick to itself) for name.

Locate the story.

Obtain *The Runaway Bunny* by Margaret Wise Brown (New York: Harper and

Row, Publishers, 1977), or one of the following:

- ▲ *We're Very Good Friends, My Father and I* by P.K. Hallinan (Nashville: Ideals Children's Books, 1990)
- ▲ *We're Very Good Friends, My Mother and I* by P.K. Hallinan (Nashville: Ideals Children's Books, 1990)
- ▲ *This Quiet Lady* by Charlotte Zolotow (New York: Greenwillow Books, 1992)
- ▲ *Daddy Makes the Best Spaghetti* by Anna Grossnickle Hines (New York: Clarion Books, 1988)
- ▲ *Blueberries for Sal* by Robert McCloskey (New York: Puffin Books, 1993)

Select a movement activity.

Use Runaway, Runaway, Runaway Bunny (p. 91) or another of your choice.

Become familiar with the prayer (p. 91).

Purchase groceries and prepare the snack (p. 93).

Gingerbread People:

- ▲ home-made or store-bought gingerbread people cookies
- ▲ milk or juice

or

Cracker People:

- ▲ crackers and sliced cheese cutouts of gingerbread people (serve both the cutouts and the remaining piece of cheese)
- ▲ milk or juice

Duplicate the Parent-Child Sharing Form (p. 216).

Preparations the Day of the Retreat

1. Gather as a team and pray.
2. Set out nametags and safety pins or tape (warning: no straight pins or strings). Have exactly as many nametags as retreatants.
3. Have each retreat team member wear a different colored nametag. This will later help the children divide into groups for their activities.
4. Atop a piano or table, create the environment in the gathering room with an arrangement of family portraits, toys, and a picture of the Holy Family.
5. Also in the gathering room, place a sample of the love coupon flower basket, a copy of *The Runaway Bunny* or book of your choice, and a Bible.
6. Gather all the materials for the craft and set out on tables in the room to be used for this activity.
7. Spread out so that at least one team member is greeting the retreatants as they arrive, one is directing parents and younger siblings to the nursery, one is

bringing retreatants and parents to the gathering room, and one is waiting in the gathering room.

8. Begin the retreat by warmly greeting the retreatants, then introducing the team members.
9. Sing together the gathering song "J-E-S-U-S" (p. 180).

Gathering Presentation

(Show family portraits and talk about them, or say:) This is a picture of my family when I was your age. And this is a picture of me now with my mom and dad. We're all a lot older now, aren't we?

Now I'm a mom and these are my children. *(Show picture.)* Families all look different. Some families have only a mother or a father. Some families have many children, and some have only one or two.

This is a picture of another family, a special family. *(Hold up picture of the Holy Family.)* It's Jesus' family. See? Jesus had a mother and father, too.

Who was Jesus' mother? *(Mary)*

Who knows who Jesus' father was? (Joseph)

I have a story about this family in God's special book. *(Hold up the Bible.)* Do you have this book at your house?

This story happened when Jesus was a little older than you. He and his mom and dad, Mary and Joseph, took a trip from their town, Nazareth, to a bigger town far away, a town called Jerusalem. But they didn't have cars when Jesus was little, so Mary, Joseph, and Jesus had to walk on this trip. Can you imagine walking all that way? Now Mary and Joseph and Jesus weren't taking this trip alone. Maybe Jesus's cousin John and his aunt Elizabeth were with them, and so were a lot of other neighbors and friends. They were all going to a Passover party.

After the party, when it was time to go home, Mary and Joseph accidentally left without Jesus. Mary thought Jesus was with Joseph, and Joseph thought he was with Mary. Mary wasn't worried because she was sure Jesus was safe with Joseph and their friends.

Joseph wasn't worried because last time he saw Jesus, Jesus was with Mary. He thought Jesus was safe, so he just kept walking home to Nazareth.

But Jesus wasn't with his mother or his father. Oh, no! Guess where he was? He had stayed behind in Jerusalem at the place where the party had been. He was busy talking to people and didn't notice his parents had left.

It was a whole day before Mary and Joseph realized that Jesus wasn't with either one of them. When Joseph caught up to Mary, he looked around for his little boy. "Mary," he asked, "Where's Jesus?"

"I thought he was with you," Mary exclaimed.

"Oh, no!" they both cried. "I wonder where he is?"

Show me how they looked. *(Put hands on cheeks and drop jaw.)*

They looked all around and asked everybody if they'd seen Jesus. Show me how they looked around for their son. *(Look to the right and left, with hand in salute position on forehead.)*

How do you think Jesus' mom and dad felt? How do you think Jesus was feeling? *(scared, worried)*

Show me what scared and worried look like. *(Bite fingernails and tremble.)*

That's how I felt one time when my little girl got lost at the amusement park. *(Or use your own story.)* She was even littler than you. We had just gotten there and all of a sudden she wasn't with us. We never even saw her walk away. I was so scared and all I could think was that I had to look for Sara till I found her. We looked and looked and finally we found her. Whew! We were so happy we hugged and hugged her.

Another time when I was exactly your age I got lost at the grocery store. I couldn't find my mom anywhere. I was over by the cereal boxes, not very far away, but I couldn't see her. I was really scared. I thought she'd never find me. But guess what? She did find me. She was looking for me the whole time.

Well, Mary and Joseph were looking for Jesus the whole time, too. They walked all the way back to the place where the Passover party had been and it was three days before they finally found him. When they did, they were so happy that they hugged and hugged him.

Even though Mary and Joseph couldn't find Jesus right away, God knew where he was the whole time. God is always with us; we can't lose God, and God can't lose us. Can you say that with me? *We can't lose God, and God can't lose us.*

So even though Mary, Joseph, and Jesus couldn't find each other for a long time, and felt worried and frightened, I think they probably talked with God about how they were feeling, don't you? Because God is always there to listen to us when we want to talk to God.

We can do that, too. Our best friend Jesus wants us to tell him how we feel. Jesus is our best friend and he loves us no matter what we say or do or feel. We can talk to Jesus about anything, anything at all.

Jesus loves us as much as our parents do. Do your mom and dad sometimes feel tired, or sick, or frustrated? Sure they do. They still love you, but they can't show you as much as they wish they could. But, you know what? The good news is that Jesus never feels tired or sick or frustrated. If our mom or dad isn't feeling well, we can always talk to Jesus. Let me show you how.

Can you stand up now? Show me how you look when you feel happy. *(Smile.)* Sometimes we clap our hands when we're happy. Can we tell Jesus when we're happy? Yes! Let's clap our hands with Jesus. *(Lead clapping.)*

Show me how you look when you feel sad. *(Look sad.)* What does it sound like? *(Boo-hoo-hoo-hoo)* Can we tell Jesus when we're sad? Yes!

Look grumpy now. *(Scowl.)* Can we tell Jesus when we feel grumpy? Let's tell Jesus right now. *(Snap fingers and shout, "Oh, rats!")*

How about frightened? Should we tell Jesus when we're scared? Yes! What does frightened look like? *(Look frightened and shake your knees.)* Let's knock our knees with Jesus.

Sometimes we feel loving. Let's hug someone we love. *(Wait.)* Wouldn't it be nice to hug Jesus, for real? Well, we can hug people who are like Jesus, can't we? Our moms or dads or our good friends or other people in our family.

Let's sing a song about sharing our feelings with Jesus.

Feelings Song
(Tune: "Frere Jacques")

Are you happy, are you happy?
Yes, I am. Yes, I am.
Clap your hands with Jesus. Clap your hands with Jesus.
He's our friend. He's our friend.

Are you sad, are you sad?
Yes, I am. Yes, I am.
Cry along with Jesus. Cry along with Jesus.
Boo-hoo-hoo. Boo-hoo-hoo.

Are you grumpy, are you grumpy?
Yes, I am. Yes, I am.
Shout along with Jesus. Shout along with Jesus.
Ooh, I'm mad. Ooh, I'm mad.

Are you frightened, are you frightened?
Yes, I am. Yes, I am.
Shake your knees with Jesus. Shake your knees with Jesus.
He's our friend. He's our friend.

Are you loving, are you loving?
Yes, I am. Yes, I am.
Hug a friend like Jesus. Hug a friend like Jesus.
He's my friend. You're my friend.

What great singing! We have some fun activities to do now while your moms and dads stay here and listen to a talk for parents. Let me show you what we'll be doing. *(Show the children the craft and story, and tell them they'll also be talking to Jesus.)*

Mommy or Daddy will pick you up when we have our snack. Time to give each other a big hug. *(Wait).*

Now look at the color of your nametag. *(Have the children leave the room with the team leader who has the same colored nametag.)* Wave goodbye.

Children's Activities

The following three children's activities run simultaneously, and the children rotate through them until they've been to all three.

Activity 1: Craft

As the children work, we talk about how Jesus is our best friend, and how he loved us first. Because Jesus loves us so much, we love each other. We're giving our love coupon baskets to our moms and dads because we love them and we know they love us, as Jesus does. Wherever there is love, Jesus is there. When we do loving things with our family, Jesus is with us.

Remember, craft time is a time of reinforcing the theme of the retreat. Far more important than what we say or do is that we share our sense of wonder, conveying our awe that Jesus is with us always. Construct Love Coupon Baskets with the children:

1. Generously coat first craft stick with glue.

2. Hold paper flower against the glue for at least 30 seconds.
3. Repeat this process on the other three sticks as each flower appears to be sticking on its own.
4. Read the words from each flower, talking with the children about ways to help their parents cash in on these coupons. Say, "When parents read the *(name the color)* flowers they will know that you want to *(teach them a song, etc.)*. Have them read you the special words at home."

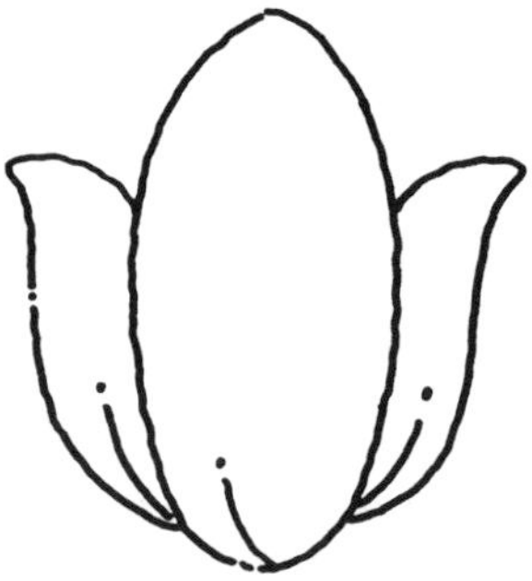

Announce to the children: Please put your love coupon basket on this table and when you and your family are ready to go home, be sure to take it with you. It's time now to go to Prayer *(or Story or Snack)*. I *(or our helper)* will walk with you.

Activity 2: Story and Movement

Story: *The Runaway Bunny* by Margaret Wise Brown (New York: Harper and Row, Publishers, 1942)

Introduce the story.

Let's read one of my favorite stories. It's about a bunny who got angry at his mom and tried to run away from her. Do you think he got lost, girls and boys? Let's read and find out.

Read the story.

(See if the children can find the bunny in each picture as he tries to hide.)

Talk about the story.

▲ That bunny couldn't hide from his mommy, could he? She wouldn't let him get lost because she loved him so much.

▲ That's the way your moms and dads are, and that's the way Jesus is. We can't lose Jesus and Jesus can't lose us. He always knows where we are and he always loves us. Jesus is our best friend.

▲ Do you remember the song we learned about sharing our feelings with Jesus? We can tell Jesus exactly how we feel and he will always love us.

(Sing the "Feelings Song," p. 88, and do the actions.)

Do the movement: Runaway, Runaway, Runaway Bunny.

This game is played like the popular game, Duck, Duck, Goose. The children sit in a friendship circle. One child walks around the outside of the circle and taps each child on the head, saying, "Runaway." When she reaches the child of her choice, she taps him on the head and says, "Bunny." This second child chases the first around the outside of the circle and tries to tag her. If she reaches the empty place and sits down without being tagged, she's safe. If he tags her first, she sits in the middle of the friendship circle for the rest of the game. Make sure each child gets a chance to play both parts.

Announce to the children: Now it's time to move to Craft *(or Prayer or Snack).* I *(or our helper)* will walk with you.

Activity 3: Prayer

Note: Lead the children into a personal encounter with Jesus by taking them on an imaginary shopping trip with Mom, Dad, or another loved adult to their favorite discount department store. By tapping into their senses, you can transform the room into this setting, where the shopping spree becomes more exciting as their imaginations take over. Here they will meet Jesus, and during prayer their friendship with him will deepen as they become familiar with him, listen to him, speak to him, and spend quiet time with him.

Lead the children.

Well! Here we are at *(name familiar discount department store in the area). (Name),* you remember where we parked the car. We're here under the light, next to the place where we return the shopping carts. Let's go—stick together so no one gets lost.

Look at the long aisles. Why don't we go to the book section first and see what good books they have for sale? *(Ask the children their preference for a book to look at, then take the imaginary book from the shelf and hand it to each child.)* Aren't these great books? What did you like about your book? Did you have a favorite picture?

Let's go down the aisle...oh, look! Up ahead. Look at the stuffed animals. Which is your favorite? *(Hand the favorite to each child. Let one or two describe what the animal looks like.)*

Let's go over to the toy department. Be careful going down this aisle. We have to walk sideways because it's so-o-o-o narrow. Careful. Follow me through these boxes...step sideways...oh, no...we have to jump over these boxes. Jump! Be careful now. They just mopped this floor, so it's still slippery. Take giant tiptoe steps. Good job!

Hey, do you see Mom or Dad? I don't see them anymore. Let's look in the next aisle...no, not there either. *(Look worried.)*

I think we'd better just sit down and wait for them to find us. I've got an idea! See that big plastic swimming pool? How about if I get it down and we sit inside it? Mom and Dad will see us when they come looking for us. *(Pantomime taking the pool off the shelf and stepping inside. Help the children step inside too, then sit down in a circle.)*

Have you ever been lost before? What did you feel like when you were lost? *(Elicit from the children the feeling of fear or worry they felt when they realized they were lost. Encourage them to talk about their experience.)*

You know, even though we don't know yet where Mommy and Daddy are, we are never really lost or alone. We have someone who loves us very much, cares for us, and is always, always with us. He's with us right now. Do you know who I'm talking about? Yes, that's right. Jesus. He's our forever friend. He's always there for us.

How about if we take a minute to be with Jesus right now? Let's all sit quietly and close our eyes. *(Allow 30-45 seconds to shift into quiet and calm.)*

Let's go into our heart rooms, children. This is a place deep inside ourselves, and Jesus lives here. See Jesus walking towards you. He's smiling and holding his arms out to you. Spend a little time looking at him. Notice what he looks like.

Jesus wants to say something to you. Listen...listen. What is he saying? *(Allow 45 seconds.)*

Now think of what you'd like to say to Jesus, because he's your best friend and he loves you so much. Talk to Jesus now in your heart room. Don't say the words out loud. *(Allow 45 seconds.)*

Jesus wants to hold you now. If it's all right with you, sit quietly with Jesus while he holds you. Know you are safe in his arms. *(Allow 45 seconds.)*

(Say softly:) You can open your eyes now, children.

(If the children are comfortable and can verbalize their prayer, ask them to share their talk with Jesus.)

What did Jesus look like? What did he say to you? Since Jesus is your best friend, what did you say to him?

Let's thank Jesus for his friendship and love, and for always being with us, even here at *(name of store).*

Oh, look, girls and boys. Mom and Dad have found us. Let's all walk back to the car together.

(If time, retrace the trip through the store to the parking lot.)

It's time to go to Story *(or Craft or Snack)* now. I *(or our helper)* will walk with you.

Snack

After the children have rotated through all three activities, we lead them to the snack room where we serve gingerbread cookies or cheese cut-out people and juice or milk. Their parents will meet them here after the children finish eating.

In the event the parents are delayed, use the maze activity on page 201.

Parent-Child Sharing Time

After the adult session, parents pick up their children in the snack room to begin their sharing time. Distribute the Parent-Child Sharing Time Form (p. 216). If weather permits, retreatants can go outside for a nature walk. If not, they might want to find a corner to sit in, parent and child together; take a walk through the church; or even spread blankets throughout the room. We allow approximately twenty minutes, asking parents and children to return to the gathering room at the appointed time for our closing.

During the parent presentation, the adult leader has suggested several questions designed to facilitate parent-child sharing:

▲ Tell me about the story you heard.
▲ What do you like about the craft you made?
▲ What was it like when you met Jesus in your heart room?
▲ What did Jesus look like?
▲ How did it feel to be with Jesus?
▲ When I met Jesus in my heart room, he said... I did...
▲ What did Jesus say to you? What did you do?

As retreatants are returning from sharing time, gather together and sing "J-E-S-U-S" (p. 180) or the "Feelings Song" (p. 88).

When all have arrived, begin the closing prayer.

Closing Prayer

Join hands in a circle and have parents and children repeat each line.

> Jesus,
> thank you for grown-ups
> who love me.
> You love me, too, Jesus.
> Let's be best friends
> and I'll talk to you
> whenever I'm happy or sad,
> whenever I'm grumpy or scared.
> And when I feel loving
> I'll hug a friend like you.
> *Amen.*

Announce to everyone: Now squeeze the hand of the special person who brought you to the retreat today.

Remind the children to take their craft home with them. Invite the children and parents to play Follow-the-Leader and lead them to the door.

7-Picnic

(1 John 4:12; Matthew 15:32-39)

Focus

We appeal to the children's experience of picnics to highlight the presence of Jesus in their lives. Picnics are special times, times when we invite those we love to break bread with us. The setting, the foods we bring, the excitement of doing this meal differently, the people with whom we share our picnic blanket all work to elevate the act of eating to something almost sacred. We focus on the refrain, "Wherever there is love, Jesus is there." Picnics are a time to look for this presence.

We stress there's no wrong way to have a picnic. It can be in the park or on the kitchen floor. It can be a breakfast picnic just as well as a lunch picnic. It can be with a large crowd or a picnic for us and our teddy bear. And we can have a winter picnic. Yes, even in the snow. It doesn't matter because picnics are times we share with people we love, and wherever there is love, Jesus is there.

Jesus went on picnics, too. We refer to the numerous times Jesus shared meals with people he loved. Then we tell the children of a particularly spectacular picnic where Jesus fed five thousand people—the miracle of the loaves and fishes. We encourage the children to think of this story every time they go on a picnic. Jesus performed this miracle to show his friends how much he loved them, and he loves us just as much. Wherever there is love, Jesus is there.

Preparations Before the Retreat

1. Meet as a team to pray, read, discuss, understand, and interiorize the focus and scriptural basis of the retreat.
2. Discern which team members will be responsible for the gathering presentation, each of the three children's activities, and the adult retreat session.
3. Choose an adult session topic from the Outlines for Parent Sessions (pp. 143-178).
4. Divide the following preparation responsibilities. Use the gifts of your community to lighten the load. Parents, teenagers, school children and senior citizens can all help prepare.

Make the nametags.
Using the teddy-bear pattern (p. 202), prepare a different color nametag for each of the four team leaders. Then, using the same four colors, prepare one nametag for each child. You should have an equal number of each color of children's nametags. You will divide into groups by colors. As the children choose their nametags, the groups are formed.

Warning: Use safety pins or tape to attach nametags. For the safety of the children, do not use straight pins or string.

Collect materials for the environment.
To arrange an attractive display on table or piano in gathering room, locate tablecloth, picnic basket, plastic or real food, thermos or jug, stuffed teddy bears, and small picnic blanket.

Prepare the craft (p. 101).
First, gather materials for Picnic Baskets:
- ▲ plastic mesh strawberry baskets, 1 per child
- ▲ extra long pipe cleaners, 1 per child
- ▲ empty 35mm film canisters, 1 per child
- ▲ checkered paper napkins, 1 per child
- ▲ white poster board

▲ construction paper: yellow, pink, tan, green, brown, red
▲ crayons or markers

Second, do the advance preparations:
1. Cut out poster-board "sandwich bread" and construction paper "sandwich fillings," "cookies," and "watermelon" (see illustrations, p. 101).
2. Cover each film canister with plain white paper.
3. Tie pipe cleaner on opposite sides of each basket to make a handle.
4. Line each basket with paper napkin.

Optional craft: Paper-Plate Food Collage
If you choose to do a paper plate collage with the children instead, you will need to precut a number of pictures of food from available magazines.

Locate the story:
Obtain *The Winter Picnic* by Robert Welber (New York, Random House, 1970) or one from the optional book list:
▲ *Frederick* by Leo Lionni (New York: Pantheon, 1967)
▲ *The Teddy Bear's Picnic* by Jimmy Kennedy (New York: Green Tiger Press, 1983)

Select a movement activity.
Use Beach Blanket Bear Bounce (p. 103) or another activity of your choice.

Become familiar with the prayer (p. 103).

Purchase groceries and prepare snack (p. 105).
Ants on a Log (see illustration at right):
▲ celery
▲ peanut butter or cream cheese
▲ raisins
▲ lemonade or hot chocolate
or
PB&J Sandwiches (cut in fourths):
▲ peanut butter
▲ jelly
▲ bread
▲ lemonade or hot chocolate

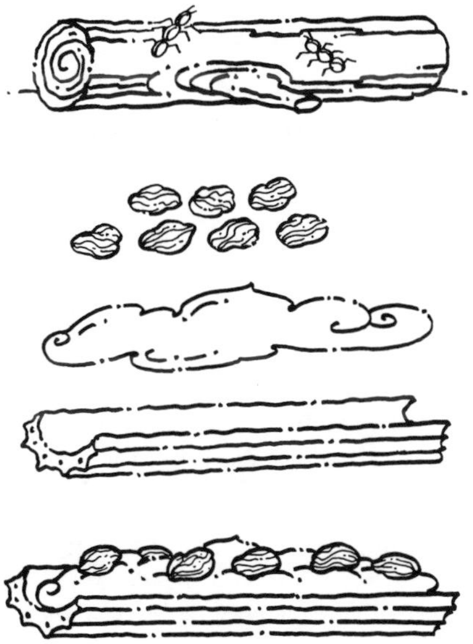

Duplicate the Parent-Child Sharing Form (p. 216).

Preparations the Day of the Retreat

1. Gather as a team and pray.
2. Set out nametags and safety pins or tape (warning: no straight pins or strings). Have exactly as many nametags as retreatants.
3. Have each retreat team member wear a different colored nametag. This will later help the children divide into groups for their activities.
4. Atop a piano or table, create the environment in the gathering room with an arrangement of tablecloth, picnic basket, plastic or real food, thermos or jug, stuffed teddy bears, and a small picnic basket.
5. Also in the gathering room, place a sample of the picnic basket craft, a copy of *The Winter Picnic* or book of your choice, and a Bible.
6. Gather all the materials for the craft and set out on tables in the room to be used for this activity.
7. Spread out so that at least one team member is greeting the retreatants as they arrive, one is directing parents and younger siblings to the nursery, one is bringing retreatants and parents to the gathering room, and one is waiting in the gathering room.
8. Begin the retreat by warmly greeting the retreatants, then introducing the team members.
9. Sing together the gathering song "J-E-S-U-S" (p. 180).

Gathering Presentation

How many of you have been on a picnic? Raise your hands.

A picnic makes eating special, doesn't it? A picnic is something we do with people we love.

Raise your hand if you've been on a picnic in a park. How about in the mountains? in your backyard? on your kitchen floor? in your bedroom?

Raise your hand if you've been on a picnic with your whole family. Raise your hand if you've been on a picnic all by yourself.

How many of you have eaten hot dogs on a picnic? How many of you have eaten cereal and orange juice on a picnic? That would be a breakfast picnic, wouldn't it?

Does it have to be sunny and warm to have a picnic? No! Did you know you could have a winter picnic outside in the snow? Raise your hand if you've ever had a winter picnic outside in the snow.

There's no right way to have a picnic, and there's no wrong way. Any time and any place you want to eat with someone special, you can have a picnic. You might want to invite a special friend to your picnic, like your teddy bear.

Or you could invite Jesus. Jesus is our best friend.

A picnic makes eating a special time. It's something we do with people we love.

And do you know what? Wherever there is love, Jesus is there.

I'm going to say that again. Wherever there is love, Jesus is there. Can you say that with me? *Wherever there is love, Jesus is there.*

So whether you have a picnic with lots of people you love, or with just your teddy bear, or all by yourself, Jesus will be there, because—wherever there is love, Jesus is there. Say that with me again. *Wherever there is love, Jesus is there.*

Do you know that Jesus went on picnics, too? I was reading about a picnic in this book. *(Hold up Bible)* Do you have this book at your house?

There are lots of stories in the Bible about Jesus eating with his friends, but one I like is about the time Jesus had a picnic with five thousand people!

Do you know how many people five thousand is? Look around this room. If this room were packed full of people, it still wouldn't be five thousand.

Well, these five thousand people had been outside with Jesus for a long time, but everyone had forgotten to bring their picnic lunches, so they were very hungry.

Jesus said, "I feel so sorry for my friends. They're hungry and they have nothing to eat." Then he had an idea. He said, "Does anyone have any bread at all?"

One of his best friends, a child, said, "I have some loaves of bread and a few small fish."

Do you think some loaves of bread and a few small fish is enough to feed five thousand people? No!

But that's what's so special about Jesus. Jesus can change things. And do you know what? He fed five thousand people with some loaves of bread and a few small fish.

He put the fish and the bread into a picnic basket like this one. *(Show the children a picnic basket.)* He gave everybody as much food as they wanted, and he never ran out of food? He fed five thousand people and he never ran out of food! Every time he took food out of the basket, more food appeared.

It was like magic, only it was Jesus' magic. It was a miracle.

Jesus fed his friends on this picnic because he loved them. And—let's say it together—*wherever there is love, Jesus is there.*

So remember that, whenever you go on a picnic with people you love, or even by yourself. Let's say it together one more time. *Wherever there is love, Jesus is there.*

Let's sing a song about going on a picnic.

Picnic Song
(Tune: "Do You Know the Muffin Man?")

Do you have a picnic lunch,
A picnic lunch, a picnic lunch,
Do you have a picnic lunch
To share with us today?
Oh, yes, I have a picnic lunch,
A picnic lunch, a picnic lunch,
Oh, yes, I have a picnic lunch
To share with you today.

Oh, do you have a best friend here,
A best friend here, a best friend here?
Oh, do you have a best friend here
To share with us today?
Oh, yes, I have a best friend here,
A best friend here, a best friend here,
Oh, yes, I have a best friend here
To share with you today.

My best friend's name is Jesus Christ,
Jesus Christ, Jesus Christ,
My best friend's name is Jesus Christ—
He's here with us today.

What great singing! We have some fun activities to do now while your moms and dads stay here and listen to a talk for parents. Let me show you what we'll be doing. *(Show the children the craft and story, and tell them they'll also be talking to Jesus.)*

Mommy or Daddy will pick you up when we have our snack. Time to give each other a big hug or a wave.

Now look at the color of your nametag. *(Have the children leave the room with the team leader who has the same colored nametag.)* Wave goodbye.

Children's Activities

The following three children's activities run simultaneously, and the children rotate among them until they've been to all three.

Activity 1: Craft

As the children work, we talk in our own words about how Jesus is their best friend and how Jesus would love to be invited the next time they have a real or pretend picnic.

Remember, craft time is time of reinforcing the theme of the retreat. Far more important than what we say or do is that we share our sense of wonder, conveying our awe that Jesus is with us always.

Construct Picnic Baskets with the children: (see illustrations)

1. Assemble "sandwich," gluing items in order: "bread," "cheese," "meat," "lettuce," "tomato," "bread."
2. Draw black seeds on "watermelon."
3. Decorate "cookies" using crayons.
4. Decorate "thermos" using crayons.
5. Helper cuts sandwich in half with adult scissors.

To simplify the craft:
Make a "peanut butter and jelly sandwich," using only red and brown, irregular shapes.

Optional craft: Paper-Plate Collage
Children construct paper-plate food collage with precut food pictures from magazines, glued onto paper plates.

Announce to the children: Let's put your picnic baskets on this table and when you and Mommy or Daddy are ready to go home, you can come in here and get your basket. It's time now to go to Prayer *(or Story or Snack)*. I *(or our helper)* will walk with you.

Activity 2: Story and Movement

Story: *The Winter Picnic* by Robert Welber (New York: Random House, 1970)

Introduce the story.
We can have a picnic in any season, at any time of day. In our story today Adam wants to make a picnic in the snow.

Read the story.

Talk about the story.

- ▲ What was the boy's name in the story? *(Adam.)*
- ▲ Do you know anyone named Adam?
- ▲ I think this story could also be about *(read from a nametag)* or about *(different name of someone in the room).*
- ▲ What was the weather like the day Adam wanted to have a picnic? *(snowy, cold)*
- ▲ Think of your last picnic. What was it like?

- ▲ Who did Adam want to come to his picnic? *(his mom)*
- ▲ Try to remember who was at your last picnic.
- ▲ Our best friend Jesus liked picnics, too. Maybe the weather was warmer when Jesus and his friends ate the bread and fish, but they had a wonderful picnic, just like you and Adam in the story. Our friend Jesus would probably like you to invite him whenever you have a picnic.

Do the movement: Beach Blanket Bear Bounce.
Using the blanket and stuffed bears from the picnic display of the gathering session, the children put one or several bears in the middle and make them bounce by moving the blanket vigorously up and down. Choose four children to hold the four corners of the blanket and demonstrate.

Explain to the children: Sometimes after we eat at a picnic we play. Our game today is Beach Blanket Bear Bounce. We need children to hold corners of the small blanket. *(choose volunteers)* Let's move our blanket up and down, all four of us, and make our bears bounce. Make sure you catch the bear on the blanket each time.

Demonstrate with three children and yourself. As you play the game, invite the children to take turns holding the corners of the blanket.

Say to them: Maybe you could teach this game to your mom or dad or your friends next time you and your best friend Jesus go on a picnic. All you need is a small blanket and a stuffed bear friend to play.

Announce to the children: It's time to go to Craft *(or Prayer or Snack)* now. I *(or our helper)* will walk with you.

Activity 3: Prayer

Note: Lead the children into a personal encounter with Jesus in the setting of a winter picnic. By tapping into their senses and imaginations, you can transform the room into a forest, a wonderful picnic place that becomes more alive as the children's imaginations take over. Here they will meet Jesus, and during their prayer their friendship with him will deepen as they become familiar with him, listen to him, speak to him, and spend quiet time with him.

Lead the children.
Do you see the tall trees above our heads? Look up and see the sun coming through the trees. Now, let's start walking through the trees to that place over there by the stream where we'll be having our picnic. Watch out for that tall grass. Better take some pretty big steps so we can get through the grass.

Wow, that was fun! I wonder what's up ahead on that hill over there. Oh, brother ...that hill is taller than I thought. Take a deep breath. Now let's take some real giant steps to climb this hill. Are you okay? Just a few more steps and we're almost to the top.

My word! Look around. You can see way off in the distance when you're up this high. Do you see the stream down there? Let's climb back down the hill and go over to the stream. Be careful. Take small steps as we go down. Try not to fall. That was a lot easier coming down, wasn't it? Easier than climbing that big hill.

Let's walk over this way...oh, no! Look, there's a deep hole. Better stay close to the wall so we don't get too near the edge of that hole. Careful. Take your time.

Whew! That was close!

Look up ahead. I see the stream. We're going to have to cross it. Watch your shoes. Step on the large rocks in the water. Careful...big, giant steps will help us here. Don't get wet. Way to go!

I've got a blanket. *(Name),* you and *(Name)* find a place on the grass here for me to spread our blanket. That's a great place. Can you hear the water in the stream? Hey, even though we're having a winter picnic, I don't feel cold, do you? I feel the sun shining on me. It feels good, doesn't it?"

(After the children have settled on the blanket near the stream, invite them to close their eyes and listen to the forest sounds. Allow 30-45 seconds, using this time to shift into quiet and calm.)

We are in our heart rooms, children. This is a place deep inside ourselves, and Jesus lives here. See Jesus walking toward you. He's smiling and holding his arms out to you. Spend a little time looking at him. Notice what he looks like.

Jesus wants to say something to you. Listen...listen. What is he saying? *(Allow 45 seconds.)*

Now think of what you'd like to say to Jesus because he's your best friend and he loves you very much. Talk to Jesus now in your heart room. Don't say the words out loud. *(Allow 45 seconds.)*

Jesus wants to hold you now. If it's all right with you, sit quietly with Jesus while he holds you. Know you are safe in his arms.

(Say softly:) You can open your eyes now, children.

(If the children are comfortable and can verbalize their prayer, ask them to share their talk with Jesus.)

What did Jesus look like? What did he say to you? Since Jesus is your best friend, what did you say to him?

(If time allows, retrace the trip through the forest back to the door of the room.)

It's time to go to Story *(or Craft or Snack)* now. I *(or our helper)* will walk with you.

Snack

After the children have rotated through all three activities, lead them to the snack room. Their parents will meet them here after the children finish eating.

(Warning: Preschoolers will not wait for hot drinks to cool. Cool hot chocolate to a safe temperature before serving.)

In the event the parents are delayed, use the Picnic Activity on page 203.

Parent-Child Sharing Time

After the adult session, parents pick up their children in the snack room to begin their sharing time. Distribute the Parent-Child Sharing Time Form (p. 216). If weather permits, retreatants can go outside for a nature walk. If not, they might want to find a corner to sit in, parent and child together; take a walk through the church; or even spread out picnic blankets throughout the room. We allow approximately twenty minutes, asking parents and children to return to the gathering room at the allotted time for our closing.

During the parent presentation, the adult leader has suggested several questions designed to facilitate parent-child sharing:

- ▲ Tell me about the story you heard.
- ▲ What do you like about the craft you made?
- ▲ What was it like when you met Jesus in your heart room?
- ▲ What did Jesus look like?
- ▲ How did it feel to be with Jesus?
- ▲ When I met Jesus in my heart room, he said... I did...
- ▲ What did Jesus say to you? What did you do?

As retreatants are returning from sharing time, gather together and sing "J-E-S-U-S" (p. 180) or the "Picnic Song" (p. 100).

When all have arrived, begin the closing prayer.

Closing Prayer

Join hands in a circle and have parents and children repeat each line.

Jesus,
you are my very best friend
and you love me.
Thank you
for inviting me
to the picnic.
We had fun.
Come home with me
and help me
to show everybody
how much I love them
because
wherever there is love,
you are there, too.
Amen.

Remind the children to take their craft home with them. Invite the children and parents to play Follow-the-Leader and lead them to the door.

8-Candle

(Luke 11:33-36)

Focus

During this season that lures children with parties and candy, costumes and decorations, we focus on the candle that lights up the jack-o'-lantern. We light a candle for the children and show them how the flame dances and flickers, as if to tell us it's happy to be with us. When we place the candle inside our carved pumpkin, the jack-o'-lantern looks brighter, happier, like he's really smiling. His joy makes us feel happy, too. We show the children the folly of covering our pumpkin with a basket. If we can't see him smile, he can't make us happy. The basket might also make the candle go out; without a candle glowing inside, the jack-o'-lantern is ordinary. It's the candle that makes the pumpkin special.

We turn now to the theology of the indwelling God. We, too, have Someone inside us who lights us up, much the way a candle illuminates a jack-o'-lantern. It's Jesus, and when we invite Jesus to dwell in us, his goodness shines forth from us. We make sure the children understand that we're all good because of our close friendship with Jesus. We can be grumpy, make mistakes, do naughty things sometimes, yet we're still good because Jesus lives in us. Being good means that people feel good when they're with us because we're so much like Jesus. It makes people want to be friends with Jesus, too. Should we wear baskets over our happy faces? No! Let us shine!

Preparations Before the Retreat

1. Meet as a team to pray, read, discuss, understand, and interiorize the focus and scriptural basis of the retreat.
2. Discern which team members will be responsible for the gathering presentation, each of the three children's activities, and the adult retreat session.
3. Choose an adult retreat topic from the Outlines for Parent Sessions (pp. 143-178).
4. Divide the following preparation responsibilities. Use the gifts of your community to lighten the load. Parents, teenagers, school children, and senior citizens can all help prepare.

Make the nametags.
Using the candle pattern (p. 204), prepare a different color nametag for each of the four team leaders. Then, using the same four colors, prepare one nametag for each child. You should have an equal number of each color of children's nametags. You will divide into groups by colors. As the children choose their nametags, the groups are formed.

Warning: Use safety pins or tape to attach nametags. For the safety of the children, do not use straight pins or string.

(Note: For an optional nametag, use the Jack-O'-Lantern pattern on p. 205. Adhere colored sticky stars—1/3 red, 1/3 green, 1/3 gold—next to child's name on orange construction-paper jack-o'-lanterns.)

Collect materials for the environment.
To arrange an attractive display on table or piano in gathering room, prepare a large jack-o'-lantern. Locate a candle to place inside and a basket large enough to cover the pumpkin.

Prepare the craft (p. 112).
First, gather materials for Mosaic Jack-O'-Lanterns:
▲ orange craft tissue paper or construction paper
▲ yellow construction paper
▲ orange or white dessert-size paper plates or pumpkin pattern (p. 206)

▲ green construction paper
▲ glue

1. If using the pumpkin pattern (p. 206), duplicate the pattern on orange paper; cut out the pumpkins.
2. Cut orange paper into a 1" squares, 30 per child.
3. Cut yellow paper into triangles (eyes, 2 per child), circles (nose, 1 per child), and ovals (mouth, 1 per child)
4. Cut green paper into 2" x 6" strips, 1 per child.

Locate the story.
Obtain *The Biggest Pumpkin Ever* by Steven Kroll (New York: Holiday House, 1984), or one of the following:
▲ *Pumpkin, Pumpkin* by Jeanne Titherington (New York: Morrow, 1990)
▲ *Halloween Surprises* by Ann Schweninger (New York: Puffin, 1986)
▲ *The Halloween Performance* by Felicia Bond (New York: Harper Collins Children's Books, 1987)

Select a movement activity.
Use Slap Jack-O'-Lantern, (p. 113) or another of your choice. If you use Slap Jack-O'-Lantern you will need a regular deck of playing cards with a small jack-o'-lantern glued to each of four jacks. If you use Candle Categories, you will need an assortment of candles in different sizes, colors, and types.

Become familiar with the prayer (p. 113).

Purchase groceries and prepare the snack (p. 115).
Pumpkin Faces (spread bread, muffins, or cookies with butter or cream cheese; add candy-corn eyes and raisin mouths):
▲ pumpkin-shaped cookies, pumpkin muffins, or round slices of pumpkin bread
▲ butter or cream cheese
▲ candy corn
▲ raisins
▲ milk or juice
or
Jack-O'-Lantern Cheese and Crackers (cut pumpkin-shaped cheese slices and serve on crackers):
▲ crackers
▲ slices of American cheese
▲ pumpkin cookie cutter.
▲ milk or juice

Duplicate the Parent-Child Sharing Form (p. 216).

Preparations the Day of the Retreat

1. Gather as a team and pray.
2. Set out nametags and safety pins or tape (warning: no straight pins or strings). Have exactly as many nametags as retreatants.
3. Have each retreat team member wear a different colored nametag. This will later help the children divide into groups for their activities.
4. Atop a piano or table, create the environment in the gathering room with an arrangement of large jack-o'-lantern, candle, and basket.
5. Also in the gathering room, place a sample of the Mosaic Jack-O'-Lantern craft, a copy of *The Biggest Pumpkin Ever* or book of your choice, and a Bible.
6. Gather all the materials for the craft and set out on tables in the room to be used for this activity.
7. Spread out so that at least one team member is greeting the retreatants as they arrive, one is directing parents and younger siblings to the nursery, one is bringing retreatants and parents to the gathering room, and one is waiting in the gathering room.
8. Begin the retreat by warmly greeting the retreatants, then introducing the team members.
9. Sing together the gathering song "J-E-S-U-S" (p. 180).

Gathering Presentation

What do you have on your nametags?

That's right, a candle *(or a jack-o'-lantern that lights up).* Look what happens when I light this real candle. It flickers and dances. It looks like it's happy, doesn't it? Maybe it's happy because we're all here together. One thing we use a candle for is to light up a jack-o'-lantern so that we can see it in the dark. See what happens? He looks happier, doesn't he? He looks brighter. He looks like he's really smiling. Doesn't this jack-o'-lantern make you feel happy? He makes us feel happy because he's so happy. Do you think we should put this basket over the pumpkin? Why not? *(Wait for answers.)* If we cover the pumpkin with a basket, the candle might go out, and then we won't see his smile. If we can't see the jack-o'-lantern, he can't make us happy with his happy smile, right? The jack-o'-lantern doesn't light itself; the candle lights up the jack-o'-lantern.

We have Someone inside us who lights us up, too. Did you know that? Jesus doesn't live up in the sky somewhere; he lives right here inside us. When we let Jesus live inside us, he lights us up. But instead of lighting us with fire, as the candle does in the pumpkin, Jesus lights us with goodness. Jesus is goodness and goodness is Jesus. Can you say that with me?

Jesus is goodness and goodness is Jesus.

We're all Jesus' special friends because we let Jesus live in us. So we're all good, as Jesus is. "Good" doesn't mean that we don't make mistakes. We all make mistakes; we're all grumpy at times; we all do naughty things sometimes. And we're still good. What "good" means is that people feel good when they're with us because we're so much like Jesus. It makes them want to be friends with Jesus, too. Would you feel good with me if I looked like this? *(Scowl.)* Would you feel good with me if I talked like this? *(Sound mean.)* How about this? *(Smile.)* I look like the jack-o'-lantern with Jesus shining in me, don't I? Should I cover my happy face with this basket? No! I want to shine!

Let's sing a song about Jesus shining in us.

I'm Gonna Let It Shine
(Tune: "I'm Gonna Let It Shine")

This little light of mine, I'm gonna let it shine.
This little light of mine, I'm gonna let it shine.
Let it shine, let it shine, let it shine.

Put it under a bushel? No! I'm gonna let it shine.
Put it under a bushel? No! I'm gonna let it shine.
Let it shine, let it shine, let it shine.

All around the neighborhood, I'm gonna let it shine.
All around the neighborhood, I'm gonna let it shine.
Let it shine, let it shine, let it shine.

Don't you dare go blow it out, I'm gonna let it shine.
Don't you dare go blow it out, I'm gonna let it shine.
Let it shine, let it shine, let it shine.

What great singing! We have some fun activities to do now while your moms and dads stay here and listen to a talk for parents. Let me show you what we'll be doing. *(Show the children the craft and story, and tell them they'll also be talking to Jesus.)* Mommy or Daddy will pick you up when we have our snack.

Time to give each other a big hug. *(Wait).*

Now look at the color of your nametag. *(Have the children leave the room with the team leader who has the same colored nametag.)* Wave goodbye.

Children's Activities

The following three children's activities run simultaneously, and the children rotate through them until they've been to all three.

Activity 1: Craft

As the children work, we talk in our own words about how Jesus is our best friend and how happy we are that he's so close to us; that he is, in fact, inside us.

Construct Mosaic Jack-O'-Lanterns with the children. (See illustration.)

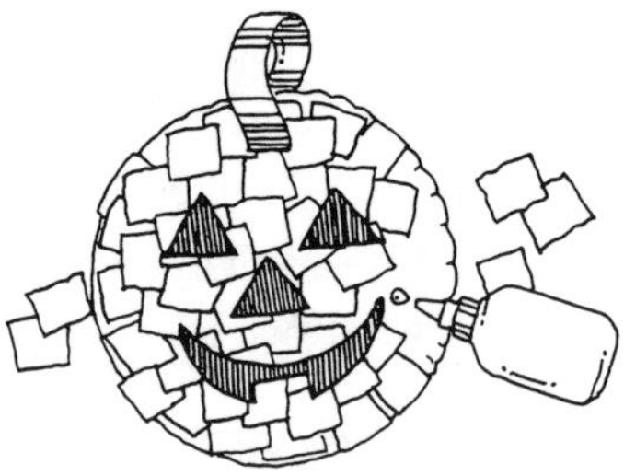

1. Children glue orange paper onto circle until covered.
2. Glue eyes, nose, and mouth on top of orange pieces.
3. Glue green strip on for stem, folding it in middle and attaching to both front and back of pumpkin.

To simplify the craft:
Glue the orange pieces and stem to the plate or pumpkin-shape ahead of time. Have the children glue on the face only.

For greater challenge:
Children glue the tissue-paper pieces onto the pumpkin base after wrapping each piece of tissue around a pencil eraser or wadding it up, creating a three-dimensional effect.

Announce to the children: Let's put your pumpkins on this table and when you and Mommy or Daddy are ready to go home, you can come in here and get it. It's time now to go to Prayer *(or Story or Snack)*. I *(or our helper)* will walk with you.

Activity 2: Story and Movement

Story: *The Biggest Pumpkin Ever* by Steven Kroll (New York: Holiday House, Inc., 1984)

Introduce the story.
The animals in this story have a wonderful time growing their garden. Because of their sharing, cooperating, and loving, something surprising happens.

Read the story.

Talk about the story.
▲ Have you ever grown a pumpkin?

- ▲ It took a lot of love for the mice in this story to take care of their growing pumpkin. That's the same kind of love our best friend Jesus shows us as we grow. Jesus takes care of us all day and all night.
- ▲ What did each of the mice want to do with the pumpkin?
- ▲ Did either one of them plan to make the pumpkin into a jack-o'-lantern?
- ▲ What does it take for a jack-o'-lantern to light up? *(a candle)*
- ▲ We can let Jesus shine in us like that candle. And when he does, we share, cooperate, and love as the mice did in the story. That's what it means to have Jesus shine in us. When we see the light shining in the jack-o'-lantern, we remember Jesus shining in us.
- ▲ Now let's make a circle and I'll show you a card game we play looking for that lit up pumpkin.

Do the movement: Slap Jack-o'-Lantern.
Use a regular deck of playing cards with a small jack-o'-lantern stuck on each of the four jacks. As the children gather around, turn the cards over one by one. Whoever sees a jack-o'-lantern can slap that card. Put those cards in a pile. Stress cooperation and not hurting each other when slapping.

Optional activity: Candle Categories
Bring 10-12 old candles. Together, group them by size *(looking for the smallest, the skinniest, etc.)*, or by color, or by type *(birthday candles, church candles, dinner candles, candles in holders, etc.)*. As the children sort the candles, talk about how Jesus lights up our life.

Announce to the children: It's time to go to Craft *(or Prayer or Snack)* now. I *(or our helper)* will walk with you.

Activity 3: Prayer

Note: Llead the children into a personal encounter with Jesus in the setting of a pumpkin patch. By tapping into their senses and imaginations, you can transform the room into a favorite place that becomes more alive as the children's imaginations take over. Here they will meet Jesus, and during prayer their friendship with him will deepen as they become familiar with him, listen to him, speak to him, and spend quiet time with him.

Lead the children.
You know, this time of year we see a lot of pumpkins. Where are some of the places you've seen pumpkins? *(Name),* do you have one at your house? Today we're going to take a trip to the pumpkin patch. Farmers grow pumpkins all together in a little patch of ground, and we call that a pumpkin patch. Sometimes

a farmer will plant a lot of strawberries together in the same place and that is called a strawberry patch. But today we're off to meet a special friend in the pumpkin patch. Before we go, let's put on our tall boots just in case there's some water or muddy ground on our way to the pumpkin patch. All right, did you put on your left boot? Now, the right boot. Great. We're ready for anything now.

Follow me down this path. Do you see the carrot tops just beginning to grow above the ground? I bet the farmer will be happy when she comes down here tomorrow to pick those juicy carrots. Careful you don't step on any of them.

I'll bet you like apples. Look, there's an apple tree up ahead. Follow me. We'll climb the hill and I can pick us each an apple.

Watch for those rocks. Step up on top of them. Careful now...that's it. Say, *(Name),* you're a good rock climber. Oh, there it is. Do you see the pumpkins up ahead? Look at all those great orange bumps. Pick out the one you would like to sit next to. Careful, don't trip. Here, how about these pumpkins in the middle? Easy now. Step over the small ones so we don't crush them. Good going.

Let's sit here in the middle. Good. Get comfortable because I told you we were going to be able to meet our good friend here. Who do you think the friend is that I've been telling you about? Jacob, do you know? That's right. Jesus. He's the friend we're going to be talking to right here in the middle of the pumpkin patch. Why don't you put your heads down? Rest them on your hands. Now let's get quiet. *(After the children have settled on the grass, invite them to close their eyes and listen to the sounds. Allow 30-45 seconds, using this time to shift into quiet and calm.)*

Now explain to them: We are in our heart rooms, children. This is a place deep inside ourselves, and Jesus lives here. See Jesus walking toward you. He's smiling and holding his arms out to you. Spend a little time looking at him. Notice what he looks like. Jesus wants to say something to you. Listen...listen. What is he saying? *(Allow 45 seconds.)*

Now think of what you'd like to say to Jesus because he's your best friend and he loves you so much.

Talk to Jesus now in your heart room. Don't say the words out loud. *(Allow 45 seconds.)* Jesus wants to hold you now. If it's all right with you, sit quietly with Jesus while he holds you. Know you are safe in his arms.

(Say softly:) You can open your eyes now, children.

(If the children are comfortable and can verbalize their prayer, ask them to share their talk with Jesus.)

What did Jesus look like?

What did he say to you? Since Jesus is your best friend, what did you say to him?

The best part is that we can come back to this pumpkin patch to talk to Jesus anytime we want. But we don't have to always come to the pumpkin patch. We can talk to Jesus anytime we become quiet on the inside.

Where are some of the places we could talk to Jesus? *(Name),* could you talk to Jesus in your bedroom? *(Name),* how about in the back seat of the car while your mom or dad is driving? *(Name),* could you talk to Jesus when you're sitting in the bathtub? Right. We can talk to Jesus anytime we want to. That's the best part about having Jesus as our best friend. He goes everywhere with us!

I think it's time we go back home. Stand up and fluff up the leaves around the pumpkin where you were sitting. Now follow me and we'll go back in a different way. Let's go past this stream. I bet the farmer uses some of this water for those pumpkins, don't you? See the stones up ahead. Let's step on them as we cross the river. Climb up this side of the hill and we can go past the apple tree where we had our treat earlier. Look down there. That's the fence we came through to get up here. Let's go back toward the fence.

It's time to go to Story *(or Craft or Snack)* now. I *(or our helper)* will walk with you.

Snack

After the children have rotated through all three activities, lead them to the snack room to enjoy pumpkin bread or cheese jack-o'-lanterns and crackers. Their parents will meet them here after the children finish eating.

In the event the parents are delayed, use the Candle Retreat Activity on page 207.

Parent-Child Sharing Time

After the adult session, parents pick up their children in the snack room to begin their sharing time. Distribute the Parent-Child Sharing Time Form (p. 216). If weather permits, retreatants can go outside for a nature walk. If not, they might want to find a corner to sit in, parent and child together; take a walk through the church; or even spread out blankets throughout the room. We allow approximately twenty minutes, asking parents and children to return to the gathering room at the appointed time for our closing. During the parent presentation, the adult leader has suggested several questions designed to facilitate parent-child sharing:

- ▲ Tell me about the story you heard.
- ▲ What do you like about the craft you made?
- ▲ What was it like when you met Jesus in your heart room?
- ▲ What did Jesus look like?
- ▲ How did it feel to be with Jesus?
- ▲ When I met Jesus in my heart room, he said... I did...
- ▲ What did Jesus say to you? What did you do?

As retreatants are returning from sharing time, gather together and sing "J-E-S-U-S" (p. 180) or "I'm Gonna Let it Shine" (p. 111). When all have arrived, begin the closing prayer.

Closing Prayer

Join hands in a circle and have parents and children repeat each line.

Jesus, we love you,
and thank you for being our best friend.
Thank you, too, for shining in me.
Help me, Jesus,
to show my goodness to everyone.
Amen.

Remind the children to take their craft home with them. Invite the children and parents to play Follow-the-Leader, leading them to the door.

9-Thanksgiving

(1 Corinthians 12:4-31)

Focus

Thanksgiving is traditionally the time we thank God for all God has given us. Today we focus on one of God's greatest gifts to us: ourselves. We wish to instill in our young retreatants an awe and appreciation of who they are. They are precious to God, to their families, and to us as Church, exactly as they are, unlike anyone else. Furthermore, each one is indispensable because they are members of God's family, the Body of Christ.

We introduce our little ones to their part in the Body of Christ, beginning with an illustration of the familiar Thanksgiving turkey. We've prepared some funny looking turkeys to demonstrate the folly of too many body parts or of one part dominating over the others. One might have all feathers, another, four legs. A third might be a turkey that is one gigantic eye surrounded by feathers. The children can talk about why this doesn't make sense.

Nor would it make any sense if our own bodies had too many, or oversized, parts. We follow the text of St. Paul's analogy of the body in his first letter to the Corinthians (1 Cor. 12:4-31) to magnify the importance of each part of our bodies, and, later, of each member of Christ's Body. The children can answer the questions Paul so beautifully posed as if he'd actually been talking to an audience of young children: "If the foot should say, 'Because I am not a hand I do not belong to the body,' it does not for this reason belong any less to the body (v. 15); and, "If the whole body were an eye, where would the hearing be?" (v. 17); and "The eye cannot say to the hand, 'I do not need you'" (v. 21)...can it? With a little discussion, the children come to realize that every single part of the body has its purpose. But no single part is all-important. People who don't have full use of their bodies, for example, know how integrally the parts of the body work together and how other body parts will compensate for nonworking parts.

Similarly, every member of a family is important. Each child in the family is unique from the others, but think how different that family would be without one of its members. Imagine how strange it would be if the family were all Francescas or only Jamals.

So it is with Christ. Since Jesus died, he doesn't have a body, only a Spirit. So we have to be Jesus' Body. Some of us are really good thinkers, so we're like Jesus' head. Some of us like to do nice things for each other, so we're Jesus' hands and feet. It's important that we all be who we are, or Jesus' Body won't work. For example, what if all of us were grown-ups? That would be as silly as if a turkey had all heads. Children are essential to the Body of Christ. And in Jesus' view, they are highly prized.

Who knows? The next time our little ones see a Thanksgiving turkey, perhaps they'll think of their importance in their own families, in God's family, in the Body of Christ.

Preparations Before the Retreat

1. Meet as a team to pray, read, discuss, understand, and interiorize the focus and scriptural basis of the retreat.
2. Discern which team members will be responsible for the gathering presentation, each of the three children's activities, and the adult session.
3. Choose a topic from the Outlines for the Parent Sessions (pp. 143-178).
4. Divide the following preparation responsibilities. Use the gifts of your community to lighten the load. Parents, teenagers, school children and senior citizens can all help prepare.

Make the nametags.
Using the hand pattern (p. 208), prepare a different color nametag for each of the four team leaders. Then, using the same four colors, prepare one nametag for each child. You should have an equal number of each color of children's nametags. On each hand, write, "*(Name)* is important in the Body of Christ." You will divide into groups by colors. As the children choose their nametags, the groups are formed.

Warning: Use safety pins or tape to attach nametags. For the safety of the children, do not use straight pins or string.

(Note: For an optional nametag, use the turkey pattern on p. 209.)

Collect materials for the environment.
To arrange an attractive display on a table or piano in the gathering place, locate lace or a tablecloth decorated for Thanksgiving, a model turkey made of paper or ceramic, and a combination of cornucopias, pilgrim figurines, colored leaves, gourds, and pumpkins. In addition, find pictures or posters of children of all ages and races. If available, locate "In His Image," the portrait of Jesus by Zdinak, which includes famous faces such as Gandhi, Martin Luther King, as well as members of the artist's family.

Prepare the gathering presentation (p. 122).
Make four different turkeys or one feltboard turkey with add-on felt parts so that the children can see three wacky turkeys (one that's all feathers, another with no eyes, and a third with four legs) and one normal turkey.

Prepare the craft (p. 125).
First, gather materials for Cardboard-Tube Napkin Rings:
▲ bathroom tissue tubes, 1 per child
▲ napkin ring decorative covering strip pattern (p. 211)
▲ turkey stickers
▲ glue
▲ stapler
▲ yarn

Second, do the advance preparations:
Because these crafts require so much preassembly, diagrams are given here, rather than with the craft activities themselves.
1. Duplicate decorative covering strips (p. 211) on white or, if possible, colored paper.

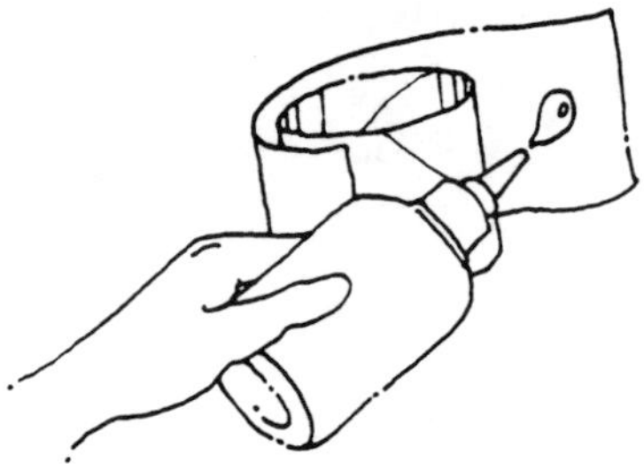

2. Cut each bathroom tissue tube into four equal parts.
3. Cut yarn into 36" lengths, 1 length per child.

Optional craft: Cornhusk Dolls

Gather materials:

▲ ivory "cornhusk" paper twist,
  16" per child (available at craft stores)
▲ floral wire, 8-12" per child (available at craft stores)
▲ 1" styrofoam balls, 1 per child *(optional)*
▲ colored markers
▲ fine-tipped black marker
▲ file folder gummed labels for nametags, 1 per child, or sample nametags (p. 211)

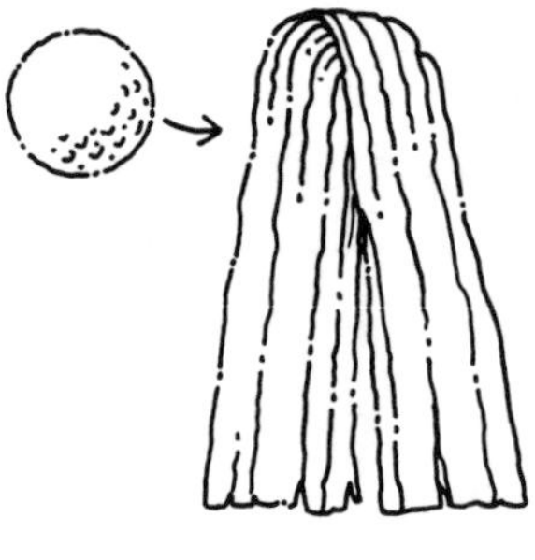

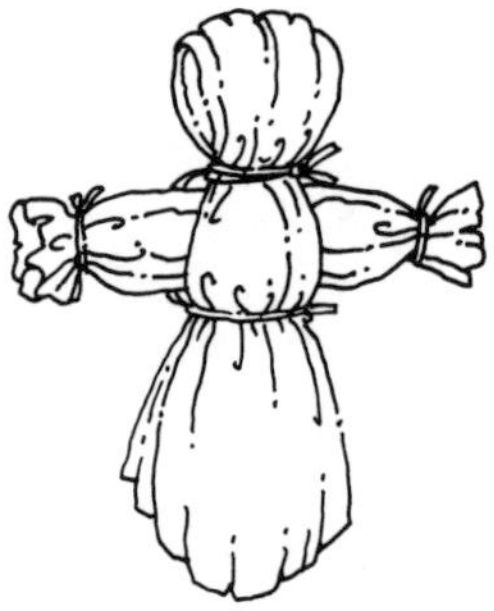

Preassemble:

1. For each doll, cut one 16" strip of paper twist into one 12" and one 4" strip.
2. Untwist both pieces so they resemble cornhusks.
3. Fold the longer piece in half, keeping the fold at the top.

4. If using styrofoam balls, slip one in between the fold now.
5. Twist 2" piece of floral wire around the "husk" 1" down to form the neck.
6. Fold the 4" piece of paper twist in half lengthwise.
7. Beneath the tied strip, insert the 4" piece between layers to form arms.
8. Twist another 2" wire below this to form the waist.
9. Attach gummed nametag now. *(Optional, see illustration.)*
10. Shape the bottom half of "husk" into long dress, or cut in half lengthwise 2" from the bottom to form legs.
11. Twist wire around arms and legs 1/2" from ends to make hands and feet.
12. Prepare adequate amounts of "girls" and "boys" for retreat group.

Locate the story.

Obtain *I Like to be Little* by Charlotte Zolotow (New York: Harper Collins, 1987), or one of the following:

▲ *When I Was Young in the Mountains* by Cynthia Rylant (New York: Dutton Children's Books, 1982)
▲ *The Important Book* by Margaret Wise Brown (New York: Harper Collins, 1990)
▲ *Here are My Hands* by Bill Martin, Jr., and John Archambault (New York: Holt, 1987)
▲ *Don't Eat Too Much Turkey* by Miriam Cohen (New York: Greenwillow, 1987)
▲ *The Foot Book* by Dr. Seuss (New York: Random House, 1968)

Select a movement activity.

Use Head, Shoulders, Knees, and Toes (p. 126) or another of your choice.

Become familiar with the prayer (p. 127).

Gather supplies:

▲ doll
▲ blanket

Purchase groceries and prepare the snack.

Ethnic Breads:

▲ variety of breads, cut in small pieces: pita, bagels, French bread, matzos, biscuits, croissants, tortillas, cornbread, sliced bread
▲ butter, honey, or jelly

or

Muffins:

▲ corn, pumpkin, or other muffins
▲ apple or white grape juice

Duplicate Parent-Child Sharing Form (p. 216).

Preparations the Day of the Retreat

1. Gather as a team and pray.
2. Set out nametags and safety pins or tape (warning: no straight pins or strings). Have exactly as many nametags as retreatants.
3. Have each retreat team member put on a different colored nametag. This will later help the children divide into groups for their activities.
4. Atop a piano or table, create the environment in the gathering room with an arrangement of Thanksgiving tablecloth, model turkey, and combination of cornucopias, pilgrim figurines, leaves, gourds, and pumpkins, pictures of children, and "In His Image," if available.
5. Also in the gathering room, place a sample of the craft, a copy of *I Like to be Little* or book of your choice, and a Bible.
6. Gather all the materials for the craft and set out on tables in the room to be used for this activity.
7. In the room where prayer will take place, put an infant doll wrapped in a blanket.
8. Spread out so that at least one team member is greeting the retreatants as they arrive, one is directing parents and younger siblings to the nursery, one is bringing retreatants and parents to the gathering room, and one is waiting in the gathering room.
9. Begin the retreat by warmly greeting the retreatants, then introducing the team members.
10. Sing together the gathering song "J-E-S-U-S" (p. 180).

Gathering Presentation

Who knows why we have Thanksgiving? *(Invite answers from the children.)*

That's right. On Thanksgiving we thank God for everything God has given us. And God has given us a lot. We have our parents, our brothers and sisters, our pets. We have lots of toys, plenty of food, and places to play. Everything we have comes from God.

But I think the best thing God ever gave us is ourselves. God made us exactly as we are, and that's why each one of us *(point around the group)* is so wonderful. Every person in this room is very important, and I want to tell you why.

First, we have to talk about turkeys. Would you believe I brought a turkey with me today? I really did. Look! *(Bring out the turkey made of only feathers.)* Here's my turkey.

What's wrong? What are you laughing at? Oh, this really is a problem. This turkey has only feathers—no head or beak. It's going to be tricky to eat, isn't it?

Well, here's a great-looking turkey. *(Hold up the one with four legs.)* Is something wrong with this turkey? *(Welcome answers.)* What's wrong with four legs? All animals have four legs, don't they? *(Let children say, "Not birds.")* I guess this turkey will have trouble walking. It will trip all over its legs because there are too many.

Oh, look. I have a beautiful turkey here. *(Show a turkey that's one large eye with feathers.)* Now don't tell me there's anything wrong with this one. Oops! Do you suppose the eye told the feet to leave? Do you suppose the eye just said, "I'm the only one that matters?" Why won't that work? *(Welcome answers.)*

Our own bodies are made up of many parts, too. In God's special book *(hold up Bible)*, a man named Paul tells us how all our body parts work together.

Read 1 Corinthians 12:14-15: "Now the body is not a single part, but many. If a foot should say, 'Because I am not a hand I do not belong to the body.'" Would the foot be right? What do you think, children? *(Pause for answers.)*

"Or if an ear should say, 'Because I am not an eye I do not belong to the body...'" (v. 16a), would it no longer be a part of the body? Do ears belong to the body, even though they're not eyes? Of course. Ears are for hearing and eyes are for seeing.

"If the whole body were an eye, where would the hearing be?" (v. 17a). *(Pause for answers.)* "If the whole body were hearing, where would the sense of smell be?" (v. 17b). *(Pause again.)*

"But as it is, God placed the parts, each one of them, in the body as he intended" (v. 18). Remember I told you that everyone in this room *(point around the group as before)* is important?

Each one of you is very important in your own family. Think what your family would be like if you weren't in it. *(Pause.)* The reason your family is so wonderful is because you are part of it. *(Pause.)*

And here's another reason why each person in this room is so important. We—all of us here—are members of Jesus' Body, the Body of Christ. We're God's family. Without any one of us here, Jesus' Body wouldn't be as wonderful as it is. It's important that we all be who we are to make Jesus' Body work. Jesus wants Carlita to be Carlita and Jenny to be Jenny. He doesn't want Tyrone to be Peter. He wants Tyrone to be Tyrone. *(Substitute the names of retreatants here.)* And

Jesus doesn't want children to be adults. He wants children to be children. Can you imagine if everybody in the world were a grown-up? That would be as silly as if a turkey had all heads and nothing else.

Children are very important members of Jesus' Body. Children are very important members of God's family. *You* are the Body of Jesus Christ. *You* are God's family.

Can you say that with me? *We are the Body of Jesus Christ. We are God's family.*

How about one more time so we'll remember? *We are the Body of Jesus Christ. We are God's family.*

Let's sing a song that reminds us that we're an important part of God's family. *(Use child retreatants' names, reading from their nametags.)*

Thanksgiving Song
(Tune: "Old MacDonald Had a Farm")

We're important, each of us
In God's family.
We're important, each of us
In God's family.
With *Carl* here and *Derek* there,
Megan, Logan, Emily, Clair.
We're important, each of us
In God's family.

(Repeat until all the young retreatants' names have been used.)

What great singing! We have some fun activities to do now while your moms and dads stay here and listen to a talk for parents. Let me show you what we'll be doing. *(Show the children the craft and story, and tell them they'll also be talking to Jesus.)*

Mommy or Daddy will pick you up when we have our snack. Time to give each other a big hug. *(Wait).*

Now look at the color of your nametag. *(Have the children leave the room with the team leader who has the same colored nametag.)* Wave goodbye.

Children's Activities

The following three children's activities run simultaneously, and the children rotate through them until they've been to all three.

Activity 1: Craft

As the children work, we talk in our own words about how important each person is to their own family and to God's family, the Body of Christ. Some of us can be like Jesus' hands by watching our little brothers and sisters. We can even be like Jesus' feet to each other, when we bring Mom something she needs or when we take out the trash. The children might add their own ideas of how we're like Jesus' Body. Our message is that we're each unique and special, and Jesus loves us exactly the way we are.

Remember, craft time is a time of reinforcing the theme of the retreat. Far more important than what we say or do is that we share our sense of wonder, conveying our awe that Jesus is with us always. Construct Cardboard-Tube Napkin Rings with the children:

1. In front of each child place four precut cardboard tube rings, five message strips, 4 turkey stickers, and one 36" string of yarn.
2. Guide children in gluing strips to cardboard rings. Put glue on one place on the cardboard tube. Glue and wrap. Then put dot of glue on paper and overlap. *(Otherwise, it's a gluey mess.)*
3. Help children apply turkey sticker to overlapping ends of message strip.
4. Instruct children to string finished rings onto 36" yarn.
5. Staple name label to yarn.
6. Tie knot.

To simplify the craft:
Make napkin rings ahead of time and show the children how to string them on yarn.

Optional activity: Cornhusk Dolls

Children simply dot eyes, nose, and mouth on face with fine black marker. Using colored markers, they decorate the doll's clothing.

Announce to the children: Let's put your napkin rings on this table and when you and Mommy or Daddy are ready to go home, you can come in here and get them. It's time now to go to Prayer *(or Story or Snack).* I *(or our helper)* will walk with you.

Activity 2: Story and Movement

Story: *I Like to be Little* by Charlotte Zolotow (New York: Harper Collins, 1987)

Introduce the story.
I remember when I was a little child your age. The thing I liked most about

being little was __________ *(Share from your own experience: riding a tricycle, watching the rain on the window pane, having someone fix your hair, playing in the sandbox.)*

In this story *(hold up book)* the little girl and her mom are talking about how fun it is to be a child. As I read, listen to how much she likes being who she is.

Read the story.

Talk about the story.

- ▲ What was your favorite part of that story? *(After each comment, ask, "Do you do that, too? It's great being a child so you can _________, isn't it?")*
- ▲ You know that part about grown-ups and birthday parties? I do know some grown-ups who haven't forgotten how to enjoy their birthdays. They have big, noisy parties, just like children do. Jesus reminds grown-ups to remember the childlike part of themselves more often and to just enjoy everything.
- ▲ Jesus loves each one of us and wants us to use all the gifts he gives us to help each other. Kids can be a big help to people, right?
- ▲ Just like our wacky turkey, the funny turkey with four feet—our world would be a strange place if there were only kids in it, or only adults in it. Kids need grown-ups and grown-ups need kids. We need all of us to be the Body of Christ.
- ▲ Come on over here and we'll play a game together.

Do the movement: Head, Shoulders, Knees, and Toes.
Remember in God's special book, the Bible, when God's friend Paul told us how important each part of the body is? Well, let's play a body game. Point to the place on your body as I say it.

Put to a tune or say the words:

> Head, shoulders, knees and toes, knees and toes
> Head, shoulders, knees and toes, knees and toes
>
> Eyes and ears and mouth and nose, mouth and nose.
> Eyes and ears and mouth and nose, mouth and nose.

Now touch your feathers. What? You don't have any? Okay, then your wattle. No wattle? That's okay, because Jesus loves you just the way you are!

Let's sing our body song again, only this time we'll sing faster. Don't forget to touch each place on your body when we say it. Ready? Faster now! *(Repeat song, faster.)*

Now it's time to move to Craft *(or Prayer or Snack).* I *(or our helper)* will walk with you.

Activity 3: Prayer

Note: Lead the children into a personal encounter with Jesus in the setting of a newborn's nursery. By tapping into their senses and imaginations, you can transform the room into a hospital, a wonderful place that becomes more alive as the children's imaginations take over. Here they will meet Jesus, and during their prayer their friendship with him will deepen as they become familiar with him, listen to him, speak to him, and spend quiet time with him.

Lead the children.

How many of you have ever been inside a hospital? Have you ever been in the nursery, where the newborn babies are sleeping and sometimes crying? Let's go on a pretend trip to the nursery right now.

Here's the elevator. Let's get inside, everyone. Okay, *(Name),* will you press the number 5? That's the floor where the nursery is located. Here we are. That didn't take long. *(Name),* would you please hold the door for us until everyone is out of the elevator? Everyone out.

Follow me down the hall, boys and girls. Wave to the nurses working at the desk. Come on down to the end of the hall. Careful. Watch out for those food carts. Hmmmmmmm. I smell something good. I think the patients are having chicken for lunch today.

Here we are. Look, can you see those beautiful babies? Look at that baby girl. She's crying because she's hungry, I think. See that baby over by the window? The little blue sign on his bassinet says his name is Alejandro. Isn't he cute? He has his tiny hand in his mouth while he's sleeping.

Come on, let's turn the corner and sit a while on those soft chairs. Oh, there's a doctor on her way to see her patient. Let's all wave to her. Here we are. Let's all sit down in a circle.

(Wait for all the children to settle in.)

Those babies were so cute, weren't they? What do you like best about newborn babies?

The doll I have inside this blanket is like the real babies we just saw. *(Unwrap the blanket and hold the doll.)* Did you notice that even when we're newborn we have beautiful bodies? Remember how tiny those babies' hands and heads and feet were? Ours were that tiny when we were newborn, too. Can you believe it?

This tiny head is very important to the baby's body, right? Even though it's small, the head is important because it holds the mouth so the baby can eat and grow. And the head holds the baby's brain inside so the baby can learn. And ears to hear, and eyes to see. This tiny head is so important. God has given us beautiful bodies that make us wonderful.

Think how important this baby is to her family! Even as tiny as she is, even though she can't talk or walk, she makes her family happy.

That's how important we are in God's family, in the Body of Jesus Christ, boys and girls. Even as little as we are, we make Jesus very happy.

Why don't we pretend we're tiny babies in a newborn nursery and our best friend Jesus comes to hold us. Want to?

Let's sit quietly and close our eyes and imagine we're lying in a bassinet.

(Give the children time to close their eyes and shift into quiet and calm. Allow 30-45 seconds.)

We are in our heart rooms, children. This is a place deep inside ourselves, and Jesus lives here. See Jesus walking toward you. He's smiling and holding his arms out to you. He picks you up and smiles at you. Spend a little time looking at him. Notice what he looks like.

Jesus wants to say something to you. Listen...listen. What is he saying? *(Allow 45 seconds.)*

Now think of what you'd like to say to Jesus because he's your best friend and he loves you so much. Talk to Jesus now in your heart room. Don't say the words out loud. *(Allow 45 seconds.)*

Jesus wants to hold you now. It's nice being like a baby again, isn't it? If it's all right with you, sit quietly with Jesus while he holds you. Know you are safe in his arms. *(Allow 30-45 seconds.)*

(Say softly:) You can open your eyes now, children.

(If the children are comfortable and can verbalize their prayer, ask them to share their talk with Jesus.)

What did Jesus look like? What did he say to you? Since Jesus is your best friend, what did you say to him?

(If time allows, sing "J-E-S-U-S," p. 180.)

Now it's time to go to Craft *(or Story or Snack)*. I *(or our helper)* will walk with you.

Snack

After the children have rotated through all three activities, we lead them to the snack room. We show the children each different type of bread, telling them that different families have their favorite breads. Their parents will meet them here after the children finish eating.

In the event the parents are delayed, use the Thanksgiving Retreat Activity on page 210.

Parent-Child Sharing Time

After the adult session, parents pick up their children in the snack room to begin their sharing time. Distribute the Parent-Child Sharing Time Form (p. 216). If weather permits, retreatants can go outside for a nature walk. If not, they might want to find a corner to sit in, parent and child together; take a walk through the church; or even spread out blankets throughout the room. We allow approximately twenty minutes, asking parents and children to return to the gathering room at the allotted time for our closing.

During the parent presentation, the adult leader has suggested several questions designed to facilitate parent-child sharing:

- ▲ Tell me about the story you heard.
- ▲ What do you like about the craft you made?
- ▲ What was it like when you met Jesus in your heart room?
- ▲ What did Jesus look like?
- ▲ How did it feel to be with Jesus?
- ▲ When I met Jesus in my heart room, he said... I did...
- ▲ What did Jesus say to you? What did you do?

Additional activity during parent-child sharing time: Face Painting
Provide face paints for parents who can create a design on their child's cheeks. Parents can talk to their child about the uniqueness of their own face-painting picture. This special child will have a picture unlike any of the other children—because this child thought of it herself and only this parent drew it. But when all the children gather together, it will make a beautiful collection of faces.

As retreatants are returning from sharing time, gather together and sing "J-E-S-U-S" (p. 180) or the "Thanksgiving Song" (p. 124).

When all have arrived, begin the closing prayer.

Closing Prayer

Join hands in a circle and have parents and children repeat each line.

Jesus,
you made me special
and you love me so much.
This Thanksgiving
I will remember to thank you
for making me me.
I'm happy
to be part
of your family.
We're best friends.
Amen.

Remind the children to take their craft home with them. Invite the children and parents to play Follow-the-Leader and lead them to the door.

10-Christmas

(Luke 2:1-20)

Focus

Many parents, concerned that their children are inundated with the commercial aspect of Christmas, seek support in focusing their children on the spirituality of this great feast. We share that concern.

Our focus is on Jesus' birthday, blending the secular with the spiritual. The goodness of Santa Claus, the loving tradition of exchanging gifts, the warmth of spending time and corresponding with friends and family, the uplifting sound of Christmas carols well-chosen are not things we wish to discard. We simply want the children to know, from a faith perspective, why we're doing it.

We point out the difference between a person's day of birth and their birthday. In the children's experience, "birthday" means parties, presents, balloons, games, noisemakers, and sugar. In reality, their day of birth was without these trappings, but was a tremendously joyful day nonetheless. Their parents had been waiting and preparing for nine months for them to be born. At this point we ask the children to spend some time with their parents hearing what their real day of birth was like. We invite adoptive parents to describe either their involvement in their child's birth or the day they brought their child home.

Jesus' real birthday, too, was a quiet, peaceful event. We emphasize this element of calm as we tell the children the Christmas story, recounted by Luke. We use the Bible as a prop, reminding the children that they can read this story at home in their own Bibles.

We talk about Advent, the time during which we get ready for Jesus' day of birth. Christmas parties, carols, cards, gifts, and Santa Claus are all ways we "bear Jesus" to the world. They're ways we love each other just as Jesus loves us.

Preparations Before the Retreat

1. Meet as a team to pray, read, discuss, understand, and interiorize the focus and scriptural basis of the retreat.
2. Discern which team members will be responsible for the gathering presentation, each of the three children's activities, and the adult session.
3. Choose a topic from the Outlines for Parents' Sessions (pp. 143-178).
4. Divide the following preparation responsibilities. Use the gifts of your community to lighten the load. Parents, teenagers, school children, and senior citizens can all help prepare.

Make the nametags.
Using the birthday-cake pattern (p. 212), prepare a different color nametag for each of the four team leaders. Then, using the same four colors, prepare one nametag for each child. On each nametag, write, "Jesus' friend: *(name)*." You should have an equal number of each color of children's nametags. You will divide into groups by colors. As the children choose their nametags, the groups are formed.

Warning: Use safety pins or tape to attach nametags. For the safety of the children, do not use straight pins or string.

(Note: For an optional nametag, use the angel pattern on p. 213.)

Collect materials for the environment.
To arrange an attractive display on table or piano in gathering room, collect "Happy Birthday" banners or streamers, balloons, party tablecloth, doll representing Jesus in manger (or nativity set), gift-wrapped box.

Prepare for the gathering presentation.

During the gathering presentation, children will use angel stick puppets prepared in advance (pattern, p. 213). Use the same pattern as the angel nametag, but attach the figure to a popsicle stick. Also needed are hay, and, if available, frankincense and myrrh for the prayer session. For the movement activity after the story, provide several nativity sets that are sturdy enough for children to handle.

Prepare the craft (p. 137).

First, gather materials for Holy Family Peanut Ornaments:

- ▲ craft sticks or Popsicle sticks, 3 per child
- ▲ 3" felt triangles in equal numbers of white, blue, and brown, 1 color of each per child
- ▲ peanuts in the shell, 3 (small, medium, large) per child
- ▲ twist ties from bread loaves or plastic storage bags, 3 per child
- ▲ craft glue
- ▲ fine-tipped felt marker
- ▲ gummed gold or silver stars, 1 per child
- ▲ yarn, ribbon, or cord, 8" per child

Second, do the advance preparation:

1. Wrap smallest peanut (Jesus) in white felt triangles and secure at "waist" with twist tie.
2. Wrap medium peanut (Mary) in blue and largest (Joseph) in brown and secure at "waist" with twist tie.
3. Leave "face" exposed.
4. Glue wooden sticks in triangle shape.
5. When dry, loop 8" piece of yarn/cord around top peak of triangle (stable) and knot for hanging.

Optional craft: Angel Stick Puppets

Children can use crayons or markers to color the angel stick puppets used in the gathering presentation and to write their names on the puppets.

Locate the story.

Obtain *The Nativity*, illustrated by Julie Vivas (San Diego: Gulliver Books, 1988), or one of the following:

- ▲ *A Christmas Story* by Brian Wildsmith (New York: Knopf, 1993)
- ▲ *B is for Bethlehem* by Isabel Wilner (New York: Puffin, 1995)
- ▲ *Hello Amigos!* by Tricia Brown (New York: Holt, 1986)
- ▲ *Christmas is a Time of Giving* by Joan Anglund Walsh (New York: Harcourt, Brace & World, Inc., 1961)

- ▲ *Birthday Presents* by Cynthia Rylant (New York: Orchard Books, 1987)
- ▲ *The Night the Angels Sang* by Allan Ross (St. Louis, Mo.: Arch Books, 1975)
- ▲ *Santa and the Christ Child* by Nicholas Bakewell (Los Angeles: Kneeling Santa, 1984)
- ▲ *Many Miles to Bethlehem* by Dina Strong (Denver: Spindle Press, 1996)

Select a movement activity.
Use the Nativity Dramatic Play (p. 139) or another of your choice.

Become familiar with the prayer (p. 139).

Purchase groceries and prepare the snack (p. 141).
Decorated Birthday Muffins:
- ▲ muffins
- ▲ honey
- ▲ festive colored sugar sprinkles
- ▲ birthday candle
- ▲ red punch or juice

or
Christmas Cookies:
- ▲ angel and star sugar cookies
- ▲ red punch or juice

Optional: "Happy Birthday" napkins, tablecloth, balloons

Duplicate the Parent-Child Sharing Form (p. 216).

Preparations the Day of the Retreat

1. Gather as a team and pray.
2. Set out nametags and safety pins or tape (warning: no straight pins or strings). Have exactly as many nametags as retreatants, plus one for each team member.
3. Have each retreat team member wear a different colored nametag. This will later help the children divide into groups for their activities.
4. Atop a piano or table, create the environment in the gathering room with an arrangement of "Happy Birthday" banners, doll representing Jesus in manger (Nativity set), gift-wrapped box, balloons, and party tablecloth.
6. Also in the gathering room, place a sample of the Holy Family Peanut Ornament, a copy of *The Nativity* or book of your choice, and a Bible.
5. Gather all the materials for the craft and set out on tables in the room to be used for this activity.

7. Spread out so that at least one team member is greeting the retreatants as they arrive, one is directing parents and younger siblings to the nursery, one is bringing retreatants and parents to the gathering room, and one is waiting in the gathering room.
8. Begin the retreat by warmly greeting the retreatants, then introducing the team members.
9. Sing together the gathering song "J-E-S-U-S" (p. 180).

Gathering Presentation

We have a very important birthday coming up. Whose birthday is it? Jesus' birthday is December 25, just ___ more days. We all have a day that's our most special day because it's our own birthday. Do you know when yours is? If you don't know, ask Mommy or Daddy right now.

Your birthday is on that day every single year.

Jesus' birthday is on December 25 and right now we're waiting for his birthday to come. The days we wait for Jesus' birthday are called Advent.

It's Advent right now. Can you say that word with me? *Advent.*

Have any of you ever been to a birthday party? What do you like best about birthday parties? *(decorations, food, presents)*

Christmas is kind of like that, too, isn't it? Christmas is Jesus' birthday party, and we celebrate with decorations, food, and presents, don't we?

That's the birthday party. But do you know what a birthday really is? It's a day that we remember the day you were born.

And guess what?

On the day you were born, the real day, there wasn't a birthday party. There were no decorations, fun foods, or presents at all. In fact, it was a quiet, ordinary day. Some of your moms even went to work on the day you were born; some of your moms vacuumed and made the beds; some of them curled up in a chair and read a book while they waited for you to be born. And your mom and dad didn't eat cake and ice cream on the day you were born. They probably ate cereal or soup, typical foods.

Some of you might have been adopted. Your parents had to wait a long time to adopt you, so you can imagine that the day they brought you home was a very happy day for them.

Ask your moms and dads right now to tell you about your real birthday, the day you were born, or about the day you were adopted? *(Allow time.)*

I would like to tell you about Jesus' real birthday, the day he was born. I read about it in this book. *(Hold up Bible.)* Do you have this book at your house?

I'm going to need your help to tell the story. There were angels at Jesus' real birthday. Would you like to be the angels? *(Pass out stick angels.)*

Even though Christmas is exciting and noisy, Jesus' real birthday—the day he was born—was actually very calm. It was a silent night. Do you know what *silent* means? Quiet. Let's see if we can make it as silent here as it was the night Jesus was born. No one say a word for just a minute. *(Wait.)*

This is what happened the day Jesus was born:

Mary and Joseph were on a trip and Jesus was in Mary's tummy. Have you ever seen a mom with a baby in her tummy? What does she look like? Well, Mary's tummy was big because it was time for Jesus to be born, and she was tired. Mary and Joseph looked for a place to sleep, but all the hotels were full.

One nice man let Mary and Joseph sleep in his stable, which is where the animals usually stay. The stable was warm and dry, and it was there—on that calm, holy night—that Jesus was born. Mary and Joseph wrapped Jesus in clean clothes and laid him in a bed they had made for him out of the animals' feedbox.

Later that night, when it was really dark, and really quiet, a whole bunch of angels appeared in the sky and started singing, quietly. Can you wave your angels in the air?

The angels were singing, "Glory to God in the highest!" But it wasn't loud singing. It was calm, holy singing.

Let's hear how those angels sounded on Jesus' birthday. Make your angels dance, and let's say together what the angels said: "Glory to God in the highest!"

And then those angels disappeared. *(Have children put their angels in their laps.)*

On the night Jesus was born, it was a quiet—silent—night. It was a calm, silent night, and a holy night. It was a holy night because Mary and Joseph were holy, and because God's holy angels were there, and because Jesus was born.

And that's the story of our best friend Jesus' real birthday.

I'll bet you've heard this song about that special night. It's called "Silent Night."

Silent Night

Silent night, holy night
All is calm, all is bright.
Round yon Virgin mother and child,
Holy Infant, so tender and mild.
Sleep in heavenly peace,
Sleep in heavenly peace.

What great singing! We have some fun activities to do now while your moms and dads stay here and listen to a talk for parents. Let me show you what we'll be doing. *(Show the children the craft and story, and tell them they'll also be talking to Jesus.)*

Mommy or Daddy will pick you up when we have our snack. Time to give each other a big hug *(Wait)*.

Now look at the color of your nametag. *(Have the children leave the room with the team leader who has the same colored nametag.)* Wave goodbye.

(Note: If using optional craft, send angel stick puppets with craft leader.)

Children's Activities

The following three children's activities run simultaneously, and the children rotate through them until they've been to all three.

Activity 1: Craft

As the children work, we talk in our own words about how happy we are to celebrate Jesus's real birthday. We remember the events of that silent, holy night.

Remember, craft time is a time of reinforcing the theme of the retreat. Far more important than what we say or do is that we share our sense of wonder, conveying our awe that Jesus is with us always.

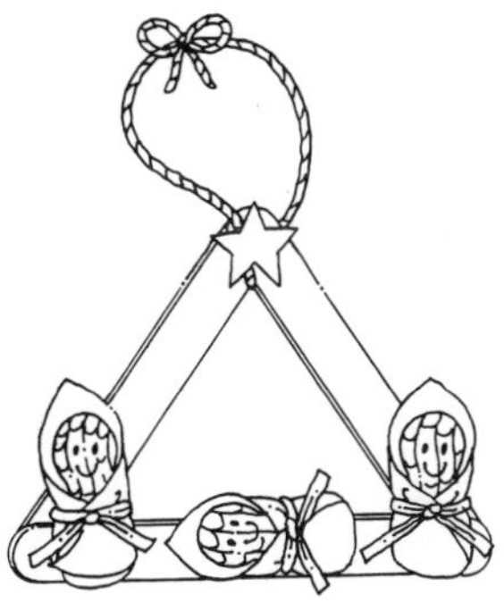

Construct Holy Family Peanut Ornaments with children (see illustration):

1. Help children write their names on the back of the stable.
2. Children stick gold or silver star on apex of stable.
3. Help children draw face on each peanut. (Plain faces look fine, too.)

4. Generously apply craft glue to bottom left corner of stable and place Mary.
5. Glue Joseph to the bottom right corner.
6. Place Jesus horizontally across the bottom of stable, between Mary and Joseph. Glue and hold securely until dry, singing "Silent Night" to pass the time as they hold the figures in place.

Optional craft: Angel Puppets
Give children colored markers to decorate the angel stick puppets. Help them write their names on them.

Announce to the children: Let's put your ornaments on this table and when you and Mommy or Daddy are ready to go home, you can come in here and get it. It's time now to go to Prayer *(or Story or Snack)*. I *(or our helper)* will walk with you.

Activity 2: Story and Movement

Story: *The Nativity*, illustrated by Julie Vivas (San Diego: Gulliver Books, 1986)

Introduce the story.
I want to share one of my favorite books with you today. The story came right out of the big Bible. Look carefully at the pictures as I read. I love these pictures.

Read the story.
(As you read, allow the children to comment on the pictures or story as they feel moved.)

Talk about the story.
What part of the story did you like most? *(Listen to several responses, affirming each.)* I'm sure glad to hear the story about Jesus' real birthday.

We have some special story-telling figures here today that you can play with. Please handle them gently as you tell the story of Jesus, Mary, Joseph, and all the shepherds and animals.

Do the movement: Nativity Dramatic Play.
Allow the children to handle and play with the figures of several nativity sets or puppets. Wooden puzzle pieces would also work. Children can choose parts and reenact the Christmas story.

Announce to the children: It's time to go to the Craft *(or Prayer or Snack)* now. I *(or our helper)* will walk with you.

Activity 3: Prayer

Note: Lead the children into a personal encounter with Jesus in the setting of Bethlehem. By tapping into their senses and imaginations, you can transform the room into that holy place, which becomes more alive as the children's imaginations take over. Here they will meet Jesus, and during their prayer their friendship with him will deepen as they become familiar with him, listen to him, speak to him, and spend quiet time with him.

Lead the children.
Today we're going on an exciting trip to a city that is far away from here. It's a little town called Bethlehem. It's on the other side of the world, but it's important to our lives because that's where Jesus was born, and that's why we celebrate Christmas. Is everyone ready?

Let's go down this small path through the fields where the shepherds are taking their sheep for the night. I'm glad the moon is so bright. We can see a lot better. Look at the stars that are out tonight! (Name), how many do you see? (Name), what do you think? How many must be in the sky tonight? I'd guess we're looking at several hundred bright stars shining tonight.

Come on...follow me closer to this cave...look! Do you see a small light inside the cave? Let's go closer. My gosh! I hear soft voices...come closer... Duck your head as we go inside the cave. Do you hear voices now?

Tip-toe after me and let's get closer to see who's inside. Look over by the wall... Do you see the baby lambs sleeping there? Let's go quietly and pet them. Feel how soft their wool is? Come on, let's see where the voices are coming from. Tip-toe behind me... I can't believe what I see!

Look, there's a beautiful baby boy lying on the fresh hay. Let's see what this is all about. Look at those shepherds standing behind the baby. They're smiling at us and telling us to come closer. Come on, let's go stand by the shepherds.

I can't believe my eyes. Look at how beautiful that newborn baby is. That must be his mother next to him in the hay. Let's go say hello. I see his dad, too. Look, he's telling us to come and sit on the hay next to the baby.

Let's sit down here. Fluff the hay so you can get closer to the baby. Listen...I hear his mother. She's telling us this is Jesus and he came to be our best friend. Look, he's smiling at us. Look how he reaches his little hand out to us.

Let's all sit down and get quiet inside. *(After the children have settled in the stable, invite them to close their eyes and listen to the sounds. Allow 30-45 seconds, using this time to shift into quiet and calm.)*

We are in our heart rooms, children. This is a place deep inside ourselves, and Jesus lives here. See Baby Jesus in his crib. He's so close to us. Say whatever you would like to to Jesus and his mom and dad. Don't say the words out loud. *(Allow 45 seconds.)*

Jesus wants to say something to you. Listen...listen. What is he saying? *(Allow 45 seconds.)*

Jesus wants to be with you now. Sit quietly with Jesus. Know you are safe with him in the stable, and with Mary and Joseph. *(Allow 45 seconds.)*

(Say softly:) You can open your eyes now, children.

(If the children are comfortable and can verbalize their prayer, ask them to share their talk with Jesus.)

Let's look around the cave. What are some of the things we've seen since we've come inside to visit Jesus? *(Name),* did you see the lambs? *(Name),* did you see the shepherds? *(Name),* what else did you notice since we got here?

Oh, did you see that? Baby Jesus started to close his eyes and fall back asleep. It's getting late, and I'm sure he's tired. His mother and dad must be, too. It's been a long day for them. Let's say goodbye.

Fluff up the hay where we were sitting. Be careful not to wake up the baby. Tiptoe behind me and we'll go back outside the cave. There are those lambs again. They slept the whole time we were here. Come on and we'll walk past the walls of the cave. Oh, look at the stars now that we're outside the cave. *(Name),* how many do you think there are now? Hundreds and hundreds of them!

I guess that's God's way of letting us know that tonight is a special night. It's the birthday of Jesus. Let's go back down the path through the field so we can tell our own mom or dad all the exciting things we've seen and heard tonight.

It's time to go to Story *(or Craft or Snack)* now. I *(or our helper)* will walk with you.

Snack

After the children have rotated through all three activities, we lead them to the snack room. Their parents will meet them here after the children finish eating.

Children might enjoy singing "Happy Birthday" to Jesus.

In the event the parents are delayed, use the Christmas Retreat Activity on page 214.

Parent-Child Sharing Time

After the adult session, parents pick up their children in the snack room to begin their sharing-time. Distribute the Parent-Child Sharing Time Form (p. 216). If weather permits, retreatants can go outside for a nature walk. If not, they might want to find a corner to sit in, parent and child together; take a walk through the church; or even spread out blankets throughout the room. We allow approximately twenty minutes, asking parents and children to return to the gathering room at the appointed time for our closing.

During the parent presentation, the adult leader has suggested several questions designed to facilitate parent-child sharing:

- ▲ Tell me about the story you heard.
- ▲ What do you like about the craft you made?

- ▲ What was it like when you met Jesus in your heart room?
- ▲ What did Jesus look like?
- ▲ How did it feel to be with Jesus?
- ▲ When I met Jesus in my heart room, he said... I did...
- ▲ What did Jesus say to you? What did you do?

As retreatants are returning from Sharing-Time, gather together and sing "J-E-S-U-S" (p. 180) or "Silent Night" (p. 137).

When all have arrived, begin the closing prayer.

Closing Prayer

Join hands in a circle and have parents and children repeat each line.

Jesus,
help us to remember
that Christmas
means you were born
so that you could be
our best friend.
We want to be
your best friend, too.
Amen.

Remind the children to take their craft home with them. Invite the children and parents to play Follow-the-Leader and lead them to the door.

Outlines for Parent Sessions

4

Parent Session 1: Forgiveness

Focus

Believers in Jesus accept and practice forgiveness. It's hard to determine which is more difficult, forgiving or accepting forgiveness, but that difficulty seems to be a reality of the human condition. The inability to accept forgiveness often stems from the inability to forgive ourselves, which in turn is rooted in the imperfect models of forgiveness in our lives. Similarly, the barriers to forgiving others spring from these same imperfect models, as well as from pride and fear. It is essential we learn to be patient with ourselves. Forgiveness is a gradual process, a healing, a transformation of heart, rather than a sudden, decisive event.

We need forgiveness, for our journey to union with God is necessarily marked with imperfections, mistakes, even failures. God is the source of forgiveness for ourselves, and the power behind our ability to forgive others. Jesus, in repeatedly forgiving, even to his last breath, enfleshed the forgiveness of God.

As parents, we also enflesh the forgiveness of God. The family is a school of forgiveness. As imperfect as our attempts will be, we must nevertheless make a conscientious effort to model forgiveness for our children. When they see their parents forgive each other, reconcile with relatives or neighbors, or ask for forgiveness, they grow up with this value themselves. When they're taught consistently to use the phrases, "I'm sorry" and "I forgive you," they learn forgiveness as a way of life. Indeed, if our children fail to give and receive forgiveness in the home, they'll have a difficult time believing God always forgives them.

The spirituality of parenting infuses the forgiveness of God into family life.

Introductions

Invite each participant to share with the large group a personal response to this question:

▲ What do you want most for your child?

Prayer

Parents will learn the Heart Room Prayer at the same time the children are entering into their own prayer at the children's sessions. The prayer itself acknowledges that some adult participants may have difficulty encountering Jesus personally, either because the idea of a personal God is unfamiliar to them, or because they've felt hurt or abandoned by God, or for a number of other reasons. We begin by leading retreatants into quieting with a gentle tone of voice.

(See p. 215 for text of the Heart Room Prayer.)

Outline

The following outline is a scaffold for constructing a talk for parents. Its foundation is the Focus (p. 143). We provide examples and anecdotes, yet attempt to give latitude to the presenter to flesh out the presentation according to his or her own gifts and life experiences. Questions for discussion are interspersed throughout the talk, allowing the wisdom and experience of the participants to embellish the speaker's words. However, it's not necessary to use all the questions. The presenter should choose which questions to use and how many, based on time limitations.

A. We need forgiveness.
   1. Life is a process of becoming true and good.
   2. We don't start at perfection. Rather, life is a series of mistakes, failures, and sins, as well as successes.
   3. Our task is to learn to live as Jesus did.
   4. We learn to live like him in the same way a child learns to crawl, walk, run, or ride a bike: we endure numerous falls, bumps, and failures.
   5. Therefore, we have much need of forgiveness.

   Ask retreatants to spend a few minutes reflecting on this question, then to share their response with the person next to them:
   ▲ What experience in your life has taught you about God's forgiveness?

   Invite two or three people to share with the whole group. If many wish to speak, limit the time by saying, "Thank you for sharing. There'll be more time later, so please keep those stories in your thoughts."

   Lead into point B.

B. God is infinite forgiveness, as the following biblical texts show:
   1. The people of Israel suffered endless failure, continually turning from God:
      a. After God's people had been led out from Egypt, they made a golden calf to worship (Ex. 32:1-9).
      b. Upon entering the promised land, the Israelites turned to worship of other gods (Judg. 2).
      c. The Northern Kingdom broke its covenant with God and set up pagan shrines under the leadership of King Jeroboam (1 Kgs. 12:26-33).

2. Yet, God's message remained constant: Come back to me (Hos. 11:1-9).
   a. Jesus said to the woman taken in adultery: "Go...[and] do not sin any more" (Jn. 8:11b).
   b. As he hung from the cross, Jesus forgave his persecutors: "Father, forgive them, they know not what they do" (Lk. 23:34).
   c. Jesus enfleshes the forgiveness of God.

C. God forgives us, so now we forgive our sister and brother.
   1. Each time we come to the eucharist we say, "We have sinned," not as self-condemnation, but as truth.
   2. Because our tender God endlessly forgives us, we learn how to do it ourselves.

Ask retreatants to meet in groups of three or four and share responses to this question:

▲ Is it easy or hard for you to forgive others? to forgive yourself? Why or why not?

Invite two or three people to share their answers with the whole group.

Lead into point D.

D. The family is a school of forgiveness.
   1. We give instruction to our children each time we say, "I'm sorry."
      a. Instruction is offered when adults forgive each other.

      Expand: Conflict is a part of any intimate relationship. While many parents try to protect children from overhearing their arguments, inevitably the children become aware of moments of conflict between their parents. Children benefit psychologically from seeing conflict resolved. It's important, therefore, that adults model forgiveness of each other to their children.

      b. Instruction is offered when parents guide their children to reconcile with siblings and friends.

      Expand: When left on their own, children tend to easily forgive one another. Hanging onto hurt and anger is more common among adults than children. Teaching children to forgive is often a matter of simply affirming their innate good will.

      Anecdote: A woman, now in her mid-twenties, used to have weekly fights with her best friend as a child. Each time, they were playing together again within hours. Forgiveness was a given. One time, however, the girl's father overheard the dispute and, in protectiveness of his daughter, ordered her to stay away from this friend who was so hurtful. The girl complied, and the two best friends parted ways. The good news is that sixteen years later, the girl remembered her childhood friend, wrote her a letter, and renewed their acquaintance. But if the father had affirmed his daughter's natural ability to forgive and move on, rather than project his own desire for avenging hurt, the unnecessary separation may not have happened.

c. Instruction is offered when adults ask forgiveness of their children: "I'm sorry, Erica. I was upset about what you did. But I didn't want to talk to you in such a harsh voice. Will you forgive me?"

   Anecdote: One hot summer day, a mother of four small children, desperate to cool off, made plans to take the children to the swimming pool. This day the children found it exceptionally difficult to cooperate. All were hot and irritable, and no one more so than the mother. After forty-five minutes of trying to enlist the children's help in finding swimsuits, gathering towels, and spreading suntan lotion, only to hear arguing about who should and should not have to do it, the mother reached the end of her rope. Her fiery eyes landed directly on the oldest son. "Will you stop this bickering?" she shrieked. And then the words of accusation poured forth. The mother watched as her son's shoulders slumped and his smile faded away. This normally lively, loving child was the picture of defeat, and the mother was overtaken with regret. She put her arms around him and said, "Tim, that wasn't fair. We're all hot and crabby and we're all having trouble pulling together. It wasn't your fault, and I made it sound like it was. I need your forgiveness." As is typical of children, Tim was generous with his forgiveness, and harmony was restored in the family.

d. Instruction is offered when parents accept apologies from their children: "I forgive you. I know you'll try not to do (say) that again."

Ask of the whole group:
▲ Have you ever asked your child to forgive you?
▲ What happened in you when you did this?

Lead into point D2.

2. Part of the message of forgiveness is that we are still good even though we did something wrong. "I don't like what you did. It was wrong." vs. "You're a bad child."

3. If our children don't learn to give and receive forgiveness in the home, they'll have a difficult time believing that God always forgives them.
4. As we grow into adulthood, it's essential to our emotional and spiritual health that we know God's forgiveness.

Reflect for a few minutes on this question, then write your response on your notepad:

▲ Who in your childhood modeled or failed to model forgiveness for you?
▲ How does this affect your vision of God as all-forgiving?

Invite retreatants to share with a partner.

Lead into point E.

E. We grow in our ability to forgive.
   1. We turn to Jesus in prayer, using our own words to speak what is in our hearts.
   2. We verbalize in prayer our sorrow and our desire to forgive.
   3. We ask for the grace to forgive.
   4. We're patient with ourselves. Forgiveness is a process, a healing, a transformation of heart, not an event.

Conclude by giving parents a question to reflect on through the week:

▲ Who in my life has hurt me? Ask God for the grace to forgive this person.

Preparations for Parent-Child Sharing Time

To set the tone for quality sharing time between parents and children, we close the parent session with an explanation of what their children have just experienced in their sessions with adult leaders. (See Parent-Child Sharing Time Form, p. 216.) Parents will find it helpful to also have a copy to refer to, as this may be the first time many parents have verbally shared a faith experience with their children.

Conclude by saying: "This quality time with you and your child alone together is the foundation of the parent-child retreat. Therefore, we request that each of you respect the time other parents are giving to their children. As tempting as it is to greet friends, we ask you to be totally present to your child for the next half-hour."

Note: We've found repeatedly that if we're not explicit, even firm, in our rationale for parent-child sharing time, the parents use this half-hour as a social time to visit with each other.

Parent Session 2: Care of You, Care of Your Child

Focus

The greatest commandments given us by a loving God say, "You shall love the Lord, your God, with all your heart...and your neighbor *as yourself*" (Mt. 22:37a, 39b, emphasis added). The second of these commandments directs us not toward selfishness, but toward a sense of self which enables us to reach out to others in a whole and healthy way. Only from a deep sense of our own worth can we hope to give of ourselves to our children.

So we begin with ourselves, the parents. Our first task is to ground ourselves in authenticity and thus let the "superparent" fallacy—being all things to all people—slide right off. To be authentic means to know who we are as people loved into being by God through Jesus and the Holy Spirit, called and gifted for the kingdom, and to act out of that truth. When we describe ourselves, we acknowledge that children are a major part of our lives, but not the totality.

Taking care of ourselves is learning to be centered in our own lives before God. Occasional solitude, while a seeming impossibility for parents of small children, is necessary to being centered, and must be integrated into parents' schedules. By reserving time for those activities which fill us with life and renew us, and by honoring each other's needs for physical and emotional space within the family, we create an environment in the home which is holy. Home, then, becomes a place where we can grow in knowledge and love of ourselves.

Prayer is the most centering, restoring of all experiences for a believing person. Centered on God, we move outward toward our children with a new power to secure them in the love of God, which is vital to their healthy development. When we give time to be present to God, and to fill ourselves with God's loving presence, we in turn can be lovingly present to our children.

Introductions

Invite each participant to share with the large group a personal response to this question:

▲ What do you like best about young children? least?

Prayer

Parents will learn the Heart Room Prayer at the same time the children are entering into their own prayer at the children's sessions. The prayer itself acknowledges that some adult participants may have difficulty encountering Jesus personally, either because the idea of a personal God is unfamiliar to them, or because they've felt hurt or abandoned by God, or for a number of other reasons. We begin by leading retreatants into quieting with a gentle tone of voice.

(See p. 215 for text of the Heart Room Prayer.)

Outline

The following outline is a scaffold for constructing a talk for parents. Its foundation is the Focus (p. 148). We provide examples and anecdotes, yet attempt to give latitude to the presenter to flesh out the presentation according to his or her own gifts and life experiences. Questions for discussion are interspersed throughout the talk, allowing the wisdom and experience of the participants to embellish the speaker's words. However, it's not necessary to use all the questions. The presenter should choose which questions to use, and how many, based on time limitations.

Taking care of mom and dad

A. Taking care of ourselves is not selfish.

1. It is absolutely necessary for parents to take care of themselves.
2. Mothers especially must confront the fallacy of the perfect wife/perfect mother who needs no one.

   Expand: The media, "supermoms" we know, and sometimes even religious leaders deliver the false message that we should be always available, utterly other-centered. A misguided understanding of how Jesus led his life, too, can shape our thinking in similar ways. The gospels tell us that Jesus was not always available to everyone: He created space for personal renewal through prayer, solitude, and spending time with close friends. Use any of these texts to illuminate this point. Jesus created time for:
   a. prayer (Lk. 22:41; Jn. 17:1; Jn. 17:9; Jn. 17:20)
   b. solitude (Mk. 1:35)
   c. friends (Jn. 2:1f; Lk. 10:38f; Jn. 11:1-3).

3. All mothers and fathers of infants, toddlers, and preschoolers are in constant demand because of the physical and emotional needs of their children.
4. In response to the silent question, "Do I even have a life?" parents must be able to answer, "Yes. And my children are a major part of it, but not all of it."
5. The life their parents have forged for themselves is something children can grow into as they mature.
6. Taking care of ourselves is learning to be centered in our own life before God.

Ask the retreatants to spend a few minutes reflecting on this question, then to share their response with the person next to them:

▲ When and how did you break out of the perfect wife/husband, mother/father mold? What was the turning point for you?

Invite two or three people to share with the whole group. If many wish to speak, limit the time by saying, "Thank you for sharing. There will be more time later, so please keep those stories in your thoughts."

Lead into point B.

B. Healthy parents in a family with small children need space.

1. Physical and emotional space, alone and uninterrupted, helps renew parents physically and emotionally.

   Expand: Creating this space clearly takes effort, and begins with establishing patterns from the start. When the children are very young, this might involve trading child-care time with other parents on a regular schedule or employing child-care providers for a fee.

2. Mutual respect between parents and children includes honoring each other's needs for time alone.

   Anecdote: As the children get older, they can help establish patterns that acknowledge and honor individual family members' needs for solitude. One family, for example, reserves a spare bedroom for anyone who needs to be alone. The signal that the room is in use is a necktie hanging from the doorknob. In this home, children and parents alike honor each other's needs by allowing private time to the one who has hung the tie.

3. When parents relieve one another from the immediate demands of the family so each can read, think, pray, talk, listen to music, and be rejuvenated, this private space in the home becomes a holy place.

C. Time away from the family can be life-giving to parents and their children.

1. Adults benefit from sharing conversation with other adults, uninterrupted by children.
2. Many churches are open to providing social and spiritual programs for parents of small children, with child-care included.
3. One spouse often takes responsibility for the children while the other one takes a morning, afternoon, or evening off.

Ask retreatants to meet in groups of three or four and share responses to this question:

▲ What do you do to establish private space within your household?

Invite two or three people to share their answers with the whole group.

Lead into point D.

D. Prayer is the most centering, restoring of all experiences for a believing person.
   1. The needs of children and household seem to take priority in a parent's life, but time for prayer is essential.
   2. Only when we're open to and centered on God can we hope to be our true selves, open and loving to others.
   3. The more centered on God we are, the more our children are affected by our faith.
   4. If we have time for our loving God, we can truly be lovingly present to our children.

Share and Invite, asking the whole group:
▲ When and where have you found time for prayer?

Taking care of the children

A. Imagine the triumph of being able to answer to God, "In my life on earth, I secured a child."
B. "Securing" a child involves five elements, each one necessary to the healthy development of children.
   1. *Acceptance* means receiving and loving each child just as he/she is.

      Anecdote: Alison, a mother of four growing boys, commented on a revelation she received from listening to other mothers speak of their children. "I used to think I should be raising them all the same," she said. "It seemed the fair thing to do. But I began noticing how my friends talked about their children—as if they were individuals with different personalities, different quirks, different needs. It made me take notice of my own boys. They really are unique!" Alison was able to let go of expectation and disappointment. It gave her the freedom to enjoy each child exactly as he is.

   2. *Love,* constant and consistent, not conditional on behavior, mirrors the stability of God's own love.
   3. *Limits and clear boundaries* provide children with true security and the freedom to grow; without this, they know chaos.

      Anecdote: A mother was taking a long car trip with her bright and physically disabled child when she heard the plea from the back seat, "I have to go to the bathroom." The mother's response, loving but firm, was, "No, Annie. You'll have to hold on for a little while." A bit later Annie asked again. "No, not yet," was her mother's response. Later, when they reached a rest stop, Annie and her mother took care of the matter.

A friend accompanying the two asked Annie's mother to explain the delay in responding to the child's request, especially since she had a disability. "Don't you see?" replied Annie's mother. "She was fine and able to wait just like any child could. I don't want to mislead her by allowing her to think her every wish has to be fulfilled immediately." This child knew true security because of the boundaries her mother set. Annie's concept of herself hinges in large part on the stability of her mother's consistent love, a love which is fair, respectful, and empowering.

4. The *forgiveness* we give and receive is basic to our faith in God. Children experience the reality of God's forgiveness in their parents and in a home where forgiving and being forgiven are commonplace.
5. *God's presence,* the promise of Jesus to be with each of us throughout our lives, is the greatest gift we can give our children. Nothing could be sweeter or more comforting for children than the understanding that Jesus has such a love for them that he wants to be with them in all of their lives—at the playground, in the bath tub, during their nap.

Reflect for a few minutes on this question, then write your response on your notepad:

▲ Think of times when you yourself were "secured" as a child, or when you "secured" a child with one or more of these gifts: acceptance, consistent love, clear boundaries, forgiveness, or God's presence.
▲ Invite two or three to share with the whole group.

Conclude by giving parents a question to reflect on through the week:

▲ Do you take care of yourself? If not, why not?
▲ What adaptations need to be made in your life to create a sacred space for you in your home?

Preparations for Parent-Child Sharing Time

To set the tone for quality sharing time between parents and children, we close the parent session with an explanation of what their children have just experienced in their sessions with adult leaders. (See Parent-Child Sharing Time Form, p. 216.) Parents will find it helpful to also have a copy to refer to, as this may be the first time many parents have verbally shared a faith experience with their children.

Conclude by saying: "This quality time with you and your child alone together is the foundation of the parent-child retreat. Therefore, we request that each of you respect the time other parents are giving to their children. As tempting as it is to greet friends, we ask you to be totally present to your child for the next half-hour."

Note: We've found repeatedly that if we're not explicit, even firm, in our rationale for parent-child sharing time, the parents use this half-hour as a social time to visit with each other.

Parent Session 3: You and Your Child Growing in Faith

Focus

The major influence in a child's faith development is his/her own parents' faith and values. Growth in how a parent prays, loves, forgives, acts, and makes decisions is key to the child's growth in faith.

What we want most for our children reveals our values. Most parents share similar desires for their children: to be happy and secure in the family, to be able to take life's hurts and eventually use them for growth, to have a strong sense of self-worth. Most of all, believers wish their children to know and love God.

This loving relationship with God is what we know as faith. In faith, we open ourselves to God, listen and speak to God, trust in the Spirit of the risen Jesus in our lives, and choose this personal Jesus as our Savior.

In faith we deepen our knowledge and understanding of God. Basic to our faith is our answer to the question, "Who is the God with whom I'm in relationship?" Our answer is continually unfolding, and in this process of exploring our personal response, we examine the images of God we already hold: father, mother, spirit, friend, shepherd, source, creator. With time and healing, we sift out false images of God: harsh judge, punisher, scorekeeper, distant one.

God's basic truths and promises are centered on our good, as reflected in the scriptures, not on punishing and testing us. Believing women and men throughout history have shared their experience of God with us in their writings and oral traditions, helping us grow in faith. Now we must trust our own experiences of God, namely how God comes to each one of us, acts in our lives, and answers our prayers. In turn, we help our children grow in faith by sharing our own faith with them: how we pray and what God is like for us.

Introductions

Invite each participant to share with the large group a personal response to this question:

▲ Describe one thing your child has taught you about God.

Prayer

Parents will learn the Heart Room Prayer at the same time the children are entering into their own prayer at the children's sessions. The prayer itself acknowledges that some adult participants may have difficulty encountering Jesus personally, either because the idea of a personal God is unfamiliar to them, or because they've felt hurt or abandoned by God, or for a number of other reasons. We begin by leading retreatants into quieting with a gentle tone of voice. (See p. 215 for text of the Heart Room Prayer.)

Outline

The following outline is a scaffold for constructing a talk for parents. Its foundation is the Focus (p. 153). We provide examples and anecdotes, yet attempt to give latitude to the presenter to flesh out the presentation according to his or her own gifts and life experiences. Questions for discussion are interspersed throughout the talk, allowing the wisdom and experience of the participants to embellish the speaker's words. However, it's not necessary to use all the questions. The presenter should choose which questions to use, and how many, based on time limitations.

A. What we want most for our children reveals our values.
  1. We want our children to be happy and secure in the family.
  2. We wish them to be healthy in mind and body.
  3. We'd rather they not be emotionally hurt, but knowing they will, we want them to be able to take life's hurts and eventually use them for growth.
  4. We hope they'll have a good sense of self-worth.
  5. We wish them to know and love God.

B. Faith is a relationship with God.
  1. In faith we hold certain sacred truths about God.

     Expand: We recognize in God the qualities of goodness, compassion, wisdom, endless forgiveness, and care of us and of all creation.

2. To live in faith means to open to and communicate with our loving God.

   Expand: Opening to God begins by acknowledging God's presence and action in our lives, either because we've experienced that grace or because we trust it to be so. In our openness, we present to God the ups and downs of our lives, the needs of our families and of the world. Growing in openness to God means then tuning into God's subtle and overt presence, appreciating how God is with us daily. The very awareness of God's love and care for us facilitates our communication with this loving God. When we open to and communicate with God, we try to "walk in God's presence" as Abraham and Sarah did (Gen 17:1).

3. In faith we trust in the presence of the risen Jesus and his Spirit in our lives.

   Expand: Jesus gave the ultimate gift to his grieving friends. Because he could no longer be with them in body, he sent his Spirit. The Spirit of Jesus is still with us today: guiding us with wisdom, comforting us in sadness, being always the source of peace, love, and joy. The presence of the risen Jesus and his Spirit in our lives has many faces. We meet him in prayer, and we know him in peace, in enlightenment, in the faces of people we love, in interactions with spouses and children, in the "lame and the halt." The goodness, beauty, and love in all things are manifestations of the risen Jesus. We trust that the risen Jesus is with us and that the Holy Spirit who led, counseled, and strengthened him will do the same for us.

4. We choose this personal Jesus as our Savior.

   Expand: Our choosing Jesus is our response to his invitation to us to be disciples. It is in his role as Savior that Jesus has made our personal relationship with God possible.

Ask retreatants to turn to the person next to them and share their response to this question:

▲ What can you say about God out of your own experience?

Invite two or three to share with the whole group.

Lead into point C.

C. In faith, we deepen our knowledge and understanding of God.
   1. We begin by asking ourselves, who is the God with whom I am in relationship?
   2. We examine the images of God that we hold: father, mother, spirit, friend, shepherd, source, creator.

3. We sift out false images of God that have come to us from misguided understanding of the scriptures or from poor teaching: that of harsh judge, punisher, scorekeeper, distant one.

   Anecdote: In their book, *Good Goats,* the Linns have created a phrase that bears repeating to ourselves and to our children: "God loves us at least as much as the person who loves us the most."[1] If this were the mantra we were to teach our children from early childhood on, we wouldn't burden them with harsh images of God that later may be difficult to erase.

4. We reflect on the experience of other believing women and men: scriptural figures, parents, mentors in the faith, friends, holy people past and present.

   Expand: We see in St. Francis of Assisi and St. Clare, for example, simplicity in living the gospel. St. Teresa of Avila had profound experiences of God in prayer. Mother Teresa in Calcutta and Dom Helder Camara in Brazil responded to the needs of the poor and desperate. Through them we discover that we come to know God in both prayer and action.

   By reading the life of Jesus, we deepen our knowledge and understanding of God. Jesus himself said, "You will come to know the Father through me." In turn, Jesus read the words of the prophets, which provide us with rich descriptions of the love and faithfulness of God.

   The experience of faith sharing groups is a powerful source of reflection on God's presence and action for many people.

5. We trust our own experience of God, namely how God comes to me, speaks to me, acts in my life, answers my prayers.

Ask retreatants to meet in groups of three or four and share responses to these questions:
▲ What false images of God have you had to discard?
▲ Do you see your children holding any of those images? Why or why not?

Invite two or three to share with the whole group. If many wish to speak, limit time by saying, "Thank you for sharing. Do keep your stories in mind so you can share them with each other at a later time."

Lead into point D.

D. God's basic truths and promises are centered on our good.

Expand: God does not test, try, or punish us. The vicissitudes of life test us. The human condition tries us. Illness, poverty, and persecution punish us.

God is the loving one who is with us, securing us through the trials and turmoils we face. God wants only good for us.

Consider these promises from the scriptures:
▲ "I am with you always, until the end of the age" (Mt. 28:20).
▲ "Fear not, for I am with you..." (Isa. 43:5a).
▲ "I have come so that you might have life and have it more abundantly" (Jn. 10:10).

E. In the scriptures, we can learn many truths of God: God loves us with an everlasting love; God is with us; God will never abandon the one who puts her/his trust in God.

Expand: Refer to any of these scriptures to illuminate point E:
▲ "I have called you by name: you are mine" (Isa. 43:1).
▲ "With age-old love I have loved you..." (Jer. 31:3b).
▲ "O Lord, you have been our refuge through all generations" (Ps. 91:1).

F. Parents help children grow in faith by sharing their own faith with their little ones.
   1. We share how we pray, including how we speak, listen, describe to God what is in our lives, ask, receive, and thank our loving God.
   2. We tell our children all about God.
      a. Our God is good, loving, always near to us.
      b. Our God made us, our world, all the animals, and our wonderful bodies as a gift to enjoy, take care of, build, share, and keep good.
      c. Our God made each person special and good.
      d. Our God is like a loving mother/father, like the most caring and kind person we know, only much more so.
      e. Our God is always kind and fair.
      f. Our God is always with us.
      g. Our God hears and understands.
      h. Our God forgives.
      i. God is our best friend.

Ask retreatants to reflect for a few minutes on either of these questions, then write their responses on their notepads:
▲ Where did you see God's face this week?
▲ How did God touch your heart this week?
▲ What does this say to you about God's promise to be with us always?

Invite two or three to share with the whole group. Be comfortable with silence at first.

Conclude by suggesting parents resolve to continue or begin sharing with their children how they talk to God.

Preparations for Parent-Child Sharing Time

To set the tone for quality sharing time between parents and children, we close the parent session with an explanation of what their children have just experienced in their sessions with adult leaders. (See Parent-Child Sharing Time Form, p. 216.) Parents will find it helpful to also have a copy to refer to, as this may be the first time many parents have verbally shared a faith experience with their children.

Conclude by saying: "This quality time with you and your child alone together is the foundation of the parent-child retreat. Therefore, we request that each of you respect the time other parents are giving to their children. As tempting as it is to greet friends, we ask you to be totally present to your child for the next half-hour."

Note: We've found repeatedly that if we're not explicit, even firm, in our rationale for parent-child sharing time, the parents use this half-hour as a social time to visit with each other.

Note

1. Dennis, Sheila, and Matthew Linn, *Good Goats*. (Mahweh, NJ: Paulist Press, 1994), 11.

Parent Session 4: Advent

Focus

Advent is a time of waiting, of expectation, of longing for the coming of Jesus. In this rich liturgical season we hear the repeated promises in the scriptures that the Messiah will come to save his people. To these are added the New Testament accounts of the promise and birth of John the Baptist, and the invitation to Mary to be the mother of God's Holy One. All of this helps to prepare believers for the celebration of Jesus' birth at Christmas. This Jesus whom we long for and meet is not a baby, nor a suffering Jesus. He is the risen Jesus, victorious over death and all evil, who is free to meet all people throughout time. He is the one who is always with us as he promised. During Advent we await a holy presence. Jesus, born of Mary, is truly God with us.

To understand the significance of Jesus' birth, we must understand God's promise. It was a promise of loving, caring presence. Never did God suggest that we be spared from the human condition. Rather, God promised to be with us through all the bittersweet happenings of our lives, helping, leading, comforting, sustaining us.

For Christians, Advent is our opportunity to enter into the mystery of God's promise as we prepare for the celebration of God's greatest gift to us, the birth of Jesus. That gift continues now in the risen Jesus. As believers, we enter into the mystery of this gift by using the weeks of Advent for prayer, reflection, and joyous family preparations for the feast of Christmas. Christians prepare for the Gift: Jesus, God with us. For believers, Advent holds meaning far more profound than four weeks of commercial hoopla.

The challenge? Despite our vision, we're surrounded with commercial glitter and excitement aimed directly at our children. Our sharing in the mystery of the gift of Jesus invites us to help our children understand Christmas. By blending secular traditions with spiritual ones, we reinforce that Jesus entered into our secular world and remains here; that times of quiet and reflection, as well as fun and excitement, bring us balance; that the sacred and the human are integrated.

Introductions

Invite each person to share with the large group their own response to this question:

▲ Who has shown you the most about God's goodness?

Prayer

Parents will learn the Heart Room Prayer at the same time the children are entering into their own prayer at the children's sessions. The prayer itself acknowledges that some adult participants may have difficulty encountering Jesus personally, either because the idea of a personal God is unfamiliar to them, or because they've felt hurt or abandoned by God, or for a number of other reasons. We begin by leading retreatants into quieting with a gentle tone of voice. (See p. 215 for text of the Heart Room Prayer.)

Outline

The following outline is a scaffold for constructing a talk for parents. Its foundation is the Focus (p. 159). We provide examples and anecdotes, yet attempt to give latitude to the presenter to flesh out the presentation according to his or her own gifts and life experiences. Questions for discussion are interspersed throughout the talk, allowing the wisdom and experience of the participants to embellish the speaker's words. However, it's not necessary to use all the questions. The presenter should choose which questions to use, and how many, based on time limitations.

A. Advent means coming, expecting someone to come, and patiently waiting for that coming.
   1. Throughout the Hebrew scriptures we hear the repeated promise that God will come and save the people.
      a. "I have witnessed the affliction of my people in Egypt... I have come down to rescue them..." (Ex. 3:7a, 8a).
      b. "Samuel said to them: 'If you with your whole heart return to the Lord...he will deliver you'" (1 Sam. 7:3).
      c. "Here comes with power the Lord God... Like a shepherd he feeds his flock..." (Isa. 40:10a, 11a).
      d. "I will bring the restoration of my people Israel..." (Am. 9:14a).
   2. Yahweh acted again and again on behalf of the chosen people.
   3. God's promise was, "I myself will come and save you."
   4. God's people, the Jews, waited with great faith and longing for God to satisfy this promise. Most of the Jews did not recognize how that promise would be fulfilled: "Behold, the virgin shall be with child and bear a son, and they shall name him Emmanuel, which means 'God is with us'" (Mt. 1:23).
   5. Jesus, born of Mary, is truly God with us.

Ask retreatants to spend a few minutes reflecting on this question, then to share their response with the person next to them:

▲ What does Advent mean to you?

Invite two or three people to share with the whole group. If many wish to speak, limit time by saying, "Thank you for sharing. Let's share more a little later on."

Lead into point B.

B. To understand the significance of Jesus's birth, we must understand God's promise.
   1. God's promise to be with us, repeated throughout the Hebrew scriptures, and fulfilled in Jesus, was a promise of loving presence. (Isa. 58:11)
   2. God did not say, "Believe in me, and nothing bad will ever happen to you."
   3. Rather, God's promise is help in what has happened, is happening, or will happen.

C. For Christians, Advent is our opportunity to enter into the mystery of God's promise as we prepare for the celebration of God's greatest gift to us, the birth of Jesus.
   1. This gift of Jesus' coming was filled with mystery in its historical context.
   2. "For God so loved the world that he gave his only Son..." (Jn. 3:16).
   3. God came to us in the flesh, Jesus, a baby with life like ours.
   4. That gift continues now in the presence of the risen Jesus.
   5. We, as believers, respond to the invitation to enter into the mystery of this gift by using the weeks of Advent for prayer, reflection, and joyous family preparations for the feast of Christmas.
   6. Advent is our time to prepare for the celebration of the Gift: Jesus, God with us.
   7. For Christians, Advent holds meaning far more profound than four weeks of commercial hoopla.

D. We help our children understand God's gift of Jesus to us by blending secular traditions with spiritual ones.
   1. To reinforce the experience of waiting, families can create an Advent wreath with evergreen boughs, to be the focal point during daily prayer and candle-lighting.

   Expand: Children's fascination with candles and love of music and story will be an enticement to join in the ritual. In some families, children take turns lighting the candles. Most children readily join in the singing of simple songs, and many older children relish the opportunity to read aloud. With the three elements of candle-lighting, song, and reading of scripture (particularly the Gospel of Luke)—and short periods of silence interspersed—children will be participants in a memorable ritual, rather than passive spectators.

2. To further emphasize the feeling of anticipation during Advent, the family can assemble their nativity scene, saving the Christ Child figure for a Christmas Eve ceremony where they place the infant in the crib.
3. Parents and children can take turns reading the account of the Savior's coming in the gospels of Matthew and Luke, then telling it and retelling it throughout Advent.

Share and Invite, asking the whole group:

▲ What good seasonal stories do your children enjoy during Advent?

Lead into point D4.

4. Christmas parties, carols, cards, and gifts are all ways we "bear" Jesus to the world by showing love to each other just as Jesus loves us.
5. Children can enter into the true spirit of the feast by also choosing, and perhaps paying for, a toy to give to a child who might not receive one otherwise.
6. In lieu of, or in addition to, material gifts, family members might give each other special acts of love (gift certificates for services, occasional compliments, expressions of affection, etc.) as a way of reflecting God's gift of Jesus to us.

Ask retreatants to meet in groups of three or four and share responses to this question:

▲ What Christmas traditions has your family established that blend the secular with the spiritual?

Invite any who desire to share their traditions with the whole group.

Lead into point D7.

7. Parents can establish a permeating atmosphere of quiet and calm in the home to balance the potentially frantic pace of the commercial season.

   Expand: The hype of Christmas can seize us before we recognize it. Our children are exposed to a myriad of television ads; their friends tell stories of indulgent Santas; relatives are anxious to bestow their gifts. While Advent should be a quiet time, our culture contradicts this. In addition to blending the secular with the spiritual, we need to explore ways to introduce quiet into the chaos.

a. Big and little people alike can benefit from an environment where they are free to ask for and receive quiet time when they need it.
b. Within such a climate, children learn to be still inside and out.

Expand: Even a simple Advent ritual at meal time can focus the family on what is true about this time of year. A few moments of silence followed by the prayer, "We remember that Jesus came and is with us now," repeated each day during Advent, brings to consciousness the need for quiet and awareness of Jesus, so necessary to offset the commercial hype.

c. In this way, Advent can be a time where all family members develop an attitude where they can listen to one another and God.

Ask retreatants to discuss:

- ▲ What do you do in your family so everyone can have quiet time?
- ▲ Do you notice a difference in attitude where family members are more present to each other because of these sacred times?

Invite two or three people to share their reflections with the whole group.

Conclude by giving parents a question to reflect on through the week:

- ▲ What do you want most for your children this Advent?

Preparation for Parent-Child Sharing Time

To set the tone for quality sharing time between parents and children, we close the parent session with an explanation of what their children have just experienced in their sessions with adult leaders. (See Parent-Child Sharing Time Form, p. 216.) Parents will find it helpful to also have a copy to refer to, as this may be the first time many parents have verbally shared a faith experience with their children.

Conclude by saying: "This quality time with you and your child alone together is the foundation of the parent-child retreat. Therefore, we request that each of you respect the time other parents are giving to their children. As tempting as it is to greet friends, we ask you to be totally present to your child for the next half-hour."

Note: We've found repeatedly that if we're not explicit, even firm, in our rationale for parent-child sharing time, the parents use this half-hour as a social time to visit with each other.

Parent Session 5: Saying 'Yes' and Saying 'No'

Note: At nearly every retreat, single parents will be present. When we speak of the role of spouse, therefore, we're sensitive to those who don't share this experience. We acknowledge this by using expressions such as, "Those who are wives..." or "Many of us have spent part or all of our adult lives in the role of wives..."

Also, while both men and women may have trouble saying "no," we find this trend to be culturally more relevant to women. Therefore, we've directed this session to women and use it when we know all the participants will be women. However, if men are present, the references to women, wives, and mothers, can be easily adapted to include and value those men who are similarly motivated in their decisions.

Focus

In making decisions in accordance with God's will, our center must be Jesus. Many of the decisions we're called on to make involve discerning whether to respond "yes" or "no" to the demands of our lives as women and mothers. Such discernment is indeed spiritual, and requires an openness to God in prayer.

We tend to define ourselves according to our roles, and as women our roles are many. Some are wives, all of us are mothers. How easy it is to see these roles as our total identity. It's within these roles that we have choices. We can choose, for example, to think of ourselves as perfect, selfless, giving wives, or as loving women who have independent lives we're excited to share with our husbands. As mothers, too, we have a choice: We can live totally other-centered lives, doing everything for our families, or we can let them know we're lovingly there for them within the context of our own rich life, which we joyously share with them. Our healthy identity hinges on an authentic understanding of who we are and where our center is.

Our primary identity is that of women centered in Jesus. We are persons in and of ourselves, created, formed, and loved into life by God. Following Jesus' command to love ourselves (Mt. 22:39), we claim and honor ourselves by accepting the freedom to take part of the day as our own to pray, be still, reflect, read, or visit. We shape plans for ourselves and live them without guilt. Honoring ourselves means we root ourselves in Jesus, allowing his Spirit to fill us and lead us.

On the other hand, when our center is ourselves, or even others, rather than

Jesus, we carry a false understanding of what a believing woman should be for those she loves. If we're centered in Jesus, we can choose between two words rather than one: "yes" or "no." Our responsibility is to pray, to search out what is true for ourselves in any situation, just as Jesus did. A prayer of discernment begins by asking the Spirit to be with us as we seek a response to the question: "What does our loving God want of me here?" We consider the scriptures, our church tradition, and the modeling of believing people we admire. We focus on what is right and authentic for us now, as we are, rather than on what might be true for us later in life, after we've grown into greater goodness and generosity. We claim our freedom to respond "yes" or "no." When we are in our center, our own truth is rooted in Jesus and his Spirit.

Introductions

Invite each person to share with the large group their own response to this question:

▲ What aspect of Jesus' life is affecting you most at this time?

Prayer

Parents will learn the Heart Room Prayer at the same time the children are entering into their own prayer at the children's sessions. The prayer itself acknowledges that some adult participants may have difficulty encountering Jesus personally, either because the idea of a personal God is unfamiliar to them, or because they've felt hurt or abandoned by God, or for a number of other reasons. We begin by leading retreatants into quieting with a gentle tone of voice. (See Appendix, p. 215 for text of the Heart Room Prayer.)

Outline

The following outline is a scaffold for constructing a talk for parents. Its foundation is the Focus (p. 164). We provide examples and anecdotes, yet attempt to give latitude to the presenter to flesh out the presentation according to his or her own gifts and life experiences. Questions for discussion are interspersed throughout the talk, allowing the wisdom and experience of the participants to embellish the speaker's words. However, it's not necessary to use all the questions. The presenter should choose which questions to use, and how many, based on time limitations.

A. We women tend to define ourselves according to our roles.
   1. As wives, we can choose to think of ourselves as the "perfect," selfless, giving wife or as a loving woman who has an independent life she is excited to share with her husband.

2. As mothers, we can live totally other-centered lives, doing everything for our families, or we can let them know we're lovingly there for them within the context of our own rich life, which we joyously share with them.
3. As women, our healthy identity hinges on an authentic understanding of who we are and where our center is.

Ask retreatants to spend a few minutes reflecting on this question, then to share their response with the person next to them:

▲ Where did you get your ideas of what a "perfect wife" and "perfect mother" were supposed to be?

Invite two or three people to share with the whole group. If many wish to speak, limit the time by saying, "Thank you for sharing. We'll have more time later."

Lead into point B.

B. Our primary identity is that of women centered in Jesus.
1. We are persons in and of ourselves.
2. Exactly as we are, we're created, formed, and loved into life by God, with God's everlasting love.
3. This loving God has commanded us, "You shall love the Lord, your God, with all your heart, and with all your soul, and with all your strength" (Deut. 6:5). "You shall love your neighbor as yourself" (Mt. 22:39b). As Christian women, we can't ignore the last part of this second command.
4. We claim and honor ourselves by allowing ourselves the freedom to take part of the day (even briefly) as our own, to pray, be still, reflect, read, or visit.
5. We further love ourselves by shaping plans for ourselves and living them without guilt.
6. Claiming and honoring ourselves means acknowledging we have a life, feelings, hopes, desires, and dreams.
7. Honoring ourselves means we root ourselves in Jesus, allowing his Spirit to fill us and lead us.

Ask retreatants to meet in groups of three or four and share responses to this question:

▲ Who has helped you come to a healthier concept of a loving woman who is wife and mother?

Invite two or three people to share their answers with the whole group.

Lead into point C.

C. When our center is ourselves and others rather than Jesus, we carry a false understanding of what a believing woman should be for those she loves.

1. Jesus tells us, "Let your 'Yes' mean 'Yes' and your 'No' mean 'No.' Anything more is from the evil one" (Mt. 5:37).
2. It's false to believe that our middle name is Yes, that we need to use it as a response to any request from children, husband, school, church, neighbors.

   Expand: Not only is saying "no" acceptable, it was Jesus himself who modeled this for us. He showed us by example that we must sort out every situation or request in order to know if "yes" or "no" is right for us. He, too, said "no." For example, many sought him for healing, but sometimes he refused such requests in order to pray, to be with the Twelve, or because he felt a call to go to another region. Use any of these texts to illuminate this point:

   a. Jesus was addressing the crowds when his mother and brothers appeared outside to speak to him. He continued to give his attention to the people (Mt. 12:46-48).
   b. The Pharisees and Sadducees asked Jesus to show them some sign in the sky. He declined (Mt. 16:1-4).
   c. James and John asked Jesus to grant their request to sit at his right and his left when he came into his glory. Jesus replied that such honor was not his to give (Mk. 10:35-40).
   d. To Pilate's surprise, Jesus refused to answer his question, "Are you the king of the Jews?" (Mk. 15:1-5).
   e. Jesus said "no" three times when the devil tempted him (Lk. 4:1-13.)

3. When we're in our center, the Spirit of Jesus gives us the freedom to choose from two responses: "yes" or "no."
4. We have a responsibility to pray, to search out what is true for ourselves in any situation.

   Expand: Being a follower of Jesus calls us to discern, to sort out as Jesus did the truth of any situation in life. Paul speaks to the Ephesians about growing up into the maturity of Christ by "living the truth in love" (4:15). It is the Spirit of Jesus that continues to center us in our truth so that we can authentically say "no" or "yes."

   In our prayer of discernment we ask the Spirit to be with us as we ask:
   ▲ What does our loving God ask of me here?

- ▲ What do the scriptures and my church teach me?
- ▲ What would believing people I admire do in this situation?
- ▲ What seems right for me *now* (not later, when I've grown in greater goodness and generosity)?
- ▲ Am I free to say "yes" or "no"?

Reflect for a few minutes on this question, then write your response on your notepad:

▲ What is your experience of saying "no"?

Invite two or three to share with the whole group. Be comfortable with silence at first.

Lead into point D.

D. If we are in our center, our own truth is rooted in Jesus and his Spirit.

1. Most of us have the experience of acting independently, relying only on our own limited resources and capabilities. The result is often struggle, worry, and floundering, even failure.

   Expand: What we learn from Jesus and his word is interdependence, not independence. We don't have to do it alone. Our loving God is with us to lead, support, clarify, strengthen, and guide. The secret then is to open to and call upon God to be with us in our life choices.

2. Choosing to live, work, pray, and work for others out of the center that is Jesus, on the other hand, can be a new source of life and freedom.
3. We learn to center in Jesus.
   a. We quiet ourselves and go to our inmost heart where Jesus dwells.
   b. We open to this loved One, speaking our heart to him.
   c. In our own words, we ask him to guide us, to be with us in all that we do.
   d. We wait for his response: Yes, this is true for me, or no, this is not right for me at this time.

Conclude by giving parents a question to reflect on through the week:

▲ What prevents you from taking time in the day to read, pray, or in other ways renew yourself?

Preparations for Parent-Child Sharing Time

To set the tone for quality sharing time between parents and children, we close the parent session with an explanation of what their children have just experienced in their sessions with adult leaders. (See Parent-Child Sharing Time Form,

p. 216.) Parents will find it helpful to also have a copy to refer to, as this may be the first time many parents have verbally shared a faith experience with their children.

Conclude by saying: "This quality time with you and your child alone together is the foundation of the parent-child retreat. Therefore, we request that each of you respect the time other parents are giving to their children. As tempting as it is to greet friends, we ask you to be totally present to your child for the next half-hour."

Note: We've found repeatedly that if we're not explicit, even firm, in our rationale for parent-child sharing time, the parents use this half-hour as a social time to visit with each other.

Parent Session 6: All One in Christ

Focus

In the family of Jesus, each of us has value, rooted in our uniqueness. We are different from, but never less than others, as Paul tells the Galatian Christians: "You are all one in Christ Jesus" (Gal. 3:28b).

St. Paul speaks of a whole new reality brought about through Jesus' life, death, and resurrection: In the kingdom of God there is no domination, no inferiority. On the contrary, all are one in the risen Jesus. All are equal in dignity and value.

The conflict arises as we try to live out this truth in a world that separates people based on differences. Communities, schools, workplaces, churches, even families, all have criteria for ranking persons better or worse, stronger or weaker, dominant or submissive. This rather twisted interpretation of uniqueness has succeeded in dividing, not unifying.

As believers in a loving God, on the other hand, we hold that each of us is unique by virtue of our being made in God's image. Each child and adult at this retreat is like no other person. Every one of us is gifted by God in our own right. Therefore, we are valued by God just as we are. Yet in the families we were raised in, and the families we're raising, children are often compared to one another in ways that are well-intentioned, but subtly devaluing.

Jesus himself encountered overt prejudices against certain persons in his day. Some people were not acceptable because of their work, their gender, their being non-Jews, their physical weakness, their personal failures against Jewish laws. Yet he accepted each person as having worth and dignity, and he invited all persons to share this new way of living.

We pass on this attitude of love and respect to our children. They will grow to love themselves to the extent that they know how their family values the uniqueness of each person. When they hear derogatory comments about neighbors, relatives, or classes of people, they are likely to intuit that they are also fair target for disparaging talk. On the other hand, when our young children think of all people as special and lovable just as they are, they grow to value themselves, too.

Introductions

Invite each person to share with the large group their own response to one of the following questions:

▲ What aspect of Jesus would you most like to introduce to your child?
▲ What aspect of Jesus has helped you most as a parent?

Prayer

Parents will learn the Heart Room Prayer at the same time the children are entering into their own prayer at the children's sessions. The prayer itself acknowledges that some adult participants may have difficulty encountering Jesus personally, either because the idea of a personal God is unfamiliar to them, or because they've felt hurt or abandoned by God, or any other number of reasons. We begin by leading retreatants into quieting with a gentle tone of voice. (See p. 215 for text of the Heart Room Prayer.)

Outline

The following outline is a scaffold for constructing a talk for parents. Its foundation is the Focus (p. 169). We provide examples and anecdotes, yet attempt to give latitude to the presenter to flesh out the presentation according to his or her own gifts and life experiences. Questions for discussion are interspersed throughout the talk, allowing the wisdom and experience of the participants to embellish the speaker's words. However, it's not necessary to use all the questions. The presenter should choose which questions to use, and how many, based on time limitations.

A. We have a powerful teaching in Galatians 3:28: "There is neither Jew nor Greek, there is neither slave nor free, there is not male and female, for you are all one in Christ Jesus."
   1. St. Paul speaks of a whole new reality brought about through Jesus' life, death, and resurrection.

2. In God's kingdom there is no domination, no superiority of men over women, one category of people, race or nationality over another.
3. In the risen Jesus all are one, all are equal in dignity and value.

B. We try to live out this truth in a world that operates not out of a sense of oneness of persons, but rather by comparisons of differences.
   1. Our society casts people in roles of better or worse, stronger or weaker.
   2. Our communities are grouped by richer or poorer.
   3. Schools, churches, and workplaces rank persons as gifted or limited, superior or inferior.

Ask retreatants to meet in groups of three or four and share responses to this question:

▲ What patterns of domination do you see in our society, church, and families?

Invite two or three to share with the whole group. If many wish to speak, limit the discussion by saying, "Thank you for sharing. It looks like we could use more time, but hold onto your ideas for later."

Lead into point C.

C. As believers in our loving God and Jesus, we hold that each person, made in God's image, is unique.
   1. Each child and adult on this retreat is like no other person.
   2. Every one of us is gifted in our own right; that is, endowed with gifts from God.
   3. We're all special just as we are.

D. Yet within families we often hear children compared to one another.
   4. "He's our brightest one."
   5. "She's so quiet, not at all like the other children."
   6. "Jimmy is on the honor roll" (said while the other children overhear, without any word of praise about them or their gifts or efforts).
   7. "Her sisters were walking and talking at this age."
   8. "Tom is really awkward at sports even though his father is such a jock."
   9. "Becky is a whiz at math even though she's a girl."

Ask retreatants to spend a few minutes reflecting on this question, then to share their response with the person next to them:

▲ How do you handle comparisons in your family?

▲ What do you do in your family to make each member know how important (s)he is to the family, the community, the church, the world?

Invite two or three to share with the whole group.

Lead into point E.

E. Jesus encountered great prejudices against certain persons in his day.
   1. Some were not acceptable because of their work (Mk. 2:14-16), their gender (Mt. 15:21f), their being non-Jews (Mk. 7:24f), their physical weaknesses (purity and temple laws), their personal failures against Jewish laws (Lk. 7:39).
   2. Yet he accepted each person as having worth and dignity.
   3. He said that all were welcome in God's kingdom.
   4. He invited all persons to share this new way of living.

F. Our children will grow up to love themselves to the extent that they know how their family values the uniqueness of each person.
   1. When children hear derogatory comments about neighbors, relatives, or classes of people, they know they're fair targets for the same kind of disparaging talk.

      Anecdote: A woman tells how she grew up hearing her favorite aunt make negative comments about people on a regular basis. Even at the time, she felt uncomfortable listening to it. But as she grew older, she found herself reluctant to spend time with this aunt. She realized, in time, that her uneasiness centered around a fear that she, too, would be criticized by this person she loved. The fear was complicated by the fact she was never quite sure what behaviors would elicit her aunt's criticism. This woman had learned to look at herself critically in light of what her aunt might perceive, rather than to see herself as predominantly good.

   2. Children who hear criticism learn to criticize—even themselves.

      Anecdote: In modeling frustration that really warrants criticism, it's important to honor the dignity of the person involved. One father learned how to state what was difficult so the children would recognize the *action* as annoying, rather than the person. One day the children witnessed a neighbor shouting unnecessarily at their dad and making unreasonable demands of him. The father walked away spewing anger about the "jerk." Then he realized the children could hear him, and he made an effort to change his tone. "Guys, that man can be nice, but right now he's acting like a jerk, and I don't like it. He's like us, I guess. Sometimes we act like jerks. But we're mostly nice. "

Expand: Equally important is the way we ourselves deal with incidents deserving of criticism. If the children haven't witnessed an unpleasant experience, there's no need to criticize in front of them. However, we need to deal with it in a healthy way so we don't internalize the anger. Like the psalmist in Psalm 83, we can take a few moments and say to God, "I want to tell you about this jerk... Be with me in this. Let me be honest and fair in the face of what he's done."

Some people have developed a habit of criticizing others. If this is the case, it might be helpful to remember that everyone has flaws, but that the good outweighs the bad. We can choose to focus on the flaws, or we can redirect the practice so we habitually see the good in everyone.

3. On the other hand, when our children think of all people as special and lovable just as they are, they grow to value themselves, too.

Invite parents to share with the whole group:

- ▲ What have you found successful ways to counter prejudice in your family or neighborhood?
- ▲ How do you help your children appreciate difference, rather than fear it or make fun of it?

Conclude by giving parents a question to reflect on through the week:

- ▲ How do the relationships I'm involved in reflect mutuality or domination?

Preparations for Parent-Child Sharing Time

To set the tone for quality sharing time between parents and children, we close the parent session with an explanation of what their children have just experienced in their sessions with adult leaders. (See Parent-Child Sharing Time Form, p. 216.) Parents will find it helpful to also have a copy to refer to, as this may be the first time many parents have verbally shared a faith experience with their children.

Conclude by saying: "This quality time with you and your child alone together is the foundation of the parent-child retreat. Therefore, we request that each of you respect the time other parents are giving to their children. As tempting as it is to greet friends, we ask you to be totally present to your child for the next half-hour."

Note: We've found repeatedly that if we're not explicit, even firm, in our rationale for parent-child sharing time, the parents use this half-hour as a social time to visit with each other.

Parent Session 7: Bless Us, O Lord

Focus

Because of our oneness in Christ Jesus, we share his power to bless. Indeed, asking for and giving blessings is part of our Christian heritage. We pray before mealtime, for example, that God will bless our food. We're generous with the expressions of affection, "God bless you" and "Bless your heart." And in the quiet of our hearts, we often ask God for blessings or ask God's blessing on another.

Blessings given and received hold several meanings. A blessing is the favor, kindness, or goodness of God poured out. The action of blessing means asking for the goodness of God to be upon a person or upon all of creation. To bless is to thank God for gifts God has so generously given us.

Made in God's image, we ourselves are a blessing. Gifted with God's endless presence, caring, guiding, and healing, and invited into relationship with God, we are the embodiment of the favor, kindness and goodness of God that is blessing. In this way, our very being is holy.

Jesus, called blessed in the scriptures (Mt. 21:9), is the blessing of God on all persons and all of creation. He is the favor of God, the kindness and goodness of God enfleshed and present to us. Jesus is our thanksgiving to God, our eucharist.

All of us in God's family have the power to bless in Jesus' name. God blessed us with the Holy Spirit, who dwells in each of us, empowering us to bless others. Indeed, all of us can call forth God's goodness on one another; all can give thanks for blessings received.

We can bless in God's name those we love and care about: spouses, children, parents, friends, the world. We can even bless places or objects. We bless in times of special need, in times of forgiveness, during crises, on special occasions, when leaving the house. All of this is in our power.

The ritual of blessing may feel awkward at first, but efforts to grow in comfort with it reap graces for the giver and the receiver. The bestowing of a blessing involves placing hands on the person and speaking out loud the desire for this person to receive a blessing from our loving God. Some grow into comfort by first blessing silently, sometimes even while the loved one sleeps, then gradually sharing the blessing aloud. Blessing—pouring out the favor, goodness, and kindness of God on those we love—nurtures healthy family life.

Introductions

Invite each person to share with the large group their own response to this question:

▲ What is your favorite season of the year? Why?

Prayer

Parents will learn the Heart Room Prayer at the same time the children are entering into their own prayer at the children's sessions. The prayer itself acknowledges that some adult participants may have difficulty encountering Jesus personally, either because the idea of a personal God is unfamiliar to them, or because they've felt hurt or abandoned by God, or for a number of other reasons. We begin by leading retreatants into quieting with a gentle tone of voice. (See p. 215 for text of the Heart Room Prayer.)

Outline

The following outline is a scaffold for constructing a talk for parents. Its foundation is the Focus (p 174). We provide examples and anecdotes, yet attempt to give latitude to the presenter to flesh out the presentation according to his or her own gifts and life experiences. Questions for discussion are interspersed throughout the talk, allowing the wisdom and experience of the participants to embellish the speaker's words. However, it's not necessary to use all the questions. The presenter should choose which questions to use, and how many, based on time limitations.

A. Asking for and giving blessings is part of our Christian heritage.
   1. We ask God to bless our food before mealtime.
   2. "God bless you" and "Bless your heart" are common terms of affection.
   3. In the quiet of our hearts, we often ask God for blessings or ask God's blessing on another.

B. To ask a blessing or to give a blessing carries several definitions.
   1. A blessing is the favor, kindness, or goodness of God poured out.
   2. To bless means to ask for the goodness of God to be upon a person.
   3. Asking for or giving a blessing means invoking God's goodness on all of creation.
   4. Blessing is thanking God for gifts received.

C. We ourselves, made in God's image, are a blessing.
   1. In Genesis 12:2 we hear, "I will bless you" and "you will be a blessing."
   2. We're a blessing because God blesses us with God's endless presence, caring, guiding, healing, inviting us into relationship.

3. Theologian Abraham Heschel has said, "Just to be is a blessing, to live is holy."

Ask retreatants to meet in groups of three or four and share responses to this question:

▲ How have you experienced God's blessing you with presence, caring, guiding, healing, and inviting you into relationship?

Invite two or three to share with the whole group.

Lead into point D.

D. Jesus is the blessing of God on all persons and creation.
   1. In Matthew 21:9 we read, "Blessed is he who comes in the name of the Lord."
   2. Jesus is the favor of God, the kindness and goodness of God enfleshed and present to us.
   3. Jesus is our thanksgiving to God, our Eucharist.

E. Ordained ministers of Jesus have special power to bless in his name, but so do all of us in God's family.
   1. The Holy Spirit is the blessing of God to us, the gift given to lead us into life.
   2. Because of the indwelling Spirit, we have the power to bless others.
   3. All can call forth God's goodness on one another.
   4. All can give thanks for blessings received.

Ask retreatants to reflect for a few minutes, then write their response on their notepad:

▲ Have Jesus and his Spirit been a blessing for you? When? How?

Invite two or three to share their responses with the whole group. Be comfortable with the silence at first.

Lead into point F.

F. We can bless in God's name all those we love and care about.
   1. We can bless our spouses—in the morning, at night, in times of special need, in times of forgiveness, during crises, anytime.
   2. We can bless our children—morning, noon, night, on special occasions, when leaving the house, in times of hurt, for special needs, during illness.
   3. We can bless friends on similar occasions.
   4. We can bless parents on even more occasions.
   5. We can bless our world and those in it in special need: individuals, couples,

families, parish communities, the hungry, the sick, the dying.

6. We can even bless places or objects.

Anecdote: Many years ago, a college woman learned about the power she had to bless others. When she married, she and her husband established the tradition of blessing each other before going to sleep. As each of their six children arrived, they, too, entered into the ritual, asking for a blessing before they went to bed, left for school, or went out to play. One evening, now twenty years after this mother had first heard of her power to bless, she found herself feeling surprised when her daughter's prom date arrived at the door. "Come in, Julio," the teenager was saying. "We have to ask my parents to bless us before we go to the dance." In this home, blessing one another was natural. The parents had taught the ritual of blessing right along with good manners and teeth brushing.

Ask of the whole group:

▲ Have you ever blessed anyone before? What awkwardness or hesitancy did you anticipate at first?

Lead into point G.

G. The ritual of blessing should be genuine, spoken from our hearts and reflecting our own personalities.

Anecdote: Most of us found or will find it awkward to bless someone for the first time. A man remembers when his father blessed him right before the son left for the service. It was uncharacteristic of Bob's father to beckon him to kneel down. Nevertheless, Bob complied. His father surprised him by saying, "Before you go to war, I must bless you." The son recognized how awkward this must have been for his father, but the words of that personal blessing have remained with him all these years: "Protect Bob through whatever happens in war, and bring him safely home to us." The blessing came directly from the father's heart in simple, natural words. His strong feeling for his son moved him to pray despite the awkwardness.

1. The ritual of blessing another begins by being still and opening ourselves to God.
2. We place a hand on the head or shoulder of the person and speak out loud our special desire for this person to receive a blessing from our loving God.
    a. O Loving God, bless this dear child with your presence this day.
    b. O Holy One, bless this dear husband with your protection and care as he sets out on this business trip. Bring him safely home.

c. O Jesus, you who have such compassion for the needy, bless all those in our city who are homeless this night.
d. Jesus, bless my mommy and daddy.
e. Try your own blessing in your own words.

Ask retreatants to make up a blessing for the person next to them. Bless that person.

Conclude by suggesting parents make an internal resolution to begin the tradition of blessing their children this week.

Preparations for Parent-Child Sharing Time

To set the tone for quality sharing time between parents and children, we close the parent session with an explanation of what their children have just experienced in their sessions with adult leaders. (See Parent-Child Sharing Time Form, p. 216.) Parents will find it helpful to also have a copy to refer to, as this may be the first time many parents have verbally shared a faith experience with their children.

Conclude by saying: "This quality time with you and your child alone together is the foundation of the parent-child retreat. Therefore, we request that each of you respect the time other parents are giving to their children. As tempting as it is to greet friends, we ask you to be totally present to your child for the next half-hour."

Note: We've found repeatedly that if we're not explicit, even firm, in our rationale for parent-child sharing time, the parents use this half-hour as a social time to visit with each other.

Appendix A

Retreat Logo Pattern

Gathering Song

J-E-S-U-S

(Tune: "Bingo")

I have a friend and he loves me,
And Jesus is his name-oh.
J-E-S-U-S, J-E-S-U-S, J-E-S-U-S,
And Jesus is his name-oh.

I have a friend and he loves me,
And Jesus is his name-oh.
(clap)-E-S-U-S, *(clap)*-E-S-U-S, *(clap)*-E-S-U-S,
And Jesus is his name-oh.

I have a friend and he loves me,
And Jesus is his name-oh.
(clap-clap)-S-U-S, *(clap-clap)*-S-U-S, *(clap-clap)*-S-U-S,
And Jesus is his name-oh.

I have a friend and he loves me,
And Jesus is his name-oh.
(clap-clap-clap)-U-S, *(clap-clap-clap)*-U-S, *(clap-clap-clap)*-U-S,
And Jesus is his name-oh.

I have a friend and he loves me,
And Jesus is his name-oh.
(clap-clap-clap-clap)-S, *(clap-clap-clap-clap)*-S, *(clap-clap-clap-clap)*-S,
And Jesus is his name-oh.

I have a friend and he loves me,
And Jesus is his name-oh.
(clap-clap-clap-clap-clap), *(clap-clap-clap-clap-clap)*, *(clap-clap-clap-clap-clap)*,
And Jesus is his name-oh.

J-E-S-U-S Poster

Make enlargements and glue onto contrasting colors of construction paper.

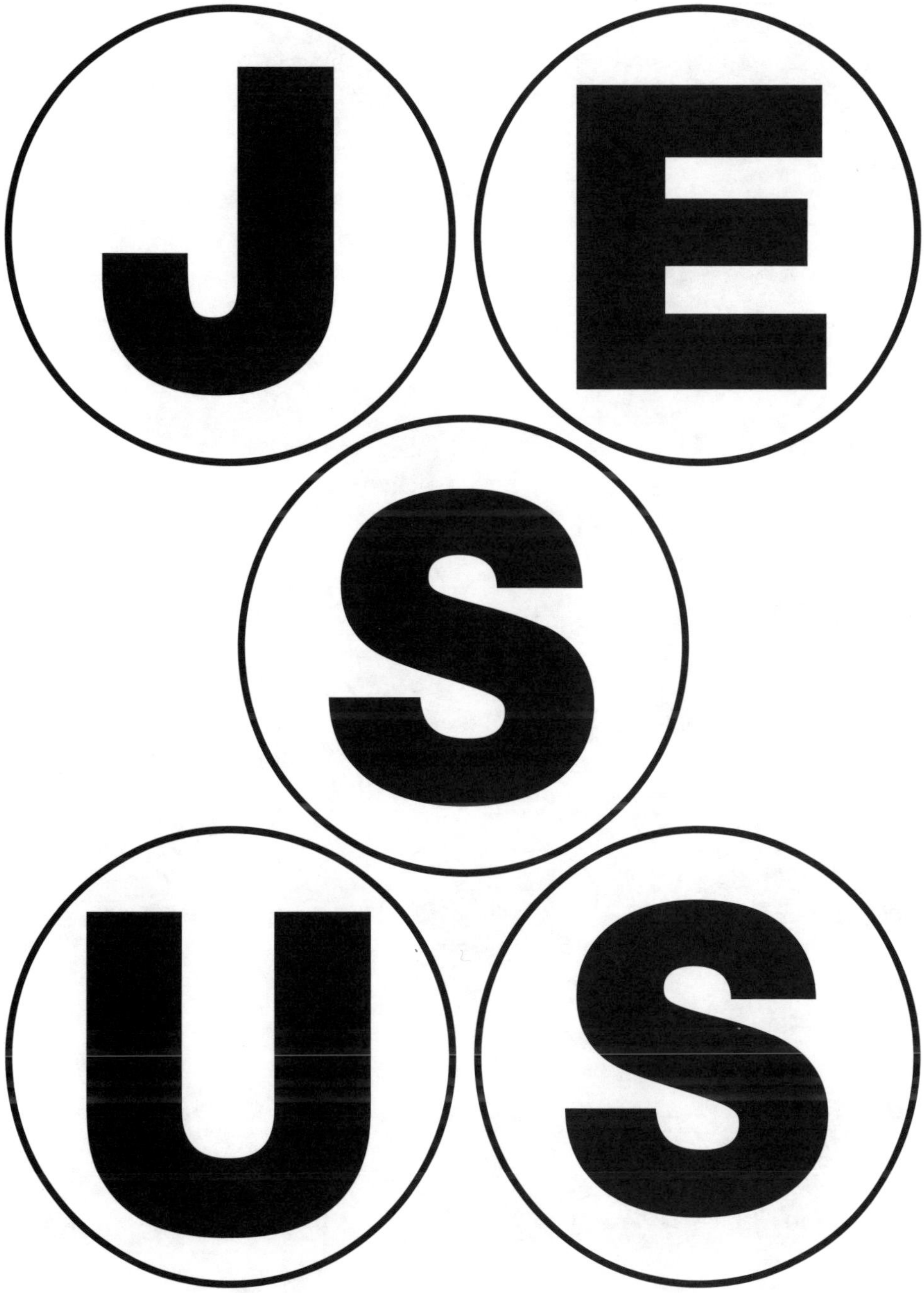

Thumbprint Designs

for posters/welcome sign (from *Great Thumbprint Drawing Book* by Ed Emberley)

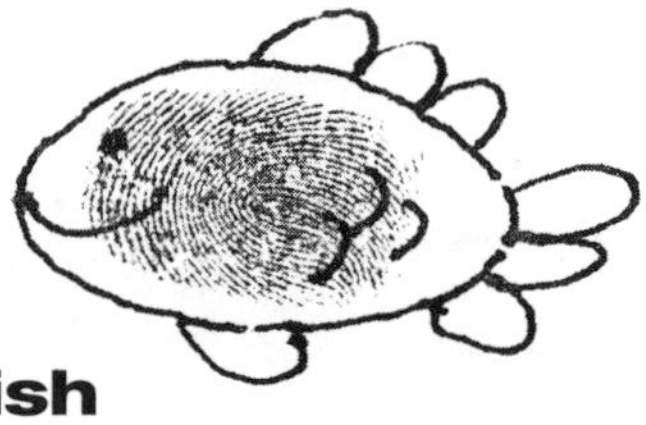

Fish

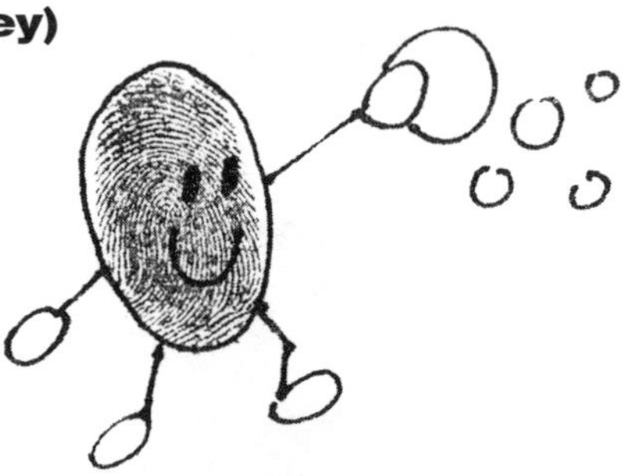

Bubbles

Valentine's Day

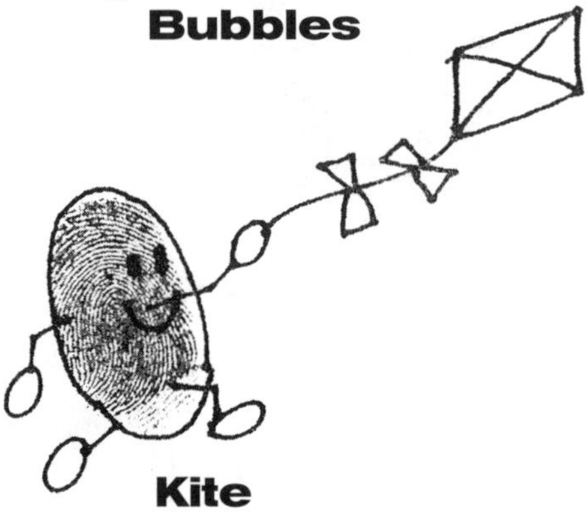

Kite

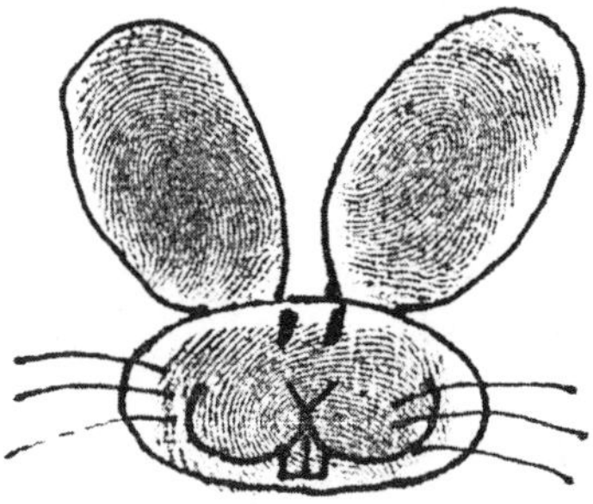

Easter

Mother's/Father's Day

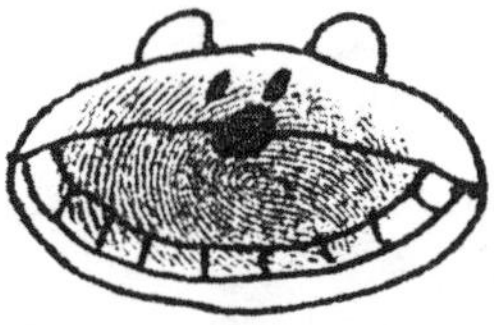

Picnic

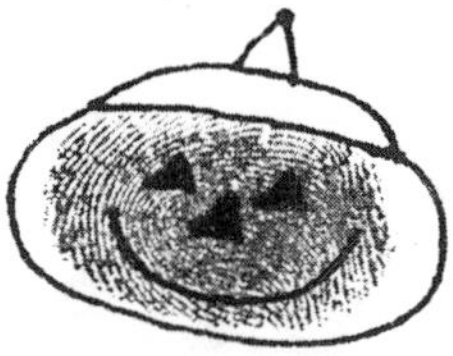

Candle

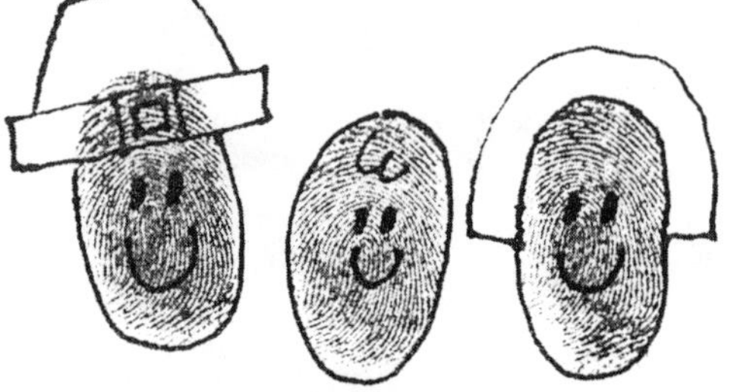

Thanksgiving

Christmas

Any Retreat

Activity Page

Jesus Friendship Hat

1. Fold a newspaper in half.
2. Fold in the corners.
3. Fold up one side. Repeat with second side.
4. Staple or tape the corners.
5. Cut along dotted lines and glue one strip (printed below) to each side of the finished hat.

1

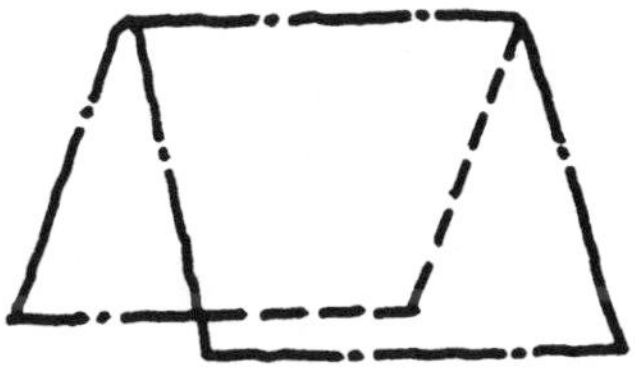

2

3

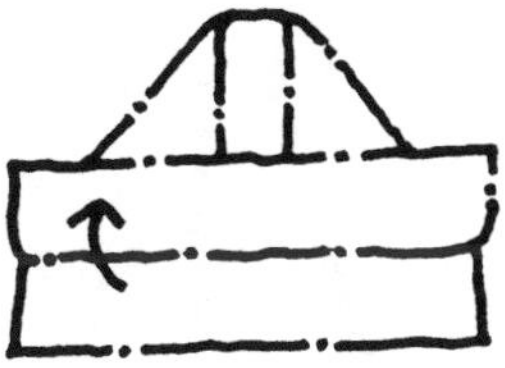

4

5

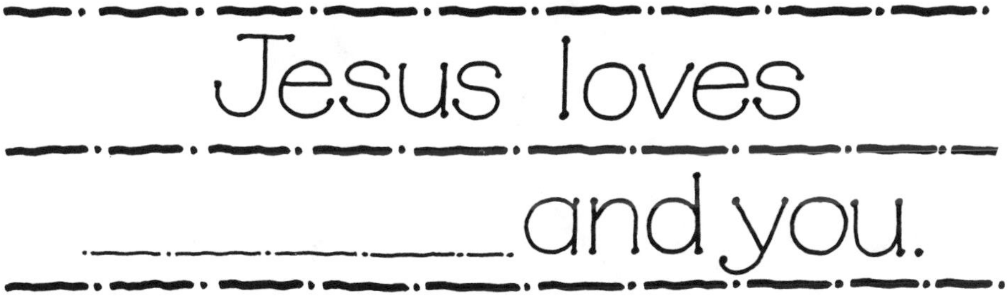

Fish Retreat

Nametag

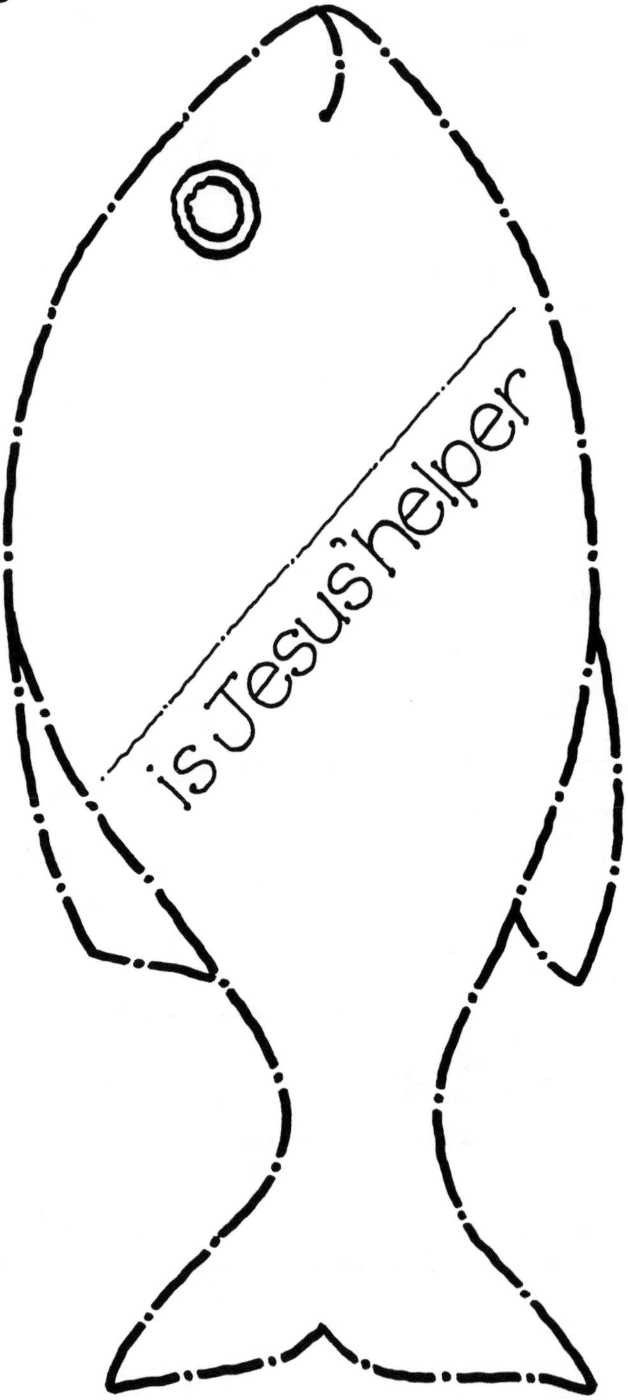

Fish Retreat

Nametag

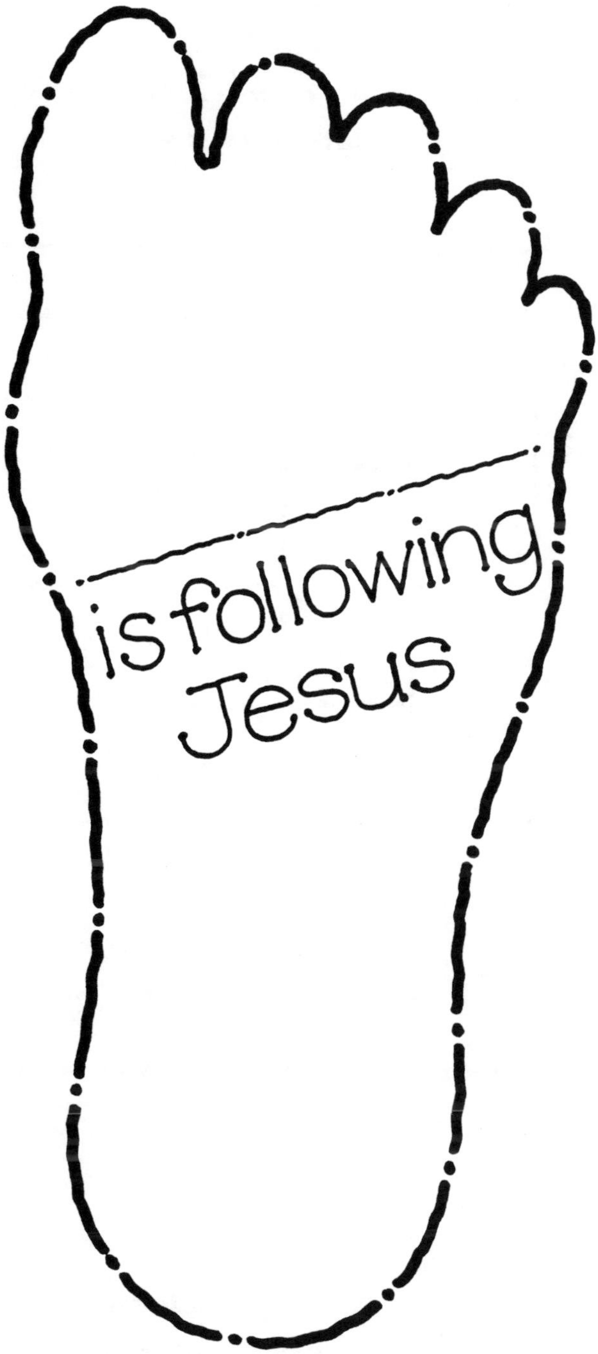

Fish Retreat

Like Jesus' helpers, follow Jesus out of the maze and tell the world about God's love.

[Jesus] said to them, "Come after me..."

—Matthew 4:19a

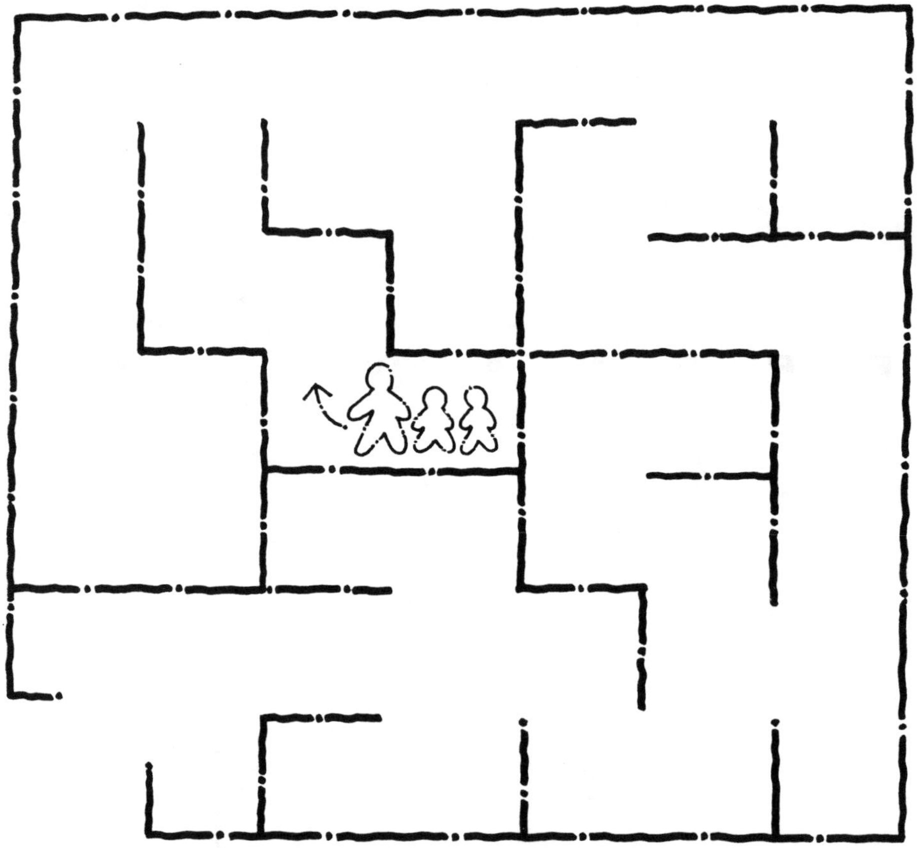

_______________ is Jesus' helper.

(child's name)

Fish Retreat

Activity Page

JESUS								
							child's name	
P	A	J	J	J	B	S		I
E	N	A	O	U	A	I		am
T	D	M	H	D	R	M		Jesus'
E	R	E	N	A	T	O		friend
R	E	S		S	H	N		and
	W				O			helper
					L			too!
					E			
					M			
					E			
					W			

Directions:

Cut along dotted lines ONLY. Punch two holes at the top. String yarn through and display.

Bubbles Retreat

Nametag

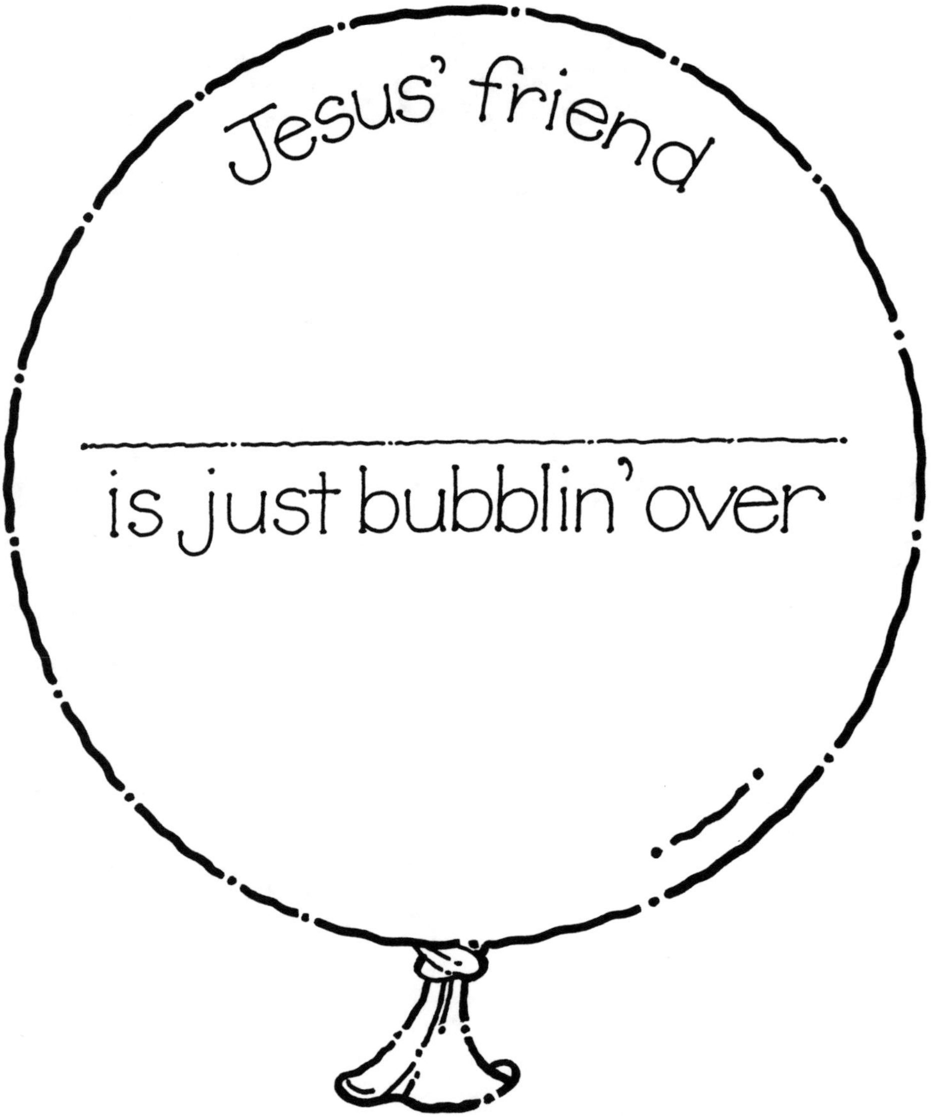

Bubbles Retreat

Nametag

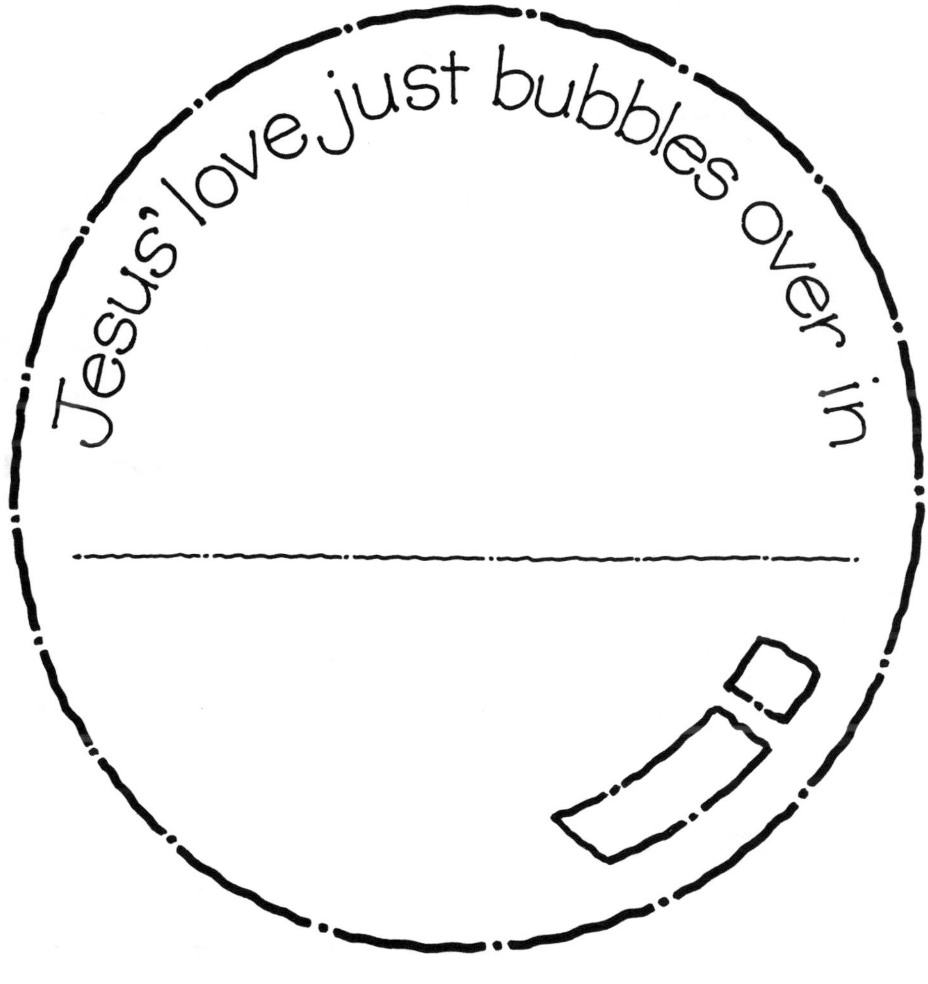
Jesus' love just bubbles over in

Bubbles Retreat

Activity Page

Love Chain:

Cut across each line. Glue, tape, or staple ends inside each other to make one chain.

Parent-child-Retreat

Jesus'

love

just

bubbles

me

over!

Child's name:

Valentine's Day Retreat

Nametag

Valentine's Day Retreat

Nametag

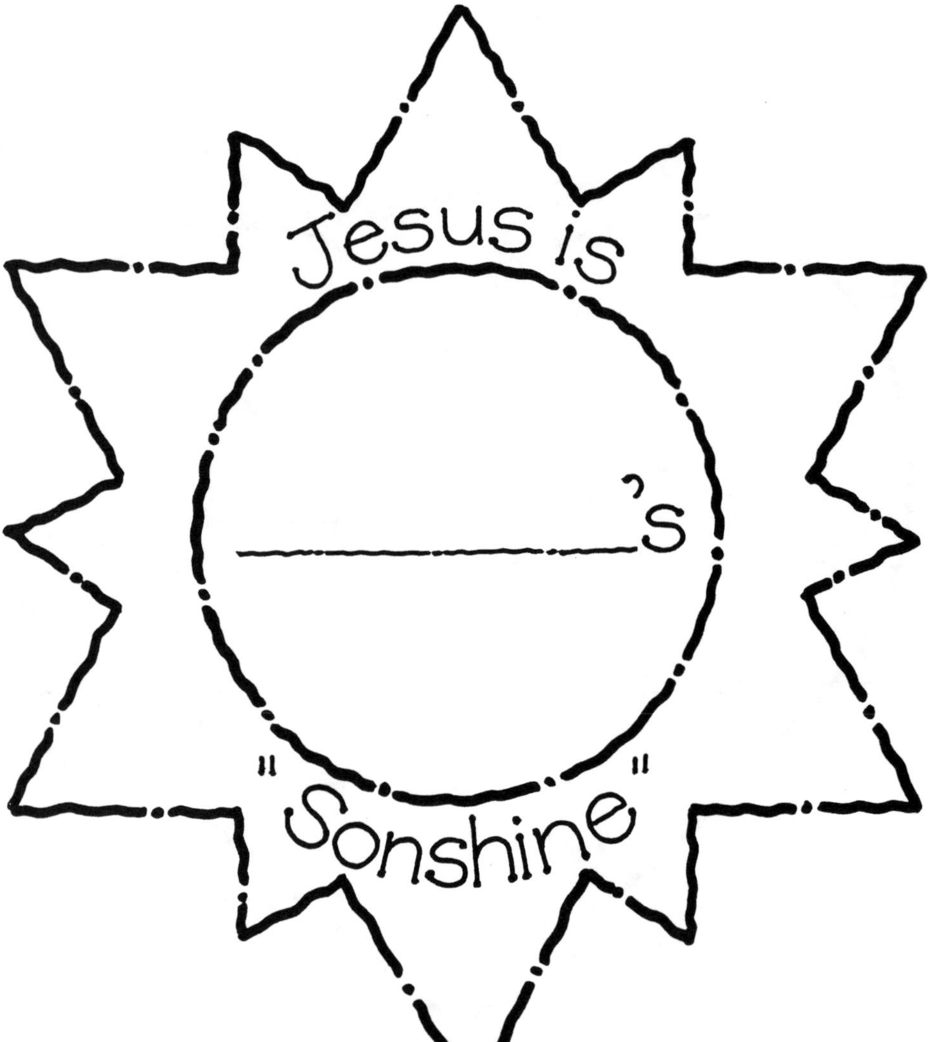

Valentine's Day Retreat

Activity Page

Name:__________________________

Cut along the dotted line at the left. Then cut out the squares and glue them into place on the friendship tree.

Kite Retreat

Nametag

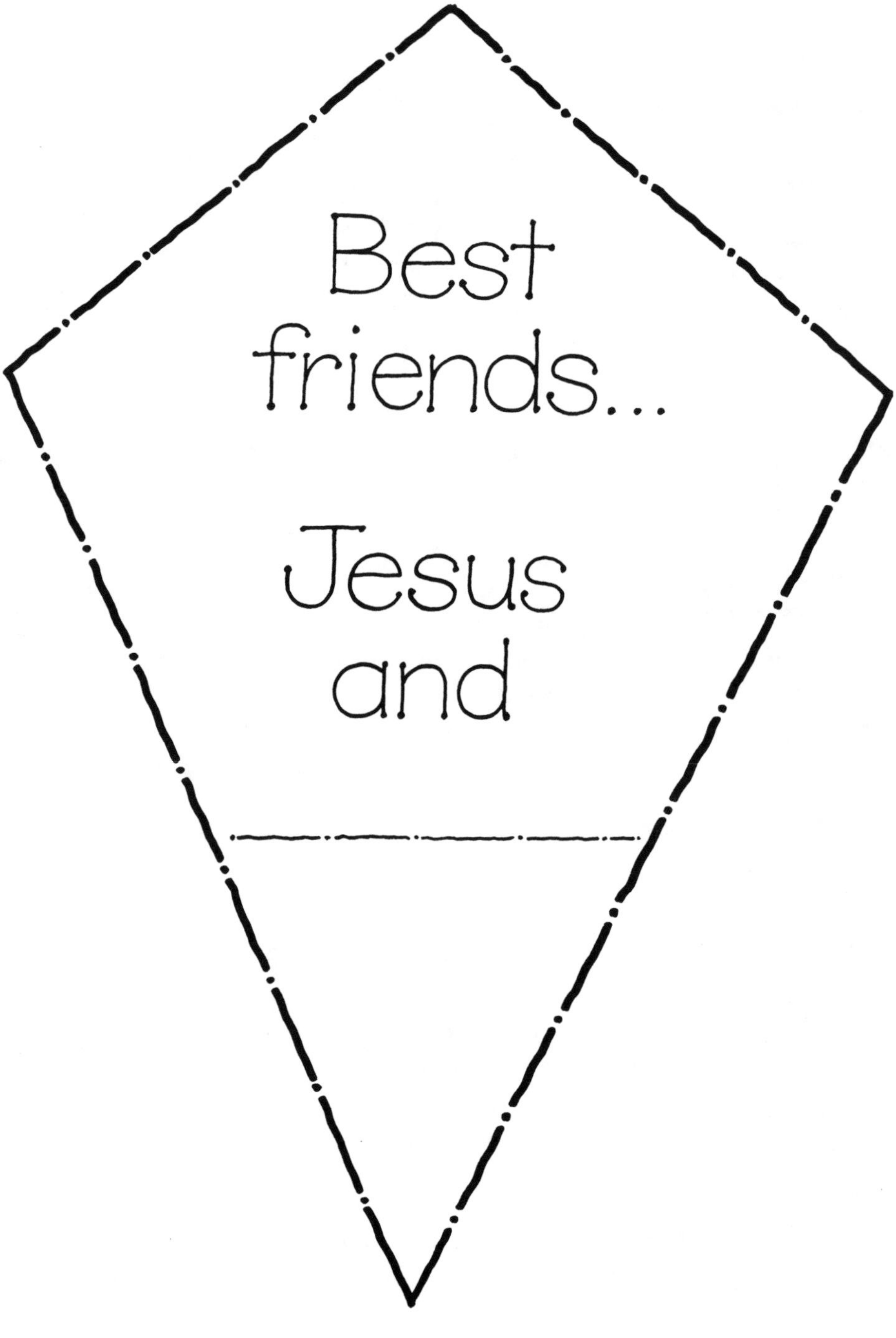

Kite Retreat

Activity Page

Jesus holds the string.

Connect the numbers and color this picture.

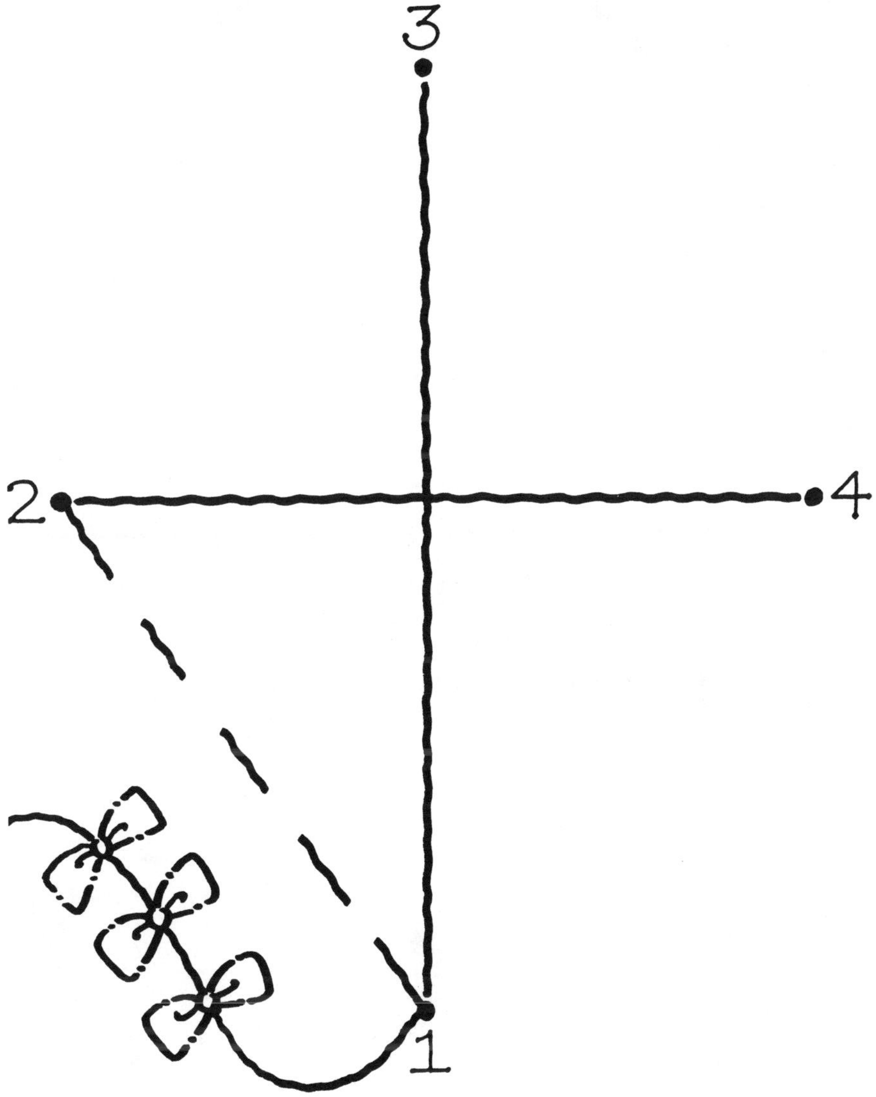

Name:______________________________

Jesus' friend

Easter Retreat

Nametag

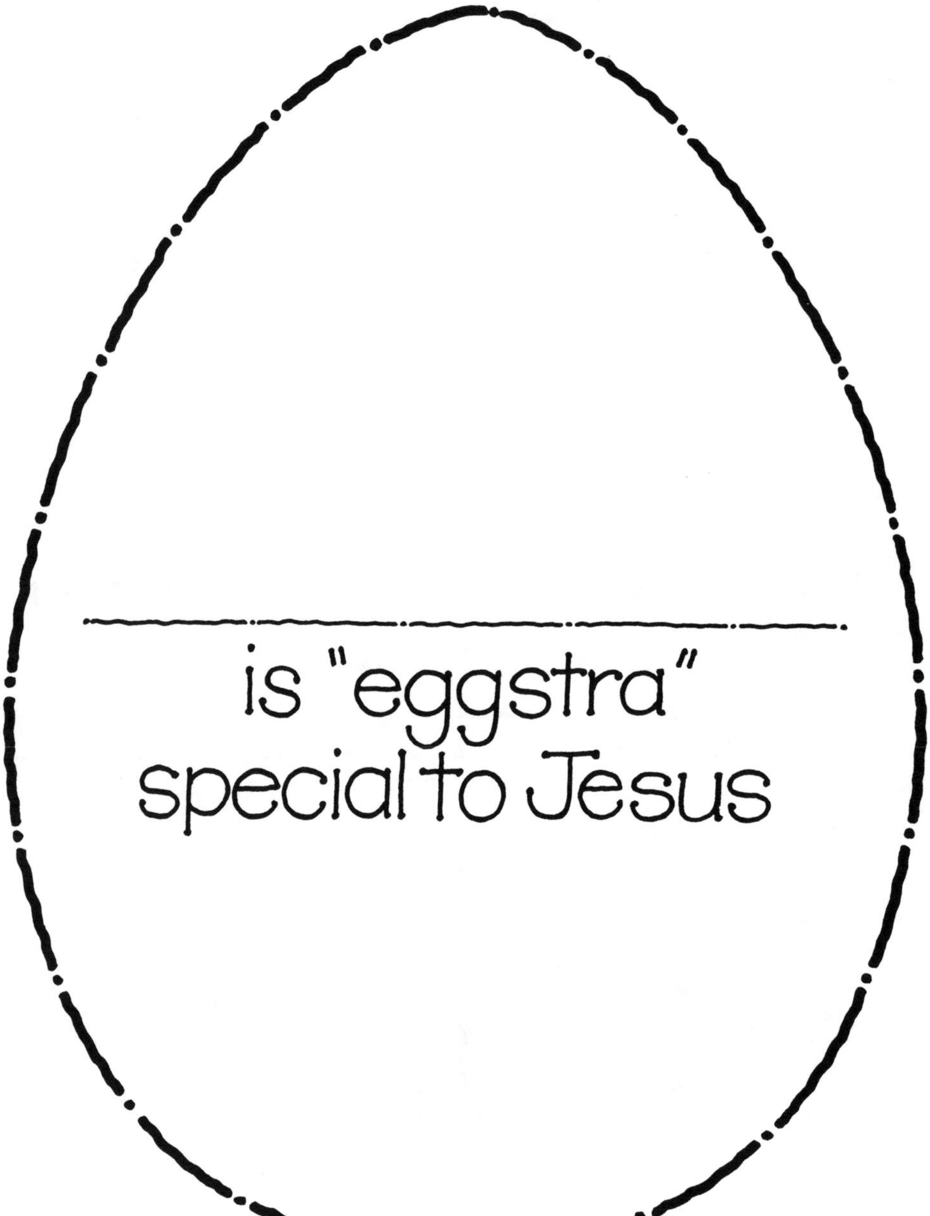
is "eggstra"
special to Jesus

Easter Retreat

Nametag

Easter Retreat

Activity Page

Faith means believing.

Connect the dots. Draw the baby chick inside the egg.

The mama hen sits patiently on the egg.

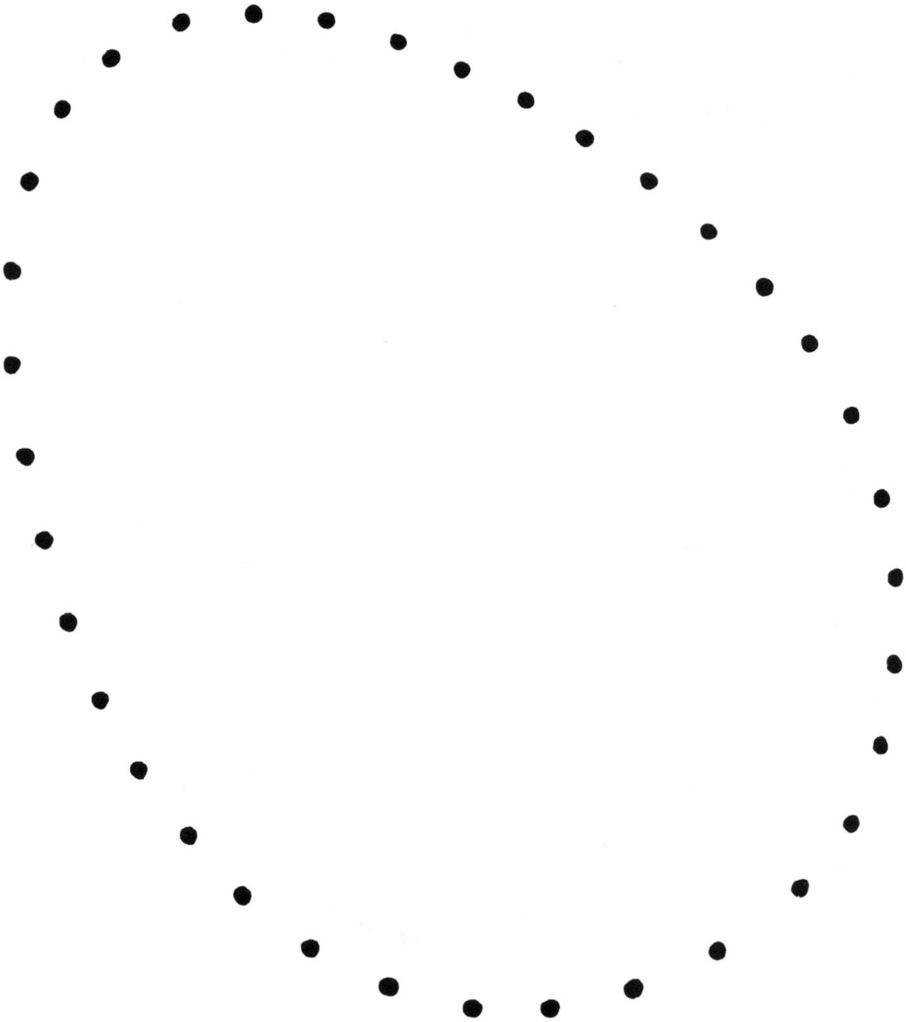

Name

____

is "egg"straordinary

Mother's Day/Father's Day Retreat

Nametag

Mother's Day/Father's Day Retreat

Nametag

Mother's Day/Father's Day Retreat

Activity Page

God gave us parents to help us.

This mom and dad are looking for their child. Color mom and dad. Draw the child in the space below. Follow the maze to bring them together.

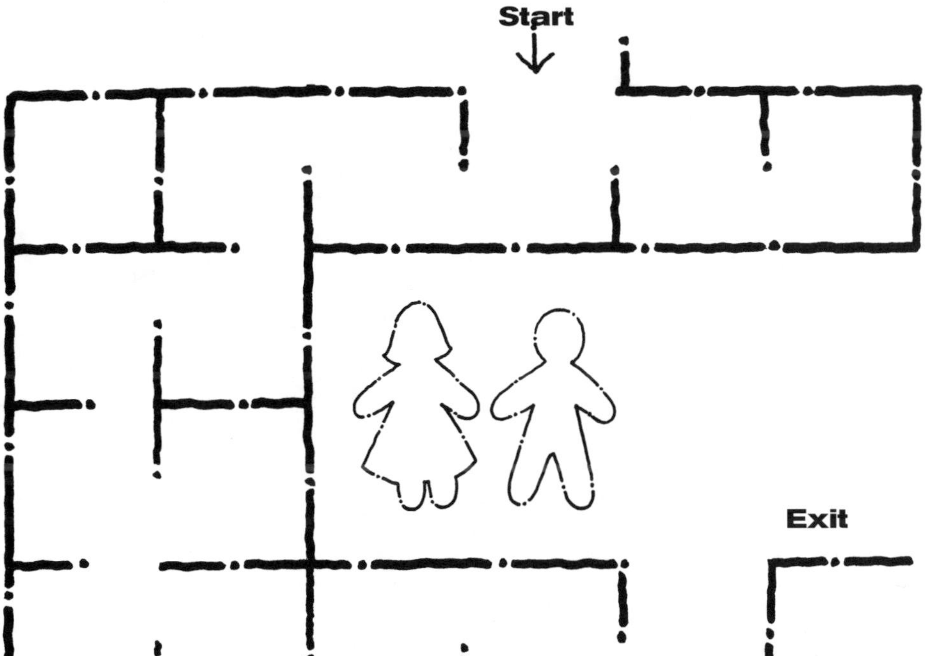

____

(name)

Picnic Retreat

Nametag

Picnic Retreat

Activity Page

Draw some bread to take on a picnic (bagels, buns, crackers, loaves, pretzels). Or, in each box, draw something you like to eat on a sandwich.

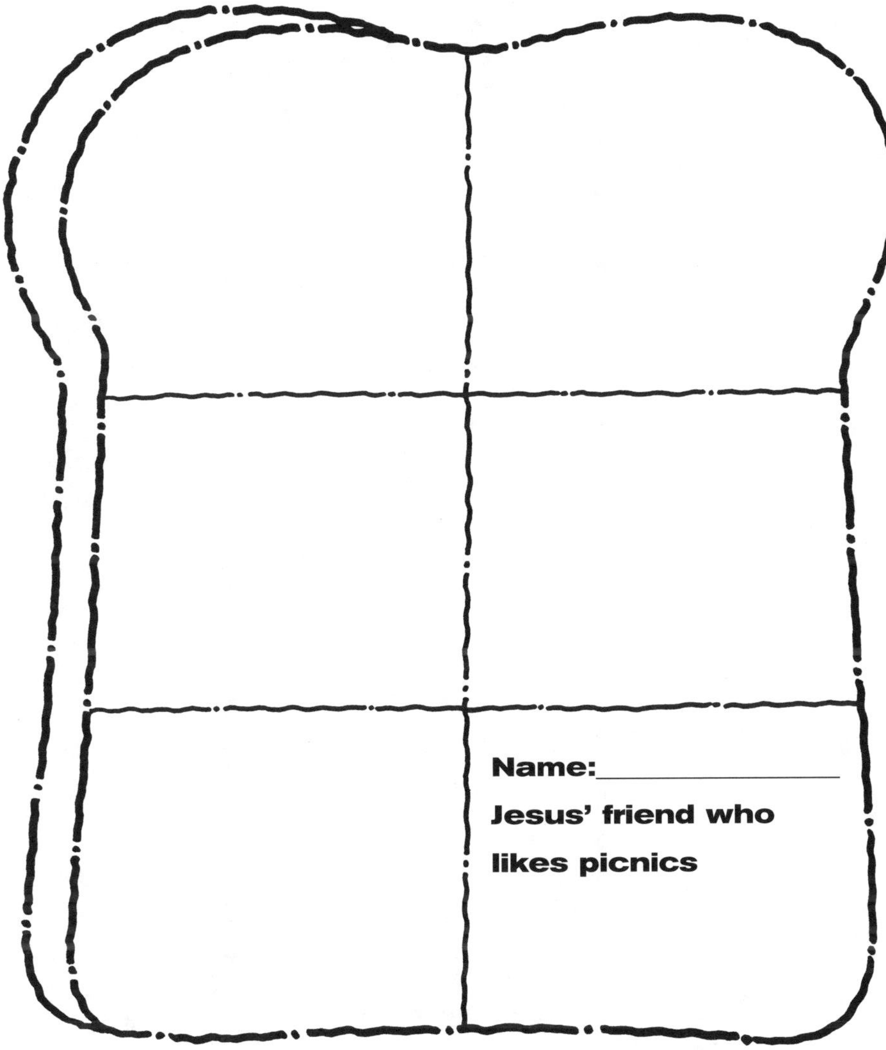

Candle Retreat

Nametag

Candle Retreat

Nametag

Candle Retreat

Mosaic Jack-O'-Lantern

(If paper plate isn't used)

Candle Retreat

Activity Page

Jesus lights us up.

Decorate this light switch cover for your home. Cut it out and tape it on a light switch.

Name:

Jesus' special light

Thanksgiving Retreat

Nametag

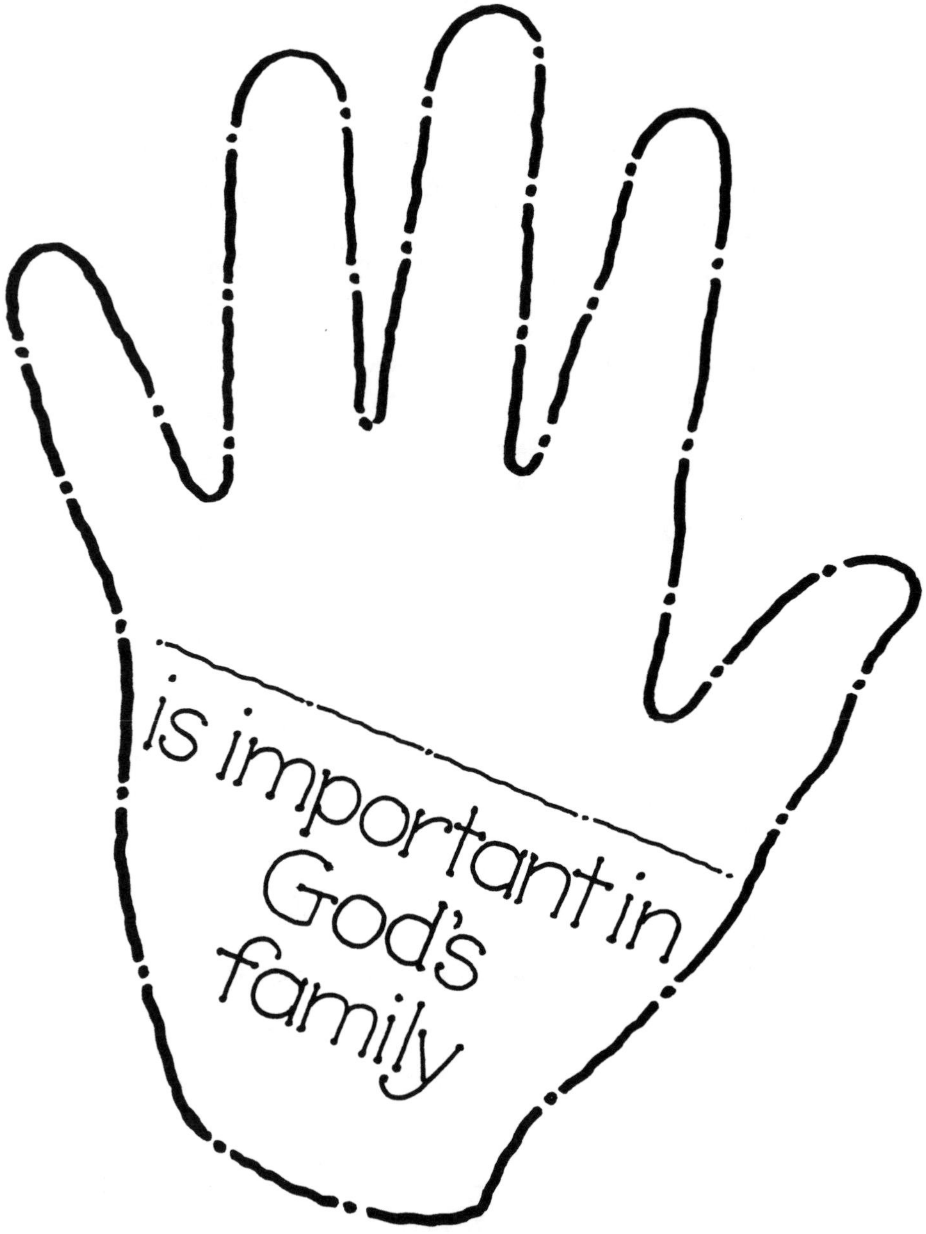
is important in God's family

Thanksgiving Retreat

Nametag

Thanksgiving Retreat

Activity Page

Jesus loved us first.

Color only the number that tells how old you were the day you came to the retreat.

Name:______________________________

Jesus loves me just the way I am!

Thanksgiving Retreat

Nametags for Cornhusk Dolls

____________________ name	is important to Jesus
____________________ name	is important to Jesus
____________________ name	is important to Jesus

Pattern for Napkin-Ring Covering Strips

Jesus loves me as I am!

I'm in God's family!

I'm important to Jesus!

I'm unique and special!

Name: ____________________

Christmas Retreat

Nametag

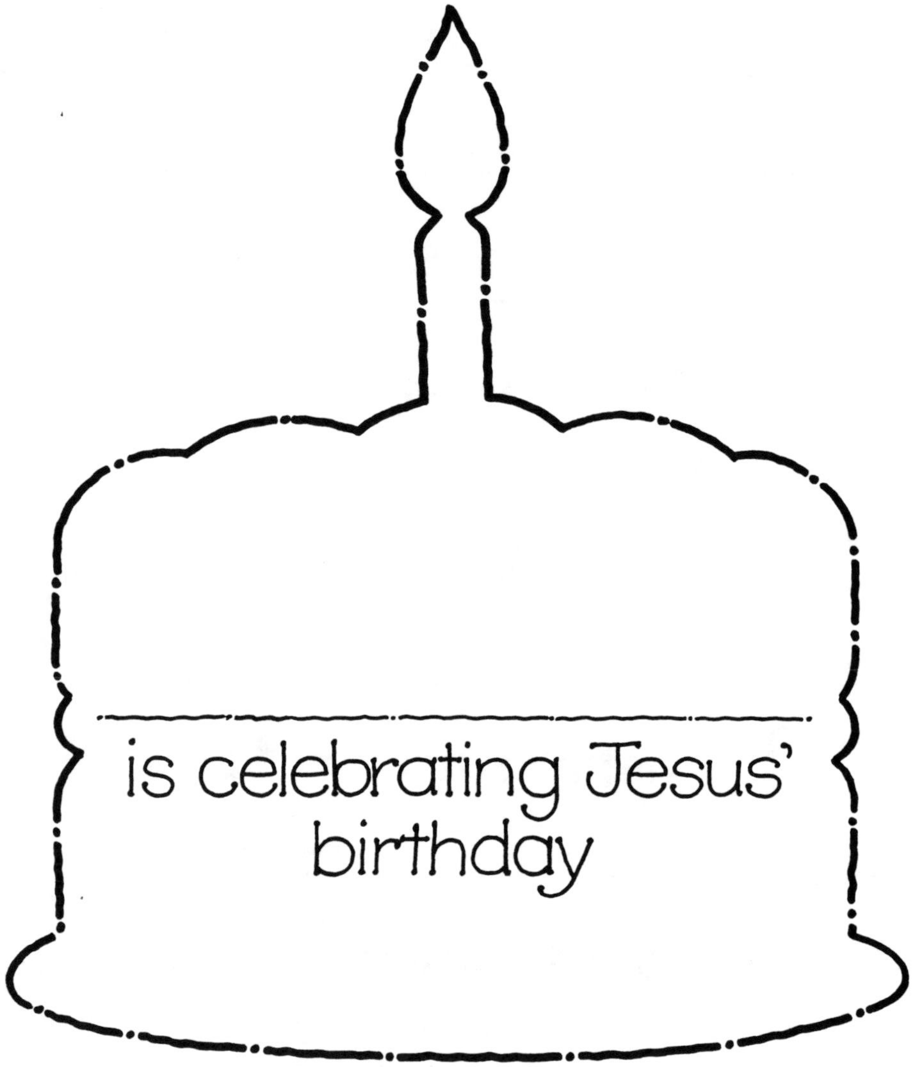
is celebrating Jesus' birthday

Christmas Retreat

Nametag

Glory to God
in the highest
and peace
to
on earth

Christmas Retreat

Activity Page

God gave us Jesus. We are gifts to each other. Everyone who loves us is a gift from God. Color in the birthday letters. Then decorate the packages.

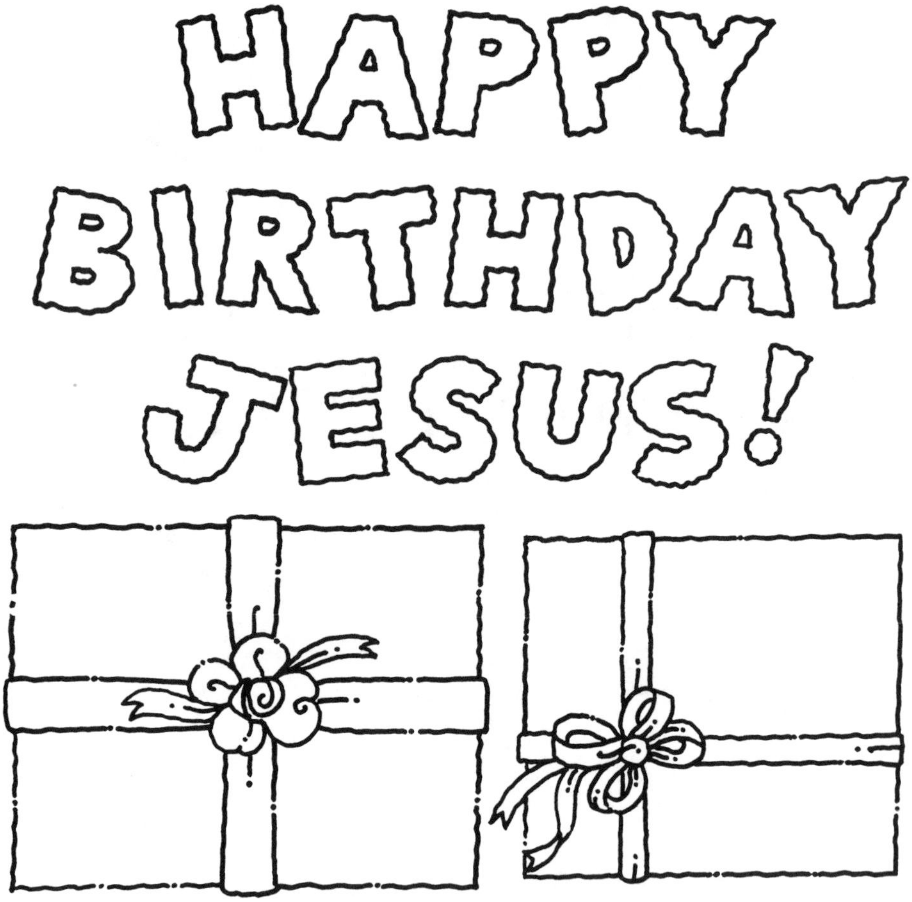

Name:______________________________

Jesus' special gift.

Parent Sessions:
Heart Room Prayer

"Close your eyes and place your feet comfortably on the floor, hands relaxed in your lap. (pause) Pay attention to your breathing. (pause) As you breathe in, breathe in the love of God. As you breathe out breathe out anything that might prevent you from focusing on God's love. (pause) Breathe in God's love; breathe out any barriers to God's love. (pause) As you breathe in, breathe in God's peace. And as you breathe out, breathe out any anxiety or worry. (pause) Breathe in God's peace; breathe out anxiety."

Wait 30 seconds, then continue:

"Visualize yourself moving down, now, into that most intimate, private place, which is your own heart. (pause) You hear a knock on the door of your heart, a door that can only be opened from the inside. You know who is knocking. It's Jesus. Go to the door and welcome Jesus in your own way."

Wait 30 seconds.

"Invite Jesus into your heart room if you can. If you can't, tell him so, openly and honestly.

Sit with Jesus now, or speak to him from a distance if you're more comfortable. Tell him what's in your heart."

Wait 1-2 minutes.

"Now close this time with Jesus. Ask him to stay with you, to dwell there in your heart room where you can always meet him."

Pause 30 seconds.

Ask each person to share with one other person something that happened in their prayer. For many, this may be the first time they've shared a faith experience. This will help them share more easily with their children later.

Parent-Child Sharing Time Form

To set the tone for quality sharing time between parents and child, duplicate this explanation and questions.

It's time now to join your child for individual sharing of your experiences today. The children have had four experiences of prayer.

▲ They've made a craft, a ______________________________.

While the children were constructing it, they talked about____________________.

▲ They heard the story_________________by____________________. It's about________________. Afterwards, they talked about the spiritual meaning of the story:______________________________.

▲ They visited Jesus in their heart room, as you did. The adult leader led the children in their imaginations to__________________ where the_______________. Afterwards, they said whatever they wanted to their best friend Jesus, in their heart rooms.

▲ They broke bread together, just as Jesus often did with his friends. Their snack was ___________________________________.

Your children may need questions to get them started sharing. Here are some suggestions.

- ▲ Tell me about the story you heard.
- ▲ What do you like about the craft you made?
- ▲ What was it like when you met Jesus in your heart room?
- ▲ What did Jesus look like?
- ▲ How did it feel to be with Jesus?
- ▲ When I met Jesus in my heart room, he said... I did...
- ▲ What did Jesus say to you? What did you do?